Nan D. Hunter is an associate prof_____ at Brooklyn Law School. S_____ ___er director of the AC_____ _____ _es- bian and Gay Rig_____ _ff attorney with the A_____ t. She has litigated ex_____ - ing the U.S. Supren_____ _irst Amendment, privac_____ _elations, and civil rights. She is the auth__ or numerous articles in the areas of gender, sexuality, and reproductive rights.

Sherryl E. Michaelson is an Assistant United States Attorney in the Central District of California* and an adjunct assistant professor of law at Southwestern University School of Law in Los Angeles. She was formerly an adjunct assistant professor of law at New York University School of Law. She served for three years as an officer in the United States Air Force. While in private practice, she litigated major lesbian and gay rights cases as a cooperating attorney with Lambda Legal Defense and Education Fund and the ACLU Lesbian and Gay Rights Project, and she has been active in community lesbian and gay rights organizations.

Thomas B. Stoddard is the executive director of Lambda Legal Defense and Education Fund, the nation's oldest and largest legal organization dedicated specifically to the rights of lesbians and gay men, and an adjunct associate professor of law at New York University School of Law. He previously served as the legislative director of the New York Civil Liberties Union and in that capacity helped to write, among other measures, the New York City ordinance outlawing discrimination on the basis of sexual orientation. He has written and spoken extensively on civil rights and civil liberties, especially as they relate to lesbians, gay men, and people with HIV disease.

*The views expressed in this book are those of the authors and do not represent the position of the United States Department of Justice.

Also in this series

AN AMERICAN CIVIL LIBERTIES UNION HANDBOOK

THE RIGHTS OF LESBIANS AND GAY MEN

THE BASIC ACLU GUIDE TO A GAY PERSON'S RIGHTS

THIRD EDITION

Nan D. Hunter
Sherryl E. Michaelson
Thomas B. Stoddard

General Editor of the Handbook Series
Norman Dorsen, President, ACLU 1976–1991

SOUTHERN ILLINOIS UNIVERSITY PRESS
CARBONDALE AND EDWARDSVILLE

Copyright © 1992 by the American Civil Liberties Union
All rights reserved
Printed in the United States of America
Production supervised by Natalia Nadraga

95 94 93 92   4 3 2 1

Library of Congress Cataloging-in-Publication Data

Hunter, Nan D.
    The rights of lesbians and gay men : the basic ACLU guide to a
gay person's rights / Nan D. Hunter, Sherryl E. Michaelson, Thomas
B. Stoddard. — 3rd ed.
        p.   cm. — (An American Civil Liberties Union handbook)
    Rev. ed. of: The Rights of gay people. 2nd ed. c1983.
    Includes bibliographical references (p.   ).
    1. Gay men—Civil rights—United States.   2. Lesbians—Civil
rights—United States.   3. Homosexuality—Law and legislation—
United States.   I. Michaelson, Sherryl E.   II. Stoddard, Thomas B.
III. American Civil Liberties Union.   IV. Rights of gay people.
V. Title.   VI. Series.
KF4754.5.Z9R54   1992
342.73'087—dc20
[347.30287]   91-40607
ISBN 0-8093-1634-X   CIP

The paper in this publication meets the minimum requirements of
American National Standard for Information Sciences—Permanence of
Paper for Printed Library Materials, ANSI Z39.48-1984. ⊗

*We dedicate this book to
Lisa, Maureen, and Walter,
who, through their love and commitment,
remind us that the movement
for full civil rights
for lesbians and gay men
is personal
as well as political*

Contents

Preface

This guide sets forth your rights under the present law and offers suggestions on how they can be protected. It is one of a continuing series of handbooks published in cooperation with the American Civil Liberties Union (ACLU).

Surrounding these publications is the hope that Americans, informed of their rights, will be encouraged to exercise them. Through their exercise, rights are given life. If they are rarely used, they may be forgotten and violations may become routine.

This guide offers no assurances that your rights will be respected. The laws may change, and in some of the subjects covered in these pages they change quite rapidly. An effort has been made to note those parts of the law where movement is taking place, but it is not always possible to predict accurately when the law *will* change.

Even if the laws remain the same, their interpretations by courts and administrative officials often vary. In a federal system such as ours, there is a built-in problem since state and federal law differ, not to speak of the confusion between states. In addition, there are wide variations in the ways in which particular courts and administrative officials will interpret the same law at any given moment.

If you encounter what you consider to be a specific abuse of your rights, you should seek legal assistance. There are a number of agencies that may help you, among them ACLU affiliate offices, but bear in mind that the ACLU is a limited-purpose organization. In many communities, there are federally funded legal service offices which provide assistance to persons who cannot afford the costs of legal representation. In general, the rights that the ACLU defends are freedom of inquiry and expression; due process of law; equal protection of the laws; and privacy. The authors in this series have discussed other rights (even though they sometimes fall outside the ACLU's usual concern) in order to provide as much guidance as possible.

These books have been planned as guides for the people directly affected: thus the question-and-answer format. (In some areas there are more detailed works available for experts.)

These guides seek to raise the major issues and inform the nonspecialist of the basic law on the subject. The authors of these books are themselves specialists who understand the need for information at "street level."

If you encounter a specific legal problem in an area discussed in one of these handbooks, show the book to your attorney. Of course, he or she will not be able to rely exclusively on the handbook to provide you with adequate representation. But if your attorney hasn't had a great deal of experience in the specific area, the handbook can provide helpful suggestions on how to proceed.

Norman Dorsen
Editor, ACLU Handbook Series
New York University School of Law

Acknowledgments

Many people have contributed to the third edition of this book. We especially want to thank the authors of the two previous editions—E. Carrington Boggan, Marilyn G. Haft, Charles Lister, and John P. Rupp—upon whose substantial labors we have built. We also owe special gratitude to Geoffrey Brown for his work on the chapter on security clearances; Gisela Caldwell for her assistance in assembling materials for the military chapter; Jay Ward Brown (unrelated to Geoffrey) for his preparation of several of the most detailed and difficult appendixes; and Teresa Matushaj and Kimberly Carr for research. Paul Hendley, Rose Patti, and Peter Cameron provided expert and invaluable clerical help.

We would be delinquent if we failed to acknowledge in addition our colleagues—especially at Lambda and the ACLU—whose advocacy made possible many of the advances described in this book.

Introduction

In a 1989 speech on the occasion of the bicentennial of the Constitution, Supreme Court Justice Thurgood Marshall noted that some Americans would "observe the anniversary with hopes not realized and promises not fulfilled." For no group is that statement more true than for lesbian and gay Americans. The law has only begun to jettison notions that a person's homosexuality reflects sinfulness or psychological disorder. Despite recent progress in some areas—including the recent repeal by Congress of the immigration statute forbidding lesbian and gay foreigners from visiting our country—as we approach the twenty-first century, the law's treatment of homosexuality seems mired in irrationality:

- In a handful of states and some cities, the law prohibits an employer from firing a person because he or she is gay; in other states, the law permits the police to arrest and prosecute that same person for private consensual sexual behavior. In a few instances, in the same state, a city law prohibits discrimination while state law authorizes prosecution.
- In some states, a lesbian mother or gay father is considered presumptively unfit to retain custody of her or his child; in other jurisdictions, lesbian or gay couples have been approved by courts to adopt a child jointly, as coparents.
- In New York, in certain housing units, the survivor of a gay or lesbian couple is treated as a family member when the partner dies and is protected from eviction even if his or her name is not on the lease; but in every state, including New York, a person can be denied visitation privileges when a seriously ill partner is hospitalized because, under the law, they are strangers.

This book—the third edition of a work first published in 1975—offers a map for navigating these erratic waters. It is written for people facing discrimination or legal uncertainty in one or more of the areas we discuss: employment, housing, family relationships, the military, protest or other expressive activities, criminal matters, security clearances, or AIDS and HIV infection. The book is not, however, a substitute for legal advice. Indeed, one warning that recurs frequently in these chapters is the need to secure competent and sympathetic counsel. But the book provides an overview for understanding general themes in legal doctrine and for starting the process of asserting rights provided by the law.

Ultimately, this is a book about the value of diversity and the right to dissent. What is remarkable is how often courts have ignored these fundamental constitutional principles when cases involve some aspect of human sexuality. For the last two decades, the antidiscrimination efforts whose results are chronicled herein reflect nothing so much as the fight to force the government and other institutions (such as employers) to adhere to these elementary precepts when dealing with issues of sexuality. The lesbian and gay civil rights movement has become both the leading edge and the lightning rod of this campaign. An increasing amount of litigation and legislation now focuses on homosexuality. How society will treat lesbians and gay men is a critical social barometer for all those who dissent from social conventions and stereotypes associated with sex and gender.

We look forward to a day when classifications based on sexual orientation will be recognized as artificial and irrelevant. In the meantime, we invite you to become part of the process by which that occurs—by claiming those rights the law has already recognized, by seeking to establish the next frontier of rights, and by supporting those brave individuals who refuse to be treated as second-class citizens. When one strips away the jargon and the procedures, the bedrock truth is that people make the law. We invite you to join the fight for justice.

THE RIGHTS OF
LESBIANS AND GAY MEN

I

Freedom of Speech and Association: The Right to Organize and Speak Out

Until the late 1960s and early 1970s, few lesbian and gay Americans spoke out about their experiences, protested inequality, or organized groups to secure their legal rights. Censorship of books, plays, and films with explicitly homosexual themes was common. Only a handful of brave individuals, gay or straight, dared to speak publicly in support of equal legal rights for lesbians and gay men.

One of the events that signaled an end to that era and marked the beginnings of the modern lesbian and gay rights movement was a dramatic shattering of silence. The Stonewall Inn, a gay bar on Christopher Street in New York's Greenwich Village, was raided by the police—a then-common occurrence—and the lesbians and gay men whom the police sought to arrest fought back in an unprecedented assertion of the right to be free from police harassment.[1] Shortly thereafter, the Gay Liberation Front was formed in New York City. It was one of the first organizations to name itself with the word "gay" (the word preferred to "homosexual" because of its self-affirming message and nonmedical origins) and to couple that term with a call for "liberation."[2]

Openly lesbian and gay organizations now exist throughout the country. Demands for an end to discrimination have become common in public discussion and the mass media, and positive images of lesbians and gay men are beginning to appear in popular culture.

With rapid shifts in public consciousness, however, has come a backlash. Many of the most venomous antigay attacks in Congress during the 1980s, for example, focused specifically on forms of speech. Congress passed an appropriations rider in one session forbidding funding for potentially lifesaving AIDS education if it "promoted or encouraged" homosexuality.[3] The Senate passed another bill that would have removed federal support for any sex education programs that described homosexuality as "normal," "natural," or "healthy."[4] Reaction to the homoerotic imagery of photographer Robert Mapplethorpe was a major factor in triggering a massive right-wing assault on the National Endowment for the Arts and led to the obscenity prosecution of a museum in Cincinnati. In the summer of 1990, four theater artists—three of them openly lesbian or gay and all four supportive of gay rights—were turned down for grants by the NEA in the midst of continuing attacks against public funding of artwork expressive of lesbian and gay themes.[5]

The tension between greater openness and tolerance on one hand and the backlash against it on the other has also shaped decision making by the courts. Thus, although fundamental First Amendment protections for speech remain perhaps the single most precious and powerful weapon in our constitutional arsenal, there are also numerous examples of failures by the law to protect full freedom of expression.

For a comprehensive discussion of free speech issues, see the ACLU handbook, *The Right to Protest* (1991).

LESBIAN AND GAY RIGHTS ADVOCACY GROUPS

Do people have a right to form organizations for the purpose of ending discrimination based on sexual orientation?

Yes. Freedom of association is a right that flows from the guarantees of freedom of assembly and speech contained in the First Amendment to the United States Constitution and the guarantee of liberty assured by the Due Process Clause of the Fourteenth Amendment. Courts have specifically acknowledged that the right of freedom of association extends to lesbian and gay organizations.[6]

Do lesbian and gay organizations have the right to incorporate?

Yes. The legal benefits of incorporation should be available to gay organizations to the same extent they are available to any other organization.[7] This principle should be recognized even in states with a sodomy law. When the Gay Activists Alliance sought to incorporate in 1972 in New York, that state had a sodomy law, and incorporation was initially rejected by the secretary of state on the grounds, among others, that "the purposes of the proposed corporation raised serious questions as to whether it may be formed to promote activities which are contrary to public policy and contrary to the penal laws of the State."[8] In overturning that denial, a New York court stated that "[i]t is well established that it is not unlawful for any individual or group of individuals to peaceably agitate for the repeal of any law."[9]

Can lesbian and gay organizations obtain federal tax-exempt and tax-deductible status?

Yes. In 1978 the Internal Revenue Service issued a ruling whereby gay organizations can obtain tax-exempt, tax-deductible status if they otherwise qualify under the tax laws.[10] Since that time, the IRS has granted tax-exempt status to many gay groups around the country.

Do lesbian and gay organizations have a right to keep the names of their members confidential?

Under most circumstances, yes. The Supreme Court has held that where, because of community temper, disclosure of the names of members of an organization might adversely affect those members, the organization is not required to disclose its membership list even if a state or local law requires it or a governmental official demands it.[11] Forcing disclosure under such circumstances violates the members' freedom of association.[12] A lesbian or gay man who fears membership in a gay organization might become known to others might not join the organization. However, the Court has enunciated exceptions to this rule. If an organization seeks tax-exempt status, for example, it may have to divulge certain information on its sources of income. Moreover, an organization that actively participates in an election campaign may be required to reveal the names of at least its major contributors under either the federal or state election laws.[13] Any gay organization faced with a demand for disclosure should seek legal advice, for these are difficult legal issues. Any organization that intends to support a particular candidate should, by all means, seek a lawyer's advice well before the campaign, so that it understands the implications of such activity.

Do lesbian and gay organizations have to reveal the names of persons who make financial contributions or pay dues to them?

Not usually. The Supreme Court has recognized that governmentally forced disclosure of contributors to organizations that espouse unpopular views can have a deterrent effect on the associational rights of the members of the organizations and has ruled that they cannot be forced to divulge such information.[14]

Do members of a lesbian and gay organization have a right to refuse to reveal their association with the organization to the government and to prospective employers?

Usually, but the right is not absolute. The Supreme Court has held that while the Constitution generally protects an individual from being forced to disclose his associational relationships, disclosure may be required when there is a state interest sufficiently compelling to overcome the individual's right to associational privacy.[15]

Public school teachers face particularly difficult problems in this area. The Supreme Court has said that a public school teacher does not give up the right to freedom of speech, belief, or association by teaching in the public schools, but he or she does have an obligation of "frankness, candor, and cooperation" in answering questions by the employing board because a teacher's work in the classroom may be sensitive and may shape the attitudes of children and adolescents.[16] In *Acanfora v. Board of Education of Montgomery County*,[17] a federal court of appeals upheld the transfer of a gay teacher from classroom to administrative duties on the ground that he failed to reveal, on a questionnaire concerning his extracurricular activities, his participation in a gay student organization while in college. The court found that the teacher had misrepresented himself in response to a legitimate question.

Consultation with an attorney is advisable when trying to decide whether or not membership in a gay organization must be disclosed on an application form or in an interview. Furthermore, it is important to remember that a right not to disclose does not constitute a right to lie. False statements in response to official inquiries may give rise to civil liability, criminal penalties, or both.

Can lesbian and gay organizations receive government funds for conducting programs and projects?

There is no barrier in the law to such funding. A number of

lesbian and gay organizations have received government grants to conduct AIDS-related prevention and education programs, for example. However, bias against such groups remains a potent obstacle in many, probably most, funding situations.

SPEECH ON CAMPUS AND IN HIGH SCHOOLS

Does the right of association under the Constitution extend to lesbian and gay student organizations at state-supported colleges and universities?

Yes. The right of freedom of association clearly extends to student organizations at state-supported institutions.[18] Federal courts have explicitly applied this right to lesbian and gay organizations at state-supported schools.[19] Official school recognition of gay organizations cannot be withheld by officials at state-supported schools merely because they do not approve of the organization. However, school officials may evaluate any student organization based on neutral factors such as the failure or refusal to abide by reasonable administrative rules and whether the organization or its members have violated state laws at functions sponsored by the organization.[20]

To what school benefits are such lesbian and gay organizations entitled?

The same benefits as any other officially recognized student organization. The benefits typically include the use of campus facilities for meetings and other appropriate purposes, including dances and other social events, and the right to use school media for the expression of ideas to the school community.[21] In addition, where a university has a system of funding student activities, a lesbian and gay student organization is entitled to funding on the same basis as all other groups.[22]

Does the freedom of association for gay students and gay student organizations extend to public high schools?

Yes. High school students, like college students, have a presumptive right to freedom of association and freedom of speech that is protected under the Constitution. Students have a right to exercise their freedom of expression on any issue, however controversial, so long as their expression does not "materially and substantially" disrupt the work and discipline of the school.[23] As a practical matter, the younger the student, the greater the authority courts will grant to school administrators to regulate student activities that function as part of the school's curriculum and speech that might be considered "disruptive."[24]

If a high school allows noncurricular clubs, must it also allow a lesbian and gay rights group?

Yes. In addition to the constitutionally based free speech claim that such a group would have, a federal law passed in 1984 prohibits a public high school that already allows noncurriculum related student groups to meet on school premises from discriminating against other students who wish to have meetings based on the "religious, political, philosophical or other content" of their speech.[25] The law covers public high schools that receive federal funds.

Can a public high school forbid participation by openly gay students in general student activities?

Presumptively not, although the law is undeveloped. In the only case on this question, a federal district court judge ruled that a gay male high school student in Rhode Island was entitled to take another male to the school prom as his date. The court accepted his argument that the proposed conduct constituted "symbolic speech" under the First Amendment and ordered the principal to permit the student and his date to attend.[26] In reaching this decision, the court upheld the principle that lesbian and gay students are entitled to the same benefits and access to student activities as other students.

Does the constitutional guarantee of the right of association extend to protect organizations at private schools?

No. The constitutional protection against interference with freedom of association applies only to public school systems and state-supported colleges and universities. The Constitution protects against action by the government (federal, state, or local), not against the actions of private organizations.

Are there any antidiscrimination laws that apply to private schools and colleges?

Yes. There are statutes that provide protection against discrimination by private as well as public entities. Some state and local civil rights laws cover private schools and prohibit discrimination based on sexual orientation. (See Appendix C for a listing of such laws.) In addition, a number of colleges and universities, both public and private, have adopted antidiscrimination policies that include sexual orientation as a prohibited basis for differential treatment. Students can seek to force the university to adhere to its own institutional policy.

Can a lesbian or gay public school teacher be dismissed or transferred to nonteaching duties for speaking about gay issues in public, outside the classroom?

Presumptively not. The Supreme Court upheld the ruling of a federal appeals court that an Oklahoma law that mandated firing school employees for "advocating" homosexuality was unconstitutional because its scope was so broad that a teacher could have been fired for making a speech outside the classroom advocating a change in the law.[27] Another federal appeals court held that the transfer of a gay teacher to nonteaching duties could not be sustained on the grounds that he appeared on television and made public statements in support of equal treatment for lesbians and gay men.[28] A similar case involving a college teacher who was fired after being quoted in several newspaper articles about gay rights also led to a victory for the teacher.[29]

The general legal standard is that while a teacher's right to freedom of speech may be balanced against the importance the state attaches to the education of its youth, a teacher's comments on public issues that are neither knowingly false nor made with reckless disregard of the truth afford no ground for dismissal when they do not impair the teacher's performance of his or her duties or interfere with the operation of the school.[30]

PROTEST SPEECH

Can the police prohibit peaceful demonstrations and pickets in support of lesbian and gay rights?

No. Such activity may not be prohibited, but it may be regulated, so long as the regulation is applied to all demonstrations and picket lines equally and without regard to the viewpoint being expressed. A city or state may establish rules for demonstrations so long as they are narrowly tailored to promote legitimate (i.e., noncensorious) public concerns, such as traffic flow.[31] Regulation is permitted as to the time, place, and manner in which demonstrations may occur. The police may, for example, limit the number of pickets in a congested area.[32] One test for the reasonableness of such regulations is whether the demonstrators are left with ample other opportunities for expressing their message.

Can the police require that protesters secure a permit prior to a demonstration or march?

Yes, so long as the criteria for the issuance of such permits are clear, neutral, and are equally applied to all applicants regardless of the point of view of the demonstration.[33]

Does the right of free speech protect persons who wear gay rights badges or buttons?

Yes. Wearing items such as armbands and buttons is a form of expression called symbolic speech. Symbolic speech is an act that, although not necessarily exclusively speech, is nonetheless a public expression of belief or opinion, and it comes within the protection of the free-speech clause of the First Amendment.[34]

COMING OUT AND POSITIVE IMAGES

Do the courts protect "coming out" speech?

Sometimes. The law is still very much in a developing state. As more and more lesbian and gay Americans choose to be open about their lives and seek not only tolerance but support for the relationships they form with partners, there will inevitably be more "coming out" speech to employers, coworkers, landlords, neighbors, and others. When the employer, landlord, or other party is a government agency, the Constitution should forbid imposing any penalty as a result of coming out. But because the law is not settled as to this important principle, it is imperative that, if possible, a lawyer's advice be sought in advance if there is reason to believe that honesty will lead to any form of government reprisal.

Is "coming out" speech considered political speech?

Sometimes. In 1979 the California Supreme Court suggested that a person's affirmation of homosexuality was analogous to the expression of a political point of view and could be protected by a California state labor law that prohibited all employers from interfering with the political activities of employees.[35] Since then, the California state attorney general has formally adopted that interpretation of the state labor code.[36] Thus, coming out speech probably cannot be the basis of a firing in the state of California.

Federal court cases, however, have yielded mixed results. One federal appeals court invalidated the firing of a county employee based on his informing his boss that he was gay and that he intended to speak as a citizen to the county commissioners on the subject of civil rights for lesbians and gay men. The court found that the speech was protected and that firing the employee because of his speech was unconstitutional.[37] In the *Acanfora* case discussed above, the press interviews, which included avowals of the teacher's own homosexuality, were found not to justify firing him (although his firing was permitted on other grounds).[38] A third, more recent case, reached the opposite conclusion. This case involved a school guidance counselor who was fired after she told her supervisor she was bisexual; the court ruled that such information is purely personal and thus not analogous to political speech and not protected under the Constitution.[39] The differing results of these cases may be reconciled by treating the first two as involving what is more traditionally thought of as political speech—i.e., addressing the county commissioners or speaking to the press—in addition to the coming out statement. The third case, on the other hand, involves coming out in a one-on-one conversation with a supervisor. Regardless, coming out speech ought to be recognized by the courts as political expression.

What are agency officials likely to claim in an attempt to fire a person who publicly affirms her or his homosexuality?

Several of the most disturbing cases have turned on the question of whether a lesbian or gay employee's actions amounted to "flaunting" homosexuality. A federal court of appeals decision in 1971 upheld the refusal of the University of Minnesota to employ a gay man as head of the university library's cataloging division on the ground that his "personal conduct, as represented in the public and University news media, [wa]s not consistent with the best interest of the university."[40] The applicant had sought a marriage license to marry another man, and the event had received much publicity. A strikingly similar case also involved a person who had tried to obtain legal recognition of gay marriage. Here, a gay activist who worked as a clerk typist for a federal agency was also fired after a highly publicized attempt to reform the marriage laws of the state of Washington. A federal appeals court (including Judge, now Supreme Court Justice, Anthony Kennedy) upheld the firing on the ground that government's interest in maintaining public confidence in the agency outweighed the employee's interest in "publicly flaunting and broadcasting his homosexual activities."[41] The federal government changed its policy after the case was decided, but the degree of the court's hostility to the gay plaintiff indicates the difficulty that even seemingly clear constitutional claims may face. Although these cases now seem dated, they have not yet been clearly overruled.

In anticipation of such an argument by an employer, it is extremely important to document that advocacy of lesbian and gay rights has no adverse impact on how a person functions on the job or on how the agency functions.

Can public transit and other state entities that accept advertising dealing with social or political issues refuse to accept advertising from gay rights organizations?

No. When a public transportation authority accepts other advertisements espousing political and social concerns, it creates a public forum, and access to such a public forum could be limited only by precise, clear regulations concerning time, place, and manner of speech. Access to such a forum may not be barred because gay rights views may be unpopular.[42]

SPEECH ABOUT SEXUALITY

Can the government stop AIDS prevention programs on the ground that they are too sexually explicit?

The government cannot prohibit the production or distribution of AIDS materials unless they are found to be obscene within the meaning of the law. However, eligibility for funding is a different question. Federal, state, and local agencies have varying rules for funding, based on the content of AIDS prevention programs. Current federal restrictions prohibit funding for materials that might be considered "offensive" to persons outside the target audience; these restrictions are under challenge in federal court.[43] State and local agencies may be more or less strict than the federal rule. Private donations and other funds from nongovernment sources, however, are not subject to these rules.

What is the legal definition of "obscenity"?
The Supreme Court has interpreted the First Amendment so that its protection of expression does not cover materials that meet the definition of obscenity. There is a three-part test for what constitutes obscenity. To be found obscene, material must run afoul of all three parts of the test: First, that to an average person applying contemporary community standards, the material taken as a whole appeals to the prurient interest; second, that the material depicts or describes in a patently offensive way certain sexual conduct as specified by state law; and, third, that the material, taken as a whole, lacks serious literary, artistic, political, or scientific value.[44]

Because this test is an interpretation of the federal Constitution, state courts are required to recognize at least that much protection for speech, but they also may interpret their state constitutions to provide more protection. In Oregon, the state supreme court has ruled that the state constitution protects sexually explicit speech to the same degree as other categories of speech and has declared that there is no obscenity exception to the free speech guarantee under that state's constitution.[45]

Are sexually explicit lesbian and gay books and films obscene?
Unless all three prongs of the test for obscenity are met, a text or image cannot be found obscene. Any material found to have serious literary, artistic, political, or scientific value, therefore, by definition cannot be adjudged obscene. An exhibition of photographs by Robert Mapplethorpe, some of which

were homoerotic, formed the basis for an obscenity prosecution
in Cincinnati in 1990, but the jury acquitted the defendants
(the museum that sponsored the exhibit and its director) of the
charge of obscenity because of the artistic value of the work.
The simple fact that materials are homoerotic is not sufficient
grounds for a legal determination that they are obscene.

NOTES

1. Truscott, *Gay Power Comes to Sheridan Square*, The Village Voice, July 3, 1969.
2. *See generally* D. Teal, *The Gay Militants* (1971); D. Altman, *Homosexual Oppression and Liberation* ch. 4 (1971).
3. Pub. L. No. 100–202, § 514 (1987).
4. The restriction was contained in an amendment to an appropriations bill governing federal health and education funds. 134 Cong. Rec. 10132 (July 27, 1988). Although the restriction was adopted by the Senate, it was later deleted before the bill became law. C. Kittredge, *Approach to Gay Life an Issue*, Boston Globe, Aug. 25, 1988, at 30.
5. For other examples of attempts to censor speech related to homosexuality, see LaMarche & Rubenstein, *The Love That Dare Not Speak: Censoring Gay Expression*, The Nation, Nov. 5, 1990, at 524.
6. *Gay Students Org. v. Bonner*, 367 F. Supp. 1088 (D.N.H.), *aff'd*, 509 F.2d 652 (1st Cir. 1974); *Gay Activists Alliance v. Lomenzo*, 38 A.D. 2d 981, 329 N.Y.S. 2d 181 (3d Dept. 1972), *aff'd*, 31 N.Y. 2d 965, 341 N.Y.S. 2d 108 (1973).
7. *Gay Activists Alliance v. Lomenzo, supra* note 6.
8. *Id.* 329 N.Y.S. 2d at 182.
9. *Id.*
10. Rev. Rul. 78–305, 1978–33 I.R.B.
11. *NAACP v. Alabama*, 357 U.S. 449 (1958).
12. *Bates v. Little Rock*, 361 U.S. 516 (1960).
13. *Buckley v. Valeo*, 424 U.S. 1 (1976).
14. *Id.*
15. *Barenblatt v. United States*, 360 U.S. 109 (1959).
16. *Beilan v. Board of Educ.*, 357 U.S. 399, 405 (1958).
17. *Acanfora v. Board of Educ. of Montgomery Cnty.*, 491 F.2d 498 (4th Cir. 1974).
18. *Healy v. James*, 408 U.S. 169 (1971); *Gay Students Org. v. Bonner, supra* note 6.
19. *Gay Students Org. v. Bonner, supra* note 6; *Gay Alliance of Students*

    v. Matthews, 544 F.2d 162 (4th Cir. 1976); *Gay Lib v. Univ. of Missouri*, 558 F.2d 848 (8th Cir. 1977), *cert. denied, sub nom. Ratchford v. Gay Lib*, 434 U.S. 1080 (1978)(with forceful dissent by Rehnquist, J.); *Student Coalition for Gay Rights v. Austin Peay State Univ.*, 477 F. Supp. 1267 (M.D. Tenn. 1979).

20. *Healy v. James, supra* note 18.

21. *Gay Students Org. v. Bonner, supra* note 6.

22. *Gay and Lesbian Student Ass'n v. Gohn*, 850 F.2d 361 (8th Cir. 1988).

23. *Tinker v. Des Moines Indep. Community School Dist.*, 393 U.S. 503 (1969).

24. See *Hazelwood School Dist. v. Kuhlmeier*, 484 U.S. 260 (1988) (school officials allowed to require deletion of articles on pregnancy and divorce from newspaper published by school journalism class); *Bethel School Dist. v. Fraser*, 478 U.S. 675 (1986) (upholding suspension of student for making "vulgar" speech, which led to disruption, to student assembly).

25. 20 U.S.C. §4071 *et seq.* (1982). School authorities can forbid only meetings which would "materially and substantially interfere with the orderly conduct of educational activities within the school." 20 U.S.C. §4071(c)(4).

26. *Fricke v. Lynch*, 491 F. Supp. 381 (D.R.I. 1980), *vacated and remanded*, 627 F.2d 1088 (1st Cir. 1981).

27. *National Gay Task Force v. Board of Educ. of Oklahoma City*, 729 F.2d 1270 (10th Cir. 1984), *aff'd by an equally divided court*, 470 U.S. 903 (1985).

28. *Acanfora v. Board of Educ., supra* note 17.

29. *Aumiller v. University of Del.*, 434 F. Supp. 1273 (D. Del. 1977).

30. *Pickering v. Board of Educ.*, 391 U.S. 563 (1968).

31. *Clark v. Community for Creative Non-Violence*, 468 U.S. 288, 293 (1984); *Grayned v. City of Rockford*, 408 U.S. 104, 115 (1972).

32. In *Olivieri v. Ward*, 801 F.2d 602 (2d Cir. 1986), for example, a federal appeals court invalidated a New York City police order that had closed the sidewalk in front of St. Patrick's Cathedral to Dignity, the organization of lesbian and gay Catholics, during the annual gay pride march. The court held that closure of the sidewalk was not justified by the threat of violence from counterdemonstrators. The court then fashioned an order requiring the police to grant equal time for demonstrating directly in front of St. Patrick's to each of the two opposing groups.

33. *Shuttlesworth v. City of Birmingham*, 394 U.S. 147 (1969).

34. *West Virginia v. Barnette*, 319 U.S. 624 (1943).

35. *Gay Law Students Ass'n v. Pacific Tel. and Tel. Co.*, 24 Cal. 3d 458, 156 Cal. Rptr. 14, 595 P.2d 592 (1979).

36. No. 85–404, 69 Ops. Atty. Gen. Cal. 80 (1986).

37. *Van Ooteghem v. Gray*, 628 F.2d 488 (5th Cir. 1980), *aff'd en banc* 654 F.2d 304 (1981), *cert. denied*, 455 U.S. 909 (1982).

38. *Acanfora v. Board of Educ.*, *supra* note 17.

39. *Rowland v. Mad River Local School Dist.*, 730 F.2d 444 (6th Cir. 1984), *cert. denied*, 470 U.S. 1009 (1985).

40. *McConnell v. Anderson*, 451 F.2d 193, 196 (8th Cir. 1971), *cert. denied*, 405 U.S. 1046 (1972).

41. *Singer v. U.S. Civil Service Comm'n*, 530 F.2d 247 (9th Cir. 1976), *vacated and remanded*, 429 U.S. 1034 (1977).

42. *Gay Activists Alliance v. Washington Metropolitan Area Transit Auth.*, 48 U.S.L.W. 2053 (D.D.C. 1979). *See also Alaska Gay Coalition v. Sullivan*, 578 P.2d 951 (Ala. 1978).

43. *Gay Men's Health Crisis v. Sullivan*, 733 F. Supp. 619 (S.D.N.Y. 1989).

44. *Miller v. California*, 413 U.S. 15 (1973).

45. *Oregon v. Henry*, 302 Or. 510, 732 P.2d 9 (1987).

II
Employment

While the past few decades have brought significant changes to the American workplace and to the rules that govern employment, the law still accords great latitude to employers.

Traditionally, an employer—at least an employer other than the government itself—could hire or fire any employee whenever it wanted and for whatever reason. This rule, known to lawyers as the "employment at will" doctrine, meant, as one court put it in 1884, that a worker could be discharged "for good cause, for no cause or even for cause morally wrong."[1]

But, happily, the employment at will doctrine is no longer the whole story. In recent years, Congress and many state and local legislatures have engrafted exceptions onto the doctrine, such as the federal Civil Rights Act of 1964, which outlaws discrimination on account of race, color, religion, sex, and national origin. Some state courts have also limited the doctrine's scope. And many employers have voluntarily adopted policies of nondiscrimination, especially large corporations. Today it would be more accurate to say that a worker can be fired for a good reason or a bad reason but not for a prohibited reason.

In most parts of the country, lesbians and gay men are still outside the protective arm of the law and still subject to the stern command of employment at will. Nonetheless, there are favorable omens, especially for employees of the government.

PRIVATE EMPLOYMENT

Can a private employer lawfully discriminate against an employee on account of his or her sexual orientation?

Unless forbidden by a state or local law, in most situations it may. There is no federal law that prevents a private employer—large or small, incorporated or unincorporated—from refusing to hire, firing, undercompensating, or otherwise treating differently any lesbian or gay employee solely because of that person's sexual orientation and regardless of aptitude or work record. Although Congress has outlawed discrimination on the basis of "race, color, religion, sex, or national origin" and, more recently, "disability,"[2] it has not yet seen fit to include sexual orientation within the reach of federal law.

Some other legislative bodies have done so. Five states— Connecticut, Hawaii, Massachusetts, New Jersey, and Wisconsin—now forbid discrimination based on sexual orientation. ("Sexual orientation" is the term most commonly used in legislation of this kind and the expression preferred by activists. The phrase "affectional or sexual preference" appears in some older laws.) And most large cities ban such discrimination, including New York, Los Angeles, Chicago, Philadelphia, Detroit, Atlanta, Boston, San Diego, San Francisco, Seattle, Minneapolis, St. Paul, Baltimore, Pittsburgh, and Washington, D.C. A large number of smaller cities, and some counties, have also acted to protect lesbians and gay men in the workplace. (For a full listing of these laws, see Appendix C.)

All in all, these statutes and ordinances cover more than one-eighth of the entire population of the United States, a remarkable accomplishment in light of the fact that before 1971 no law of this sort existed anywhere.

Are persons living in a place without such a law totally without recourse?

Not necessarily. If there is a written contract with the employer, and that contract limits the circumstances of the employee's discharge, the employee may be able to sue the employer for breach of contract. If, in a union shop, the agreement between the union and the employer requires "just cause" for termination or sets forth certain procedural guarantees that were disregarded by the employer, there may also be a claim.

There may be other arguments as well, depending on the state and whether the courts there have been sympathetic to challenges to the employment at will doctrine. Some state courts have invalidated dismissals that, in their eyes, violate "public policy."[3] Others have read into each employment relationship an "implied covenant of good faith and fair dealing."[4] Still others have inferred from the particular circumstances of employment a promise that the employee would not be fired arbitrarily.[5] Very few lesbian or gay plaintiffs have ever succeeded on claims of this sort, but state courts seem increasingly open to such assertions.[6]

Inventive lawyers and tenacious plaintiffs can make startling changes in the law. In 1979 the California Supreme Court rendered a remarkable opinion striking down the discriminatory employment practices of Pacific Telephone and Telegraph Company, the local subsidiary at that time of AT&T. Pacific Telephone was a private company, and California had no statute barring discrimination on account of sexual orientation, but the court accepted an ingenious theory offered by the plaintiffs' lawyers that arose from the special nature of the company's business. Pacific Telephone, while private, was, according to the court, a "state-protected monopoly or quasi-monopoly" and was therefore obligated under the state constitution, as well as various state statutes, to "avoid arbitrary employment discrimination."[7]

In some circumstances, discrimination related to a worker's sexual orientation may also constitute discrimination of another kind. The dismissal of a lesbian who is divorced and, in addition, HIV-positive could lead to claims of sex discrimination, marital-status discrimination, and disability discrimination, depending on the facts surrounding the dismissal. (See chapter 8, "The Rights of People with HIV Disease," for a more thorough discussion of how disability and handicap discrimination laws protect people with AIDS and HIV.) In California firing someone because he or she came out to an employer or worked for the passage of gay-rights legislation, among other things, would probably violate the state's labor code, which prohibits employers from interfering with their employee's political activities.[8]

It is best, in any event, to consult with a lawyer who specializes in employment discrimination whenever such discrimination arises or is anticipated.

What action can be taken if a person suffers discrimination and lives in a place that outlaws sexual-orientation discrimination?

Again, a lawyer should be sought, if possible. All records that relate to the employment and dismissal, including any performance appraisals and any general personnel documents, such as a handbook, should be provided to the lawyer. The greatest barrier to success in most employment discrimination cases is the lack of sufficient proof. Generally, the burden is on the worker to prove that the discriminatory act resulted from a forbidden motive, not on the employer to show that it arose from another, permissible cause.

In some jurisdictions, a lawyer is not necessary to formally challenge discrimination. A form can be filed at a human rights commission or similar agency; there may be a small fee. The worker then waits for a response from the employer, who is notified of the allegations by the agency. Even under these circumstances, it is best to speak first with a lawyer who is able to explain all the available options.

Is it discrimination if a person is fired for talking about being gay, for wearing a button, or for holding his or her lover's hand in public?

Gay people are entitled to to be treated in the same way, and judged according to the same standards, as their heterosexual colleagues. The rules that govern the workplace must be applied in an evenhanded way. What is permissible, and what is not, depends largely on the context. Lesbian and gay employees should be able, for example, to have pictures of their lovers on their desks if heterosexual employees are permitted similar pictures of their spouses and families. If, however, the company prohibits personal photographs of all kinds on the desks of all employees, a denial to the gay employee is not discriminatory—merely unreasonable.

Some older cases maintain that lesbians and gay men, even when otherwise protected from discrimination, may not "flaunt" their homosexuality. In one opinion rendered in 1976, a federal appellate court upheld the dismissal of a clerk typist for the federal Equal Employment Opportunity Commission (exquisite irony!) because he had engaged, in its words, in "open flaunting and careless display of unorthodox sexual conduct in public." His "flaunting" consisted in part of writing a letter to the commission that said, "I work for the E.E.O.C. and am openly Gay," and of instituting a lawsuit seeking the right to marry another man.[9] There has been little recent precedent on this question, and it is unclear how modern courts would look at it. At its core, the reference to "flaunting" in the older cases reflects nothing more than a desire to suppress gay people and a total violation of the principle of evenhandedness articulated above.

Can an employer offer benefits to married employees—such as health benefits for spouses—that are denied to single employees, and therefore lesbian and gay employees?

Many employers offer special benefits to employees who are married—from health insurance to bereavement leave—and such benefits can substantially increase the compensation those employees receive. In several recent cases, lesbian and gay employees have challenged the legality of such plans, claiming that they amount to discrimination on account of sexual orientation (since gay couples are denied the right to marry and are therefore unable to obtain the benefits through that avenue) or discrimination on account of marital status. The only appellate decision on this question, rendered in 1985 by a court in California, rejected both arguments.[10] Other cases are pending.

PUBLIC EMPLOYMENT

Can the government discriminate against its employees on account of their sexual orientation?

As a general rule, no. Governmental employers—whether local, state, or federal—are subject to constitutional requirements providing for fair treatment of all individuals. The government need not act identically toward all people, but it must, at a minimum, act rationally and not capriciously. (Note the contrast of this rule with the employment at will doctrine covering private employers.)

In 1969 the U.S. Court of Appeals for the District of Columbia, perhaps the second most important federal court in the country, specifically addressed the issue of homosexuality and federal employment in the case of a man who had been fired by the National Aeronautics and Space Administration for "immoral conduct." The man, Clifford Norton, had been arrested by officers of the morals squad of the District of Columbia Police Department for a traffic violation after they observed him attempting to make the acquaintance of another man in Lafayette Square, directly across from the White House. The court overturned the dismissal, declaring that it could not take place without "some reasonably foreseeable, specific connection between [the] employee's potentially embarrassing conduct and the efficiency of the service." It also rejected the idea that an assertion of "immorality" by itself could justify a termination.

> We are not prepared to say that the Commission could not reasonably find appellant's homosexual advance to be "immoral," "indecent," or "notoriously disgraceful" under dominant conventional norms. But the notion that it could be an appropriate function of the federal bureaucracy to enforce the majority's conventional codes of conduct in the private lives of its employees is at war with elementary concepts of liberty, privacy, and diversity.[11]

On the basis of this and other decisions, the Civil Service Commission issued, in December of 1973, the following directive to federal supervisors.

> You may not find a person unsuitable for Federal employment merely because that person is a homosexual or has engaged in homosexual acts, nor may such exclusion be based on a conclusion that a homosexual person might bring the public service into public contempt. You are, however, permitted to dismiss a person or find him or her unsuitable for Federal employment where the evidence establishes that such person's homosexual conduct affects job fitness—excluding from such consideration, however, unsubstantiated conclusions concerning possible embarrassment to the Federal Service.[12]

This directive, the substance of which is still in effect, recognizes that the suitability of employees must be determined individually and not on the supposed characteristics of an entire class of people. It is no guarantee of job security, but it constitutes a substantial improvement in the law.

In 1978 Congress enacted the Civil Service Reform Act. Although the act makes no specific mention of homosexuality, it does state that supervisors may not discriminate "on the basis of conduct which does not adversely affect the performance of the employee or applicant or the performance of others."[13] This statutory change would seem to enhance further the employment rights of federal workers who are lesbian or gay.

In the late 1940s and early 1950s, in the cold-war frenzy fostered by Senator Joseph McCarthy and others, at least 1,700 federal workers lost their jobs on allegations of homosexuality.[14]

Against that backdrop, the present policies of the Civil Service Commission represent a virtual revolution in the law.

Aren't there some federal departments and agencies that still explicitly discriminate against lesbians and gay men?

Indeed there are. All the branches of the military still exclude gay people from enlistment, alleging that "homosexuality is incompatible with military service."[15] The mere admission that one is gay will lead to rejection or expulsion. Unlike the Department of Defense, the FBI and the CIA claim to evaluate candidates for employment individually, but gay men and lesbians are almost invariably turned down, purportedly because of security concerns.[16]

Many individuals have challenged these policies of exclusion through lawsuits, but the courts have so far, with minor exceptions, declined to overturn them, accepting at face value the government's claims that these agencies are special and that lesbians and gay men represent threats to national security and to internal discipline.[17] Ultimately, however, the policies will almost certainly fall since they rest on nothing more substantial than the prejudices and canards that once permeated all of federal employment. In time, the principles in the *Norton* case, described above, will extend to these agencies as well.

To what degree can state and local governments discriminate against lesbians and gay men?

The constitutional precept of evenhandedness applies to state and local governments just as it does the federal government. Indeed, the fifty states have constitutions of their own that reinforce the idea that government should not act arbitrarily or irrationally. Thus what the *Norton* case said about the federal government should apply with equal force to state and local agencies. (In a number of states, governors have issued executive orders specifically declaring that lesbians and gay men are entitled to equal treatment in state employment.[18])

The courts, however, have not always been openminded or consistent in reviewing these issues. In 1981, for instance, a federal district court in Texas validated the refusal of the Dallas Police Department to hire an openly gay man to work in its property room. "There is legitimate concern about tension between known and active homosexuals and others who detest homosexuals," wrote the judge. "There are also legitimate doubts about a homosexual's ability to gain the trust and respect of the personnel with whom he works," he added.[19]

Eventually, such an opinion will come to be seen as an outdated curiosity. In the meantime, government employees at all levels should exercise prudence, while keeping in mind that they enjoy—at least theoretically—constitutional protections denied workers in the private sector.

Can a public school fire or refuse to hire a lesbian or gay teacher solely on account of that person's sexual orientation?

The answer should be "no," for the reasons articulated in the *Norton* case, but the law on this issue is inconsistent—indeed, baldly contradictory.

Some school systems, like that of the District of Columbia and New York City, explicitly prohibit discrimination against a teacher on account of sexual orientation. And some courts have explicitly vindicated the rights of gay teachers. The most respected and significant opinion on this subject was issued in 1969 by the Supreme Court of California. In that case, *Morrison v. State Board of Education*, the court held that the state could not revoke a teaching license on the ground of homosexual conduct unless it could demonstrate "unfitness to teach." The court then set forth the following factors for consideration by the state:

> the likelihood that the conduct may have adversely affected students or fellow teachers, the degree of such adversity anticipated, the proximity or remoteness in time of the conduct, the type of teaching certificate held by the party involved, the extenuating or aggravating circumstances, if any, surrounding the conduct, the praiseworthiness or blameworthiness of the motives resulting in the conduct, the likelihood of the recurrence of the questioned conduct, and the extent to which disciplinary action may inflict an adverse impact or chilling effect upon the constitutional rights of the teacher involved or other teachers.

The court stressed that any finding of unfitness had to be supported by factual evidence and could not rest on general suppositions of impropriety or "immorality."[20]

Morrison may be the most authoritative opinion on this issue, but, sadly, it has been distorted, misunderstood, and even disregarded by authorities in other states. Eight years after *Morrison,* the Supreme Court of Washington upheld the dismissal of a "known homosexual" by a high school in Tacoma, Washington, accepting without question the conclusion of the trial court that the mere fact of his homosexuality, once known by students and other teachers, "impaired" his efficiency.[21] Several years later, the federal courts sustained the firing of a guidance counselor by a school system in southern Ohio because she had told a secretary and several teaching colleagues that she was bisexual.[22] And in 1983 the attorney general of West Virginia rendered a written opinion expressing his official view that a school board may discharge for "immorality" a teacher who is lesbian or gay since, as he averred, "lesbianism and homosexuality are forms of immorality in most West Virginia communities."[23]

It is important to add that in virtually all states, criminal convictions for certain crimes—including, among others, those involving serious sexual misconduct—will lead automatically to the revocation of a teaching license.[24]

Of all public employees, teachers are the most susceptible to dismissal and discrimination. The myths that gay people molest and recruit children, although completely without basis, still haunt the profession. Thus, even in states with explicit legal protections like California, care and common sense are advisable.

Can a state deny a professional or occupational license on account of an applicant's sexual orientation?

In general, no. Candidates for such licenses—covering everything from the practice of law to massage therapy—must usually show they possess "good moral character." In the past, before the modern gay rights movement, the "good moral character" requirement posed a problem for any lesbian or gay man since, as the teaching cases above show, homosexuality was automatically assumed to preclude a finding of moral fitness. These days are largely, but not entirely over, at least for occupations *not* involving the care of children.

The Supreme Court declared in 1957 in a case involving an applicant to the bar of New Mexico: "A state can require high standards or qualifications, such as good moral character or proficiency in its law, before it admits an applicant to the bar, but any qualification must have a rational connection with the applicant's fitness or capacity to practice law."[25] Lower courts have now explicitly extended that precedent to lesbians and gay men.[26] As the Florida Supreme Court stated prosaically in 1981, "Private noncommercial sex acts between consenting adults are not relevant to prove fitness to practice law."[27]

NOTES

1. *Payne v. Western Atl. R.R.*, 81 Tenn. 507, 519–20 (1884), *rev'd on other grounds sub nom. Hutton v. Watters,* 132 Tenn. 527, 179 S.W. 134 (1915).

2. *See* Civil Rights Act of 1964, 42 U.S.C. § 2000e–2 and Americans with Disabilities Act of 1990, 42 U.S.C. § 12112. These two statutes only apply to employers with 15 or more employees. The courts have uniformly rejected the argument that the term "sex" in the Civil Rights Act of 1964 should cover sexual-orientation discrimination; *see, e.g., DeSantis v. Pacific Tel. & Tel. Co.*, 608 F.2d 327 (9th Cir. 1979) and *Smith v. Liberty Mut. Ins. Co.*, 569 F.2d 325 (5th Cir. 1978).

3. *See, e.g., Peterman v. International Bhd. of Teamsters,* 174 Cal. App. 2d 184, 344 P.2d 25 (1959)(dismissal based on employee's refusal to perjure himself violates public policy); *Payne v. Rozendaal*, 147 Vt. 488, 520 A.2d 586 (1986)(termination of an employee based solely on age violates public policy).

4. *See Cleary v. American Airlines, Inc.*, 111 Cal. App. 3d 443, 453, 168 Cal. Rptr. 722, 728 (2d Dist. 1980). *See also Fortune v. National Cash Register Co.*, 373 Mass. 96, 364 N.E.2d 1251 (1977). *Cf. Criscione v. Sears Roebuck & Co.*, 66 Ill. App. 3d 664, 384 N.E.2d 91 (1st Dist. 1978).

5. *See, e.g., Toussaint v. Blue Cross & Blue Shield of Mich.*, 408 Mich. 579, 292 N.W.2d 880 (1980); *Rabago-Alvarez v. Dart Industries, Inc.*, 55 Cal. 3d 91, 127 Cal. Rptr. 222 (1976).

6. In June of 1991, a judge in Alameda County, California, awarded $5.3 million to a gay man who had been fired by the Shell Oil Co. in violation of explicit assurances by it that no one would be fired for activities outside the work place. See San Francisco Chronicle, June 18, 1991, at A16. In *Madsen v. Erwin*, 395 Mass. 715, 481 N.E.2d 1160 (1985), the Supreme Judicial Court of Massachusetts rejected most of the unjust dismissal claims against the *Christian Science Monitor* brought by a writer who had been fired by the newspaper

because of her admission that she was gay, largely on the ground that the defendant was engaged in a religious enterprise and was therefore insulated by the First Amendment's religious guarantees. The court's focus on the religious character of her employer implies that such claims might prevail against a secular defendant.

7. *Gay Law Students Ass'n v. Pacific Tel. & Tel. Co.*, 24 Cal. 3d 458, 595 P.2d 592, 156 Cal. Rptr. 14 (1979).

8. *See* Cal. Lab. Code §§ 1101, 1102. *See generally Fort v. Civil Serv. Comm'n*, 61 Cal. 2d 331 (1964); *Gay Law Students Ass'n, supra* note 7, 24 Cal. 3d at 486, 595 P.2d at 609, 156 Cal. Rptr. at 31 (1979). In 1986 the attorney general of California issued a written opinion expressing his view that these provisions of the Labor Code protect not only lesbians and gay men who engage in overt political activity, but also those who have not actually declared or acted upon their political beliefs. *See* 69 Op. Att. Gen. Cal. 80 (1986). *See also Soroka v. Dayton Hudson Corp.*, 235 Cal. App. 3d 654, 1 Cal Rptr. 2d 77 (1st Dist. 1991) (appeal pending) ("These statutes . . . prohibit a private employer from discriminating against an employee on the basis of his or her sexual orientation").

9. *Singer v. United States Civil Serv. Comm'n*, 530 F.2d 247 (9th Cir. 1976) *vacated*, 429 U.S. 1034 (1977). The case was subsequently remanded to the Civil Service Commission for reconsideration in light of new regulations relating to an employee's "suitability" for employment; *see* Rivera, *Our Straight-Laced Judges: The Legal Position of Homosexual Persons in the United States*, 30 Hastings L.J. 799, 822–25 (1979). For a similar opinion, see *McConnell v. Anderson*, 451 F.2d 193 (8th Cir. 1971).

10. *Hinman v. Department of Personnel Admin.*, 167 Cal. App. 3d 516, 213 Cal. Rptr. 410 (1985).

11. *Norton v. Macy*, 417 F.2d 1161 (D.C. Cir. 1969).

12. *Civil Service Bulletin*, Dec. 21, 1973, quoted in *Ashton v. Civiletti*, 613 F.2d 923, 927 (D.C. Cir. 1979).

13. 5 U.S.C. § 2302(b)(10).

14. *See* J. D'Emilio, *Sexual Politics, Sexual Communities: The Making of a Homosexual Minority in the United States 1940–1970* 44 (1983).

15. *See* ch. 4 ("The Armed Services").

16. *See, e.g., Padula v. Webster*, 822 F.2d 97 (D.C. Cir. 1987)(F.B.I. policies and practices); and *Dubbs v. Central Intelligence Agency*, 866 F.2d 1114 (9th Cir. 1989) (C.I.A. policies and practices). *See also* ch. 3 ("Security Clearances").

17. *See, e.g., Beller v. Middendorf*, 632 F.2d 788 (9th Cir. 1980), *cert. denied*, 452 U.S. 905 (1981)(military generally); *Dronenburg v. Zech*, 741 F.2d 1388 (D.C. Cir. 1984)(navy); *ben-Shalom v. Marsh*, 881 F.2d

454 (7th Cir. 1989)(army); *Padula v. Webster*, 822 F.2d 97 (D.C. Cir. 1987)(F.B.I.). For an unusual example of a successful challenge, see *Watkins v. U.S. Army*, 875 F.2d 699 (9th Cir. 1989)(en banc), *cert. denied*, 111 S. Ct. 384 (1990)(Army is equitably estopped from barring plaintiff's reenlistment since it has had full knowledge of his homosexuality and repeatedly permitted previous enlistments).

18. As of this writing, California, Minnesota, New Jersey, New Mexico, New York, Ohio, Pennsylvania, Rhode Island, and Washington have such executive orders. *See* Appendix C.

19. *See Childers v. Dallas Police Dep't*, 513 F. Supp. 134 (N.D. Tex. 1981).

20. *See Morrison v. State Board of Education*, 1 Cal. 3d 214, 461 P.2d 375, 82 Cal. Rptr. 175 (1969). In two subsequent cases, the California Supreme Court elaborated upon the principles set forth in *Morrison*. In *Pettit v. State Board of Education*, 10 Cal. 3d 29, 513 P.2d 889, 109 Cal. Rptr. 665 (1973), the court upheld the license revocation of a teacher who had engaged in three separate acts of oral sex with men other than her husband at a private party and also appeared on television in partial disguise to talk about "nonconventional sexual life styles"; the court distinguished *Morrison* by asserting the teacher's alleged "total lack of concern for privacy, decorum or preservation of her dignity and reputation." In *Board of Education v. Jack M.*, 19 Cal. 3d 691, 566 P.2d 602, 139 Cal. Rptr. 700 (1977), the court overturned the dismissal of a gay man who had been arrested but not convicted of lewd conduct for allegedly soliciting a police officer in a public restroom; the court stressed the teacher's long and unblemished teaching record, declaring that "[p]roof of the commission of a criminal act does not alone demonstrate the unfitness of the teacher, but is simply one of the factors to be considered." For another important appellate decision upholding the constitutional rights of gay teachers, see *National Gay Task Force v. Board of Education*, 729 F.2d 1270 (10th Cir. 1984), *aff'd by an equally divided Court*, 470 U.S. 903 (1985)(portion of Oklahoma statute authorizing the dismissal of a teacher for the mere advocacy of gay rights violates the First Amendment).

21. *See Gaylord v. Tacoma School Dist. No. 10*, 88 Wash. 2d 286, 559 P.2d 1340, *cert. denied*, 434 U.S. 879 (1977). For a similar case, see *Safransky v. State Personnel Bd.*, 62 Wis. 2d 464, 215 N.W.2d 379 (1974)(upholding the dismissal of a gay man as the houseparent of a state-run home for mentally retarded boys on the ground that he failed to project, in the words of the court, "the orthodoxy of male heterosexuality").

22. *See Rowland v. Mad River Local School Dist.*, 730 F.2d 444 (6th Cir.

1984), *cert. denied*, 470 U.S. 1099 (1985). Justice Brennan, joined by Justice Marshall, issued a passionate dissenting opinion to the Supreme Court's refusal to consider this case. He wrote, "[D]iscrimination against homosexuals or bisexuals based solely on their sexual preference raises significant constitutional questions under both prongs of our settled equal protection analysis." 470 U.S. at 1014.

23. *See* Op. Att. Gen. W. Va., slip op. (Feb. 24, 1983).

24. *See, e.g.*, Cal. Ed. Code §§ 44425, 44010. Crimes requiring automatic revocation of a teaching license in California include unlawful sexual intercourse with a female under 18, incest, sodomy with another person under 18, lewd and lascivious acts with a child under 14, oral copulation with another person under 18, and disorderly conduct involving the solicitation to engage in lewd or dissolute conduct in public.

25. *See Schware v. Board of Bar Examiners*, 353 U.S. 232 (1957).

26. *See, e.g., Application of Kimball*, 33 N.Y.2d 586, 347 N.Y.S.2d 453, 301 N.E.2d 436 (1973); *Florida Board of Bar Examiners Re N.R.S.*, 403 So. 2d 1315 (Fla. 1981).

27. *N.R.S., supra* note 26, at 1317.

III

Security Clearances

Certain federal employees and certain employees in the private sector are required to have security clearances if they need access to classified documents in the course of their work. The jobs from which openly gay men and lesbian women have been most uniformly excluded in recent times have been those involving access to information classified by the government.

The federal government's policy of requiring security clearances for a wide range of jobs and of denying clearance to known or suspected homosexuals has its roots in the post-World War II period. Prior to that time, with the exception of the military, neither the federal government nor private employers routinely inquired into the sexual orientation of employees. In the anti-Communist hysteria of the late 1940s and 1950s, this situation changed dramatically. During the cold-war period a concerted campaign developed to exclude lesbians and gay men from important jobs in the federal government.[1] That campaign has continued, although there are signs that the situation is changing.

Perhaps the most salient change is that most security clearances for gay applicants are regularly (if not routinely) granted. This has come about because lesbian and gay Americans have had the courage to be honest about their homosexuality. As a result, the primary governmental argument against according them security clearances—that gay people are greater security risks because they are more liable to blackmail—has lost most of its force.[2] A dramatic indication of the weakness of that contention was the admission in 1991 by Secretary of Defense Richard Cheney that "it was a bit of an old chestnut."[3]

In lieu of the traditional blackmail rationale, the government increasingly relies on claims that "indirect blackmail" is possible. It asserts that although openly gay people are themselves not at risk for blackmail, their acquaintances may be, and that threats of exposure directed at friends and lovers may provide a means for hostile governments to acquire information from lesbians and gay men holding security clearances.[4]

At the same time, with respect to employment generally—

as opposed to obtaining a security clearance for such employment—there are certain ambiguities that create a treacherous situation for gay people. On the job, open affirmations of homosexuality or bisexuality may legally lead to dismissal.[5] There exists a fine line between the personal honesty that invalidates a blackmail rationale and either a desire to keep one's intimate life private or, on the other hand, an openness of expression that may lead to charges that the individual is "embarrassing" an employer. Thus, an openly gay worker seeking a security clearance is faced with a catch–22: being honest enough not to be liable to blackmail, but not so honest that statements are found to be disruptive.

What is a security clearance?
It is a license from a department or agency of the federal government giving its holder access to classified information he or she has a need to know.

What kinds of security clearances are there?
The type of security clearance depends on the governmental agency or department involved. The most frequently sought levels of classification are confidential, secret, top secret, and sensitive compartmentalized information (SCI).

Who is required to have a government-issued security clearance?
Federal employees who occupy a "sensitive" position, defined as "any position . . . the occupant of which could bring about, by virtue of the nature of the position, a material adverse effect on the national security."[6] The heads of federal departments and agencies must ensure that all permanent occupants of such positions have a security clearance. In addition, the program covers various private-sector industries engaged in defense-related research and manufacturing activities. At the end of 1983, approximately 2,725,000 government civilian and military personnel had security clearances, as did 1,500,000 employees of private contracting firms.

How is the security-clearance program for federal employees administered?
Most federal departments and agencies rely on the Defense

Investigative Service to conduct security investigations, although some (including the Department of Energy, the State Department, and the Federal Bureau of Investigation) have their own security-clearance programs.

Have lesbians and gay men been able to secure and retain security clearances?

Yes. Most agencies that grant clearances, including the Department of Defense and the Department of Energy, no longer automatically exclude lesbians and gay men because of their sexual orientation.[7] The most recalcitrant departments were the so-called police agencies (including the CIA and the FBI) that continued to apply apparently per se antigay rules.[8] In 1991, however, the CIA agreed to settle a lawsuit challenging its policy by reconsidering an openly lesbian applicant for a security clearance and treating homosexual conduct and associations on the same basis as heterosexual activities.[9]

At present, nearly all gay applicants can get ordinary secret and top secret clearances; the army and the National Security Agency have granted only a few SCI clearances to gay workers. Lesbians and gay men are routinely subjected to expanded investigations, however. These expanded investigations can, as a practical matter, disqualify lesbian and gay applicants even if no security concerns are revealed because they may take so long to complete that the employer has to select another worker who can go forward with a project with less delay. Unfortunately, the policy of ordering expanded investigations whenever an applicant is gay has been upheld by the courts.[10]

What is the legal basis for denial of a security clearance?

Federal departments and agencies are directed to deny applications for security clearances in cases in which the clearance official "cannot affirmatively determine that it is clearly consistent with the national interest to grant a security clearance."[11]

How does evidence of homosexuality usually come to the attention of security investigators?

Applicants are asked to provide detailed information on required forms. For example, applicants are asked if they were discharged from the military under other than honorable conditions, have ever been convicted of breaking the law, have forfeited collateral, or are presently subject to a criminal proceeding. Medical questions include whether applicants have ever been treated for a mental illness. Answers to any of these questions may provide a basis for more direct and detailed inquiries into homosexual conduct.

In addition, the Office of Personnel Management and others responsible for monitoring the access of federal employees to classified information almost always check arrest and court records and the files of other state and federal agencies, including those of the FBI. This information is supplemented by personal interviews with the applicant and her or his acquaintances. Direct questions about homosexual conduct may be asked if any answers give rise to suspicion.

Membership in gay organizations is used as evidence of possible homosexual conduct. Military discharges are also used, even those that are technically "honorable" but are recorded as being related to homosexual orientation.

Evidence of homosexual conduct may also arise in connection with the updating or upgrading of a security clearance already possessed by an employee. The investigation conducted in those circumstances closely resembles the initial investigation. At one time such investigations were initiated after a reported arrest or after a person was observed in a place known to be frequented by lesbians or gay men.

How is the present industrial security program administered?

The initial processing of industrial security clearance requests is done by the Defense Industrial Security Clearance Office (DISCO) in Columbus, Ohio. DISCO is also responsible for updating and upgrading industrial security clearances and follows essentially the same procedures in such cases as it does for the initial application. If DISCO is unable to make a determination, it contacts the Directorate for Industrial Security Clearance Review (DISCR) in Arlington, Virginia, for a final decision.

What are the significant steps in the processing of an industrial security clearance?

If DISCO approves the application, employer and employee are notified. If it makes an adverse recommendation, the application is referred to DISCR. The matter is then either returned to DISCO for further consideration or retained by DISCR. If the application is retained by DISCR, a further investigation by one of the security divisions of a branch of the military may be conducted. The applicant is often required to respond to written questions; interviews with the applicant and his or her acquaintances are also required. After DISCR makes its decision, a Statement of Reasons is issued if that decision is unfavorable to the applicant.[12]

The applicant has a right to file a written reply to the charges and to a hearing at his or her request. The applicant may be accompanied by counsel before the hearing examiner and may introduce evidence and present witnesses on his or her own behalf. Adverse witnesses may be crossexamined.

If the examiner rules against the applicant the decision may be referred to the appeal board, which makes its decision based exclusively upon the written record as transmitted to it by the hearing examiner. If the appeal board sustains the prior decision to revoke or deny a security clearance, the applicant's only remaining avenue of appeal is through a lawsuit against the government in the courts.

Security clearances usually take at least six months for gay people when all goes well. Depending on the circumstances it is not unusual for more time to elapse (sometimes, although rarely, as long as a year and a half) between the filing of the initial application and the issuance of a final decision.[13]

Is access to classified information permitted during this period?

Without an outstanding security clearance, the answer is almost invariably no. Rarely if ever are temporary clearances granted during the pendency of the review process. If an employer performs mostly government-related contract work, an applicant may not be able to work for that employer until the application is granted. During the updating or upgrading of a security clearance, an employee will generally be permitted to continue to hold that clearance during the review process, depending on the seriousness of the reservations motivating DISCO to recommend against its continuance and on the extent of the employee's willingness to cooperate with the investigation.

If a question is raised regarding a clearance on grounds of homosexual conduct, what should be done?

An applicant for a security clearance should first contact a lawyer or a gay organization with experience in such matters. If an employee holds a security clearance and a question is raised concerning sexual orientation, the employee should not respond to any inquiry, no matter how innocent it may appear, before consulting a lawyer.

If the issue is raised, should sexual orientation be denied?

Absolutely not, although unless the issue is raised by someone else, a person need not volunteer the information. Most fundamentally, a person should never give inaccurate answers in the course of a security investigation. Questions should be answered truthfully or not at all.

Generally speaking, the best policy for gay people under investigation for security clearances is openness and honesty. For example, failure to list membership in any organization, gay or nongay, is one ground for denial of a security clearance that courts are likely to uphold since such failure constitutes a falsification indicating a desire to conceal one's homosexuality.

What about family members or friends who may be interviewed as part of a security investigation?

Family members and acquaintances should be advised to tell the truth. If they know the person under investigation is gay, they should be advised to tell that to government investigators, if asked, since their knowledge will negate an inference of susceptibility to blackmail.

NOTES

1. *See* J. D'Emilio, "The Homosexual Menace: The Politics of Sexuality in Cold War America" in *Passion and Power: A History of Sexuality* 226–40 (Peiss and Simmons eds. 1989).
2. It is also worth noting that in the approximately 40 years in which the federal government has had security clearance programs in effect, there has been not one instance of successful blackmail of an American for espionage in which homosexuality was involved, although there have been espionage cases of blackmail involving heterosexual affairs. *Hear-*

ings on Security Clearances before the Subcomm. on the Civil Service of the House Comm. on Post Office and Civil Service and the Sub-comm. on Constitutional Rights of the House Comm. on the Judiciary, 101st Cong., 1st Sess. (1989) (statement of Franklin E. Kameny).

3. *Cheney Cites Problems with Anti-Homosexual Rule*, Washington Post, Aug. 1, 1991, at A7.

4. *See, e.g., High Tech Gays v. DISCO*, 895 F.2d 563 (9th Cir. 1990).

5. For private sector employees, there is little employment protection outside the states and cities where civil rights laws cover sexual orientation. *See* ch. 2. Even for government employees, "too much" honesty has led to firings. *See Rowland v. Mad River Local School Dist.*, 730 F.2d 444 (6th Cir. 1984) *cert. denied*, 470 U.S. 1009 (1985). *Singer v. U.S. Civil Service Comm'n.*, 530 F.2d 247 (9th Cir. 1976), *vacated and remanded*, 429 U.S. 1034 (1977).

6. Exec. Order No. 10,450, 18 Fed. Reg. 2489 (1953), as amended by Exec. Order No. 11,785, 39 Fed. Reg. 20053 (1974).

7. In 1987 a Defense Department spokesperson noted that homosexuality is not necessarily a bar to clearance and was quoted as saying that "we clear homosexuals year in and year out." Rice, *Lesbian Fights Demotion by Defense Department*, San Francisco Recorder, May 8, 1987, at 1,3.

8. *See, e.g., Dubbs v. CIA*, 866 F.2d 1114 (9th Cir. 1989); *Padula v. Webster*, 822 F.2d 97 (D.C. Cir. 1987).

9. *Dubbs v. Central Intelligence Agency*, No. C85–4379 EFL (N.D. Ca. June 17, 1991).

10. *See High Tech Gays v. DISCO, supra* note 3.

11. 32 C.F.R. 155.2(c), 7(a)(1990).

12. In the case of certain special access clearances no such written notice or Statement of Reasons is made.

13. For a more detailed (although dated) examination of industrial security clearance procedures, see Note, *Security Clearance for Homosexuals*, 25 Stan. L. Rev. 403, 406 *et seq.* (1973). *See also High Tech Gays, supra* note 3, at 565–69.

IV

The Armed Services

Countless lesbians and gay men have served honorably in the armed services in times of peace and war, and many are still in uniform. Nevertheless, the Department of Defense persists in characterizing homosexuality as incompatible with military service and vigorously attempts to exclude lesbians, gay men, and bisexuals from its ranks.

The discussion that follows will examine the major pitfalls faced by lesbians and gay men in the military. While the prospects for entering or remaining in the service as an openly gay man or lesbian are not encouraging, it is important to realize that service members need not sacrifice all of their constitutional rights while in military service and that the assistance of a lawyer or other qualified person can help to ensure those rights will be respected should sexual orientation become an issue.

What is the official military policy regarding lesbian and gay service members?

Department of Defense regulations provide:

Homosexuality is incompatible with military service. The presence in the military environment of persons who engage in homosexual conduct or who, by their statements, demonstrate a propensity to engage in homosexual conduct, seriously impairs the accomplishment of the military mission. The presence of such members adversely affects the ability of the Military Services to maintain discipline, good order, and morale; to foster mutual trust and confidence among service members; to ensure the integrity of the system of rank and command; to facilitate assignment and worldwide deployment of service members who frequently must live and work under close conditions affording minimal privacy; to recruit and retain members of the Military Services; to maintain the public acceptability of military service; and to prevent breaches of security.[1]

Based on the foregoing policy, the Department of Defense requires the discharge of any service member who, prior to or during military service: (1) "has engaged in, attempted to engage in, or solicited another to engage in a homosexual act"; (2) "has stated that he or she is a homosexual or bisexual"; or (3) "has married or attempted to marry a person known to be of the same biological sex."[2] A "homosexual act" is defined by the regulations as any "bodily contact, actively undertaken or passively permitted, between members of the same sex for the purpose of satisfying sexual desires." This discharge policy applies to both active duty service members and reservists.

Are there any exceptions to this policy requiring discharge?
Discharge is mandatory in all cases in which the service member is identified by the military as a homosexual or bisexual. The military's policy does permit exceptions to the requirement of discharge, but the exceptions are extremely narrow and rarely used and apply only where a person who commits or attempts to commit homosexual acts is found not to be a homosexual or bisexual. Thus, a person found to have engaged in, attempted to engage in, or solicited another to engage in a homosexual act may be retained in the military only if an administrative discharge board, with the approval of the officer designated by the secretary of the member's branch of service to act as the separation authority for that branch, makes *all* of the following findings:

(1) The conduct is a departure from the member's usual and customary behavior and, under all the circumstances, is unlikely to recur;

(2) The conduct was not accomplished by the use of force, coercion, or intimidation by the member during a period of military service;

(3) Under the particular circumstances of the case, the member's "continued presence in the Service is consistent with the interest of the Service in proper discipline, good order, and morale"; and

(4) The member does not desire to engage in or intend to engage in homosexual acts.[3]

Individuals who are being discharged because they have stated that they are homosexuals or bisexuals may remain in the service only if the administrative discharge board finds that, in fact, the member is not a homosexual or bisexual. A person being discharged for attempting to marry an individual of the same biological sex may be retained only if the board finds both that the service member is not a homosexual or bisexual and that the purpose of the marriage or attempted marriage was to avoid or terminate military service.

For these purposes, the regulations define a "homosexual" or "bisexual" as a person who "engages in, desires to engage in, or intends to engage in homosexual acts." The service member bears the burden of proving that she or he is not a homosexual or bisexual.[4]

A service member suspected of homosexuality may be discharged under other discharge provisions where circumstances warrant.[5] This is most likely to occur if the military determines that the service member fraudulently enlisted—i.e., lied in response to the questions concerning preservice homosexual conduct or "tendencies" on his or her enlistment application—or if the member is determined to be unsuitable for military service for other reasons—for example, drug or alcohol abuse or other misconduct.[6]

Can a person be court-martialed for being a homosexual?
No, but a service member may be court-martialed for conduct involving homosexuality. If the service member is alleged to have engaged in sodomy or in "indecent acts," or if the member's homosexual conduct is alleged to have violated military proscriptions against fraternization between superiors and subordinates or otherwise to have compromised good order and discipline,[7] the military may elect not to discharge the member administratively but instead to subject the member to trial by court-martial.[8]

Article 125 of the Uniform Code of Military Justice provides that any service member "who engages in unnatural carnal copulation with another person of the same or opposite sex or with an animal is guilty of sodomy. Penetration, however slight, is sufficient to complete the offense."[9] The article applies to both heterosexual and homosexual oral and anal intercourse and makes no distinction between married and unmarried partners.[10] However, the Air Force Court of Military Review recently held the constitutional right to privacy barred application of the article to "heterosexual, noncommercial, private acts of oral sex between consenting adults."[11] The government has appealed this ruling to the Court of Military Appeals.[12]

In the absence of aggravating circumstances, violation of Article 125 is punishable by dishonorable discharge (or, in the case of officers, dismissal from the service), total forfeiture of pay and allowances, fine, and confinement at hard labor for five years.[13] The so-called general articles (Article 134, prohibiting "all conduct of a nature to bring discredit upon the armed forces," and Article 133, prohibiting "conduct unbecoming an officer and a gentleman") may also be used to penalize service members accused of homosexual conduct.[14]

Fraudulent enlistment or appointment is also a crime under the Uniform Code of Military Justice, punishable by dishonorable discharge or dismissal, forfeiture of all pay and allowances, fine, and confinement for two years.[15]

Because military retirees remain subject to the Uniform Code of Military Justice, lesbians and gay men may be subject to prosecution for homosexual conduct even after they have left active military duty.[16] Moreover, a previous requirement that conduct committed by a military member in a civilian setting could not be the subject of a court-martial unless shown to be military-related has now been abolished.[17] Consequently, any conduct by a member of the military—including off-base, off-duty, same-sex relationships with civilians—may now be subject to prosecution by court-martial.

Are discharge or court-martial the only actions the military may take against suspected "homosexuals"?

No. Although discharge and court-martial are the most serious actions, the military may take or threaten other consequences as well. For example, when an individual who has received scholarship funding from the Reserve Officer Training Corps (ROTC) is discharged because of homosexuality, the military may threaten to compel repayment of the scholarship. However, negative publicity and intervention from members of Congress has led the military to back down recently in several such cases.[18]

In addition, homosexuality and certain forms of sexual conduct may be the basis for denial of a security clearance.[19] Lesbian and gay service members are often first identified by the military and referred for administrative discharge through investigations performed pursuant to applications for security clearances.

What kind of discharge can a person expect to receive if discharged for homosexuality?

There are three characterizations that may be applied to administrative discharges. An honorable discharge is appropriate "when the quality of the member's service generally has met the standards of acceptable conduct and performance of duty for military personnel, or is otherwise so meritorious that any other characterization would be clearly inappropriate." A general (under honorable conditions) discharge is awarded if the member's service "has been honest and faithful," but "significant negative aspects of the member's conduct or performance of duty outweigh positive aspects of the member's military record." A discharge under other than honorable conditions (OTH), formerly called the undesirable discharge, may be issued when the reason for separation is based upon one or more acts or omissions or upon a pattern of behavior that "constitutes a significant departure from the conduct expected of members of the Military Services."[20] Except in cases of fraudulent enlistment, an OTH discharge may not be imposed for homosexuality unless an administrative discharge board finds that, *during the member's current term of service,* the member has attempted, solicited, or committed a homosexual act in one or more of the following aggravating circumstances: "[b]y using force, coercion, or intimidation"; "[w]ith a person under 16 years of age"; "[w]ith a subordinate in circumstances that violate customary military superior-subordinate relationships"; "[o]penly in public view"; "[f]or compensation"; "[a]board a military vessel or aircraft"; or in "another location subject to military control under aggravating circumstances . . . that have an adverse impact on discipline, good order, or morale comparable to the impact of such activity aboard a vessel or aircraft."[21]

A service member who has not yet completed his or her first 180 days of continuous active duty may be issued an entry level separation in lieu of any of the foregoing characterized discharges.[22]

In addition to the various categories of administrative discharge, two types of punitive discharges may be imposed, but only pursuant to court-martial conviction. Bad conduct discharges may be given by either special or general courts-martial, while the dishonorable discharge (or its analog for officers, dismissal from the service) is the most stigmatizing form of discharge and can be imposed only by sentence of a general court martial.[23]

During the five-year period encompassing fiscal years 1985 through 1989, very few discharges (less than one percent) were on grounds related to homosexuality. Of the discharges that were issued for homosexuality, approximately 56 percent were honorable discharges, nearly 29 percent were general, and just under 7 percent were OTH discharges. The Department of Defense reported no bad conduct or dishonorable discharges for homosexuality during those years. Although these figures reflect improvement over times past when thousands of gay men and lesbians received undesirable or dishonorable discharges, they compare less favorably to overall discharges for the same period, 74 percent of which were fully honorable.[24]

What are the consequences of receiving a discharge less than fully honorable?

Recipients of anything less than a fully honorable discharge may be barred from some federal and state jobs and may encounter difficulty in obtaining civilian employment, particularly where a government-issued security clearance is required.[25] Recipients of OTH, bad conduct, and dishonorable discharges also forfeit their rights to receive payment for accrued leave, to be buried in a national cemetery, and to retain uniforms, ribbons, medals, and service bars.[26]

Numerous other service-related benefits—such as educational benefits, vocational rehabilitation, loans, special housing, hospitalization, outpatient medical and dental treatment, pensions and compensation for service-connected injuries or disabilities—are denied to recipients of dishonorable discharges and are available to the recipients of bad conduct and OTH discharges only if approved by the administering agency, usually the Veterans' Administration (VA), on a case-by-case basis.[27] Recent changes in regulations now make most persons with OTH or undesirable discharges for homosexuality eligible for VA benefits, unless aggravating circumstances were involved.[28]

How many service members are discharged from the military for homosexuality each year?

The most recent available data show that the military discharged a total of 6,670 enlisted service members and 102 officers for homosexuality in fiscal years 1985 through 1989.[29] Enlisted discharges for homosexuality declined moderately in comparison with the total number of discharges during the five-year period, while the relative rate of officer discharges for homosexuality gradually increased over the same period.

Are all of the services alike in their treatment of persons suspected of homosexuality?

All of the services are subject to the same Department of Defense policy mandating the discharge of homosexuals, although each branch has its own regulations to implement that policy.[30] However, recently published figures indicate that the services differ widely both in their rates of discharge for homosexuality and in their treatment of those discharged for that reason. The Navy discharges a much higher percentage of its enlisted members (.71 percent) than either the Army (.29 percent) or the Marines (.25 percent), while the Air Force discharge rate (.41 percent) falls in the middle.[31] The Air Force (.14 percent) and Navy (.12 percent) discharge officers for homosexuality at three to four times the rate of the Army (.03 percent) and Marine Corps (.04 percent).[32]

The Navy was the most liberal in granting honorable discharges (68 percent) to those discharged for homosexuality, while the Army gave the fewest honorable discharges (40 percent). In contrast, the Marine Corps was the most punitive in imposing OTH discharges for homosexuality (12 percent), while the Air Force had the lowest rate of OTH discharges (2 percent).[33] Significantly, for all branches except the Navy, those discharged for homosexuality were much less likely to receive Honorable discharges and significantly more likely to receive OTH discharges than the average service member being discharged.[34]

Are lesbians and gay men treated alike under the military policy?

While the policy on its face applies equally to gay men and lesbians (as do the relevant provisions of the Uniform Code of Military Justice), it appears that the military is particularly aggressive in enforcing the policy against women. During the five-year period including fiscal years 1985 through 1989, Marine Corps enlisted women were more than seven times more likely than their male counterparts to be discharged for homosexuality. Homosexuality discharge rates for women were more than double than that of men in each of the other services.[35]

This disparity in discharge rates for men and women appears to be no accident. Newspapers recently reported the disclosure of a message from the commander of the Navy's Atlantic surface fleet to the officers in charge of nearly two hundred ships and forty shore installations in the eastern half of the nation, ordering them to vigorously root out lesbian sailors even though they are generally "hard-working, career-oriented, willing to put in long hours on the job and among the command's top performers."[36]

It would also appear that the military is far from colorblind in its implementation of the homosexual discharge policy. Although blacks are generally slightly less likely than whites to find themselves discharged for homosexuality, those blacks who are discharged for homosexuality are significantly less likely than their white counterparts to receive honorable discharges and substantially more apt to receive OTH discharges.[37]

Is the military's policy effective in eliminating lesbians and gay men from the armed services?

To the contrary, the military succeeds in "weeding out" only a small percentage of the lesbians, gay men, and bisexuals who serve in this country's armed forces. Because the military's policy of exclusion requires lesbian and gay service members to conceal their sexual preference in order to avoid discharge, it is difficult to quantify with any precision their representation in the armed services. However, one study indicates that gay men are as likely as their heterosexual counterparts to enter the military and that lesbians are significantly more likely to enlist than are heterosexual women.[38] Thus, the military's own studies have concluded that approximately 10 percent of military service members are exclusively or predominantly homosexual in their adult sexual conduct and that as many as 46 percent of servicemen and more than 28 percent of servicewomen have engaged in "homosexual conduct" as defined by the military discharge regulations.[39]

Most service members who are discharged for homosexuality are not detected until they have served for some time. A study of the 4,914 men who were separated from the Army and the Air Force on the grounds of homosexuality during the period of 1981 through 1987 reported that only 28 percent were discharged in their first year; 72 percent continued to serve at least two years, almost 32 percent served more than three years, and 17 percent served five years or more before being discharged for homosexuality.[40]

The vast majority of lesbians and gay men in the military complete their terms of service undetected and are honorably discharged.[41]

How much does the military's policy of discharging lesbians and gay men cost the taxpayers each year?

A General Accounting Office report published in 1984 in response to congressional inquiries indicates that nearly $18 million is wasted each year by discharging service members for homosexuality. Of that total, more than $17.5 million, or roughly $12,300 per person, represents the cost of recruiting and training people who will ultimately be discharged as homosexuals. Another $370,000, or $230 per person, is spent each year on investigations and on processing the discharges. These figures do not include the cost of defending the military policy against challenges brought in the courts.[42]

Is the military's policy based on legitimate concern for national security—for instance, the potential for blackmail?

No. The military's own studies have concluded that homosexuality has no relationship to the ability of an individual to perform military service and that there are no data to prove that lesbians and gay men pose any special security risk. As early as 1957, the Navy's Crittenden Report acknowledged that the notion that homosexual individuals pose a security risk was "without sound basis in fact. . . . [N]o intelligence agency, as far as can be learned, adduced any factual data . . . to support these opinions."[43] Recent Department of Defense studies have concluded that "[i]n the 30 years since the Crittenden report was submitted, no new data have been presented that would refute its conclusion that homosexuals are not greater security risks than heterosexuals."[44] The military's policy seems to be rooted in the same kind of stereotypes and prejudice that led the armed forces for many years to exclude minorities and women from the military.[45]

Have any courts found the military's policy of excluding or discharging lesbians and gay men to be unconstitutional?

Despite several widely publicized court rulings questioning the constitutionality of the military's antigay policies, most courts considering the issue have upheld the constitutionality of the current regulations, at least as applied to homosexual conduct.[46] Indeed, since the adoption of the new regulations mandating discharge of all homosexuals, there has been only one case in which a discharge for homosexuality was overturned. In *Watkins v. United States Army*,[47] the court ruled—without considering whether the military's policy itself was constitutional—that equitable rules of fairness barred the Army from discharging or preventing the reenlistment of the member for homosexuality after fourteen years of service when the Army had been informed that Watkins was gay at the time he was drafted and had previously considered his homosexuality several times at administrative discharge boards, when changing his reenlistment category, and in reviewing his security clearance and, each time, had decided to retain him.[48]

The extent to which speech alone can justify discharge when there is no evidence of homosexual conduct is unclear. Two appellate courts have expressly considered this question. In *benShalom v. Secretary of the Army*,[49] the trial court found that the Army's discharge of a reserve sergeant violated her First Amendment rights to free speech and association because the discharge was based solely on her statement that she was a lesbian and not on any sexual conduct on her part. This decision, however, was reversed on appeal. The appellate court held that even if the new regulations, which required discharge of those professing the "desire" to engage in homosexual acts, chilled constitutionally protected speech, they were not unconstitutional.[50] Similarly, in *Pruitt v. Cheney*,[51] a federal appellate court in California considered a First Amendment challenge to the discharge of an Army Reserve officer. The Army's investigation began in response to the officer's statements, reported in a newspaper, concerning her efforts to reconcile her sexual preference with her spirituality. The evidence against the officer consisted entirely of her statements identifying herself as a lesbian.[52] The court nevertheless held that the officer's discharge was based not on her speech but on her identity as a lesbian, of which her admissions (in the newspaper and elsewhere) were permissible evidence and, therefore, that her discharge was not barred by her right to free speech.[53]

However, *Pruitt* and other pending cases offer some hope for change. Despite its rejection of the First Amendment challenge to the discharge in *Pruitt*, the federal appellate court in that case also rejected the Army's generic claims that homosexuality is inconsistent with military service. The case was sent back to the district court, where the Army will be required to justify with hard evidence its policy that the presence of lesbian and gay soldiers adversely affects the military mission.[54] Another case, in which a Naval Academy midshipman was forced to resign weeks before his scheduled graduation, based solely on his admission that he was a homosexual, is now pending before a federal appeals court in the District of Columbia.[55]

What circumstances trigger an investigation of a serviceman or woman for homosexual involvement?

On rare occasions, the process begins because someone has been observed engaging in sexual relations with a person of the same sex.[56] Sometimes an individual will turn himself or herself in to military authorities, hoping to be discharged or seeking guidance. Because the military does not recognize the principle of "privileged communications" between physicians and patients, military doctors, psychiatrists, psychologists, social workers, and other medical personnel are under an affirmative obligation to report evidence of homosexuality to military commanders.[57] Despite recognition of a privilege for communications with clergy,[58] some military chaplains have been known to compromise the confidences of service members seeking guidance concerning their sexual orientation.[59]

Most often an individual's name surfaces in connection with another case. An allegation or admission of homosexuality on the part of one individual often results in extensive investigations of everyone associated with that person.[60] Once an investigation has begun, it is not uncommon for it to develop into a purge or witchhunt.[61]

How are charges involving homosexuality generally investigated?

Tactics reportedly used by military investigators include surveillance of gay and lesbian bars and community groups, following suspected homosexuals off base, opening letters from secured mailboxes, and leaking word of investigations to military colleagues.[62]

Investigators—with or without a warrant or the member's permission—may search quarters, lockers, and personal belongings for incriminating evidence (magazines, letters, advertisements, pictures, address books, and so forth). A person under investigation should not consent to such a search (even if the agents produce a warrant) but should insist on seeing a lawyer.

The most significant part of the investigative process is the personal interrogation conducted by investigative agents. The interrogation may last several hours or stretch over several days.

> Interrogators attempt to force confessions, present written statements of guilt ready to be signed by the [target of the investigation], and threaten loss of custody or family estrangement if [targets] will not comply. In a chapter on interrogations, the NIS manual on procedures states, "It is considerably easier to successfully interrogate the anxious subject whom the interrogator observes is on the verge of losing self control, than the calm, collected individual who is in excellent self control."[63]

Investigators will often attempt to destroy mutual trust between lovers and among peers in order to pressure service members to "confess" and to provide the names of other lesbians and gay men. Those who refuse to participate or who testify on behalf of colleagues accused of homosexuality may be reassigned to less desirable duty, reduced in rank, or investigated themselves.

Investigators may try to convince a person under investigation that he or she really does not need to see a lawyer prior to speaking with them; that everything will be fine once he or she cooperates; that the investigators will help to provide medical assistance; that they already have all the information they need but would like to clarify a few details; that no one need know of the military's action if the person being investigated cooperates; and that without cooperation, the maximum penalty is likely to be imposed (i.e., a referral for a trial by court-martial and a punitive discharge). Often, there are two investigative agents present at the interrogation: one who attempts to gain the subject's confidence as a "good guy" and the other who plays the role of the "bad guy." They may try to persuade the person under investigation to take a lie-detector test. *This invitation should be refused.*[64]

A service member may be required to report to investigative offices, but, as discussed below, the member cannot be required to answer questions or make statements that will be incriminating. If a lawyer has not been consulted, the service member should not submit to the interrogation at all.

At what point is the person suspected of homosexual involvement informed that an investigation is being conducted or about to be initiated?

An informal investigation, including surveillance and questioning of friends and acquaintances, may progress for some time before the individual is informed that he or she is suspected of homosexual involvement. At the time a formal investigation is begun, the individual suspected of homosexual involvement may be summoned to appear before a commanding officer or, more often, before the investigative agent involved in the case and informed of the pending investigation.

If a person is called before a commanding officer or investigator, what rights are available?

During every stage of the process, beginning with initial questioning, an individual has certain basic rights, which include the following:

1. To be informed of the specific "offenses" of which he or she is accused.
2. To remain silent.
3. To be informed that anything said may be used against him or her.

4. To have the advice and assistance of either an ap-
    pointed military lawyer or civilian counsel retained at
    personal expense and to consult with a lawyer prior to
    responding to charges.[65]

**If, after being informed of these rights, a person decides to
speak to an investigator anyway, can he or she assert these
rights later?**

To some extent. While the individual may cease answering
questions and exercise the right to remain silent at any time,
once she or he has confessed there may be little a lawyer can
do to help. If the confession was obtained before the individual
was informed of his or her rights, an attorney can attempt to
preclude its use if the case proceeds to trial by court-martial.
However, in an attempt to undo damage done during any time
the person has waived her or his rights, the person will have the
burden of showing the previous waiver should be invalidated.

It is rarely in one's best interest to answer questions or make
admissions to military authorities concerning sexual orientation
or behavior. The best advice is not to waive rights in the first
place, particularly the right to consult with an attorney before
doing anything else.

**If referred to a psychiatrist, will any statements made be
kept confidential?**

No. As noted above, military law does not recognize the
principle of privileged communications in relationships between military doctors and patients.[66] It is best to assume any
statements made to a psychiatrist or medical officer will find
their way into the psychiatrist's report and will be used against
the person under investigation.

What happens once the investigation has been completed?

An informal investigation may be concluded without the
subject's ever having been notified that it was being carried on.
Once a formal investigation of an enlisted member has been
completed, the member will be informed that (1) the evidence
did not support the charges that were made and that the charges
were consequently dropped, or (2) the charge has been referred
for trial by general or special court-martial, or (3) an administrative discharge appears to be warranted.[67] In the latter case, the

member will be notified of his or her rights in relation to the administrative discharge proceeding.[68]

What rights does an enlisted member have before an administrative discharge board?

Enlisted members have the right to notice of certain facts prior to appearing before an administrative discharge board. This includes the right to notice of

- the basis of the proposed separation, including the circumstances upon which the action is based and a reference to the applicable regulations.
- whether the proposed separation could result in discharge or release from active duty or the reserves and the form and least favorable characterization of the proposed separation.
- a "reasonable period of time," not less than two days, in which to respond to the notification of rights and to request a hearing before the administrative discharge board.

The board itself must be composed of at least three experienced commissioned, warrant, or noncommissioned officers, all of whom must be senior to the member who is the subject of the discharge proceedings.

During the proceedings, enlisted members have the right to:

- submit written statements on their behalf and, if being discharged for homosexuality, to appear in person before the board to testify on their own behalf.
- consult with and be represented before the administrative board by qualified military counsel or by civilian counsel of the member's choosing retained at his or her personal expense.
- question any witness who appears before the board. However, since the military may use the affidavits or written statements of witnesses against the member without calling the witness to testify at the hearing, the member may not actually have the opportunity to crossexamine all witnesses whose statements are being used against him or her.

- present witnesses to testify on the member's behalf and to introduce other evidence in his or her favor. However, the board cannot compel civilian witnesses to appear, and the military will pay for the travel of a witness only if the commander finds that the personal appearance of the witness is essential.
- present argument prior to the close of the case.

The board's recommendations are determined behind closed doors. However, its findings and recommendations must be reported to the separation authority, usually a general or flag officer, appointed by the secretary of the applicable service branch. A written record, but not necessarily a verbatim record of the board's proceedings, must be kept if discharge is recommended. The member has a right to receive a copy of the board's statement of facts and recommendations. The member also has the right to obtain copies of all unclassified documents that will be forwarded to the separation authority in support of the proposed separation and to a summary of all such classified documents.

If an OTH discharge is recommended, the record of the board's proceedings must be reviewed by a judge-advocate or civilian attorney employed by the military department prior to action by the separation authority.[69]

What procedure is followed once the administrative discharge board has made its findings and recommendations?

Once the record of proceedings is turned over to the separation authority, it is reviewed to determine whether there is sufficient evidence to verify the allegations charged as the basis for separation. If the separation authority agrees with the board's recommendation of separation or retention, the case is concluded and the board's recommendation is put into effect. If the separation authority finds that, despite a board's recommendation of separation, the allegations of homosexuality have not been adequately proved or the member falls within one of the narrow exceptions to the discharge policy discussed above, it may order the member retained. The separation authority may also order a more favorable character of discharge than the board has recommended, but it may not give a member a less favorable type of discharge than that recommended by the board. Finally, if the board has recommended retention, but the separation authority disagrees, it may forward the case to the secretary of the service branch involved, with a recommendation for separation. The secretary must then decide whether the member will be separated or retained. When a case is forwarded to the secretary and the secretary orders separation, the characterization of service must be honorable or general, or an entry level separation.[70]

How does the procedure differ for officers?

Officers who have completed their probationary periods have somewhat greater procedural protections afforded to them.[71] In general, if a military commander finds that an investigation has produced sufficient evidence to charge an officer with homosexuality, the officer will be ordered to show cause before a board of inquiry why his or her commission should be retained. The board of inquiry must be composed of at least three officers, all of whom must hold grade O–5 or above and must be senior to the officer appearing before the board. The officer has the right to receive written notice, at least thirty days in advance of the convening of the board of inquiry, of the reasons why he or she is being charged and of the character of discharge recommended. The officer's rights before a board of inquiry are similar to those of an enlisted member before an administrative discharge board. If the board's findings are adverse, the officer has a right to receive a copy of the board's findings and recommendations and to present a written rebuttal to a board of review.

At any time during the proceedings, the officer may resign from the service or request voluntary retirement (if otherwise eligible to retire). However, the officer may be involuntarily discharged only by action of the secretary of the applicable military department and only if removal is recommended by the board of inquiry.[72]

What procedures are available for postseparation review of an administrative discharge?

Often the possibility of postseparation upgrade is used by investigators to persuade service members to waive their rights and accept a less than honorable discharge. Postseparation review is an uphill battle with no guarantee of success. While some members have won upgrades of their discharges, no one should accept a discharge characterization lower than that to which he or she may be entitled in the hope of someday having it upgraded.

Two relatively distinct administrative bodies have authority to review administrative discharges. The Discharge Review Board (DRB) of the service involved has the authority to review administrative discharges[73] on its own initiative, although it almost never does so; cases almost always are brought before the DRBs by the individual who has been discharged.[74] The DRBs may review and upgrade the character of a discharge or change the reason for discharge, but they are not authorized to revoke a discharge, order reinstatement, or grant back pay.[75] The procedures before the DRB are much the same as those of administrative discharge boards, except that the veteran has no right to counsel appointed at the expense of the government.

One of the primary factors considered by DRBs in determining whether the character of discharge is appropriate is change in military policy.[76] Because the adoption of the Defense Department policy on homosexuality included the directive that OTH discharges were to be awarded only in cases involving specified aggravating circumstances, any veteran who received an OTH or undesirable discharge for homosexuality where such circumstances were not present should consult with an attorney about applying for a discharge review.

Each branch of the military also has a Board for the Correction of Military Records (BCMR), staffed by civilians, which handles appeals from decisions made by the DRBs and also deals with demands for reinstatement and back pay.[77] The BCMRs have very rarely acted favorably on demands for reinstatement or back pay. Hearings before the BCMRs are discretionary and are rarely granted, but full relief may be granted without a hearing. If a hearing is granted, the procedures utilized by the BCMRs closely resemble those utilized by the DRBs and administrative discharge boards.

Can a conviction after trial by court-martial, or from an adverse decision by a DRB or a BCMR, be appealed?

Yes. Every general or special court-martial resulting in a punitive (bad conduct or dishonorable) discharge is automatically referred to a Court of Military Review and may in some instances be further reviewed by the Court of Military Appeals, or even by the United States Supreme Court.[78] On the completion of a military appellate review, the constitutionality of court-martial convictions may also be challenged in the federal courts.[79]

Similarly, after all military administrative remedies have been exhausted or are shown to be fruitless, administrative discharges can be challenged in the federal courts on four grounds: (1) absence of statutory authority to discharge; (2) the arbitrary or capricious nature of the decision; (3) the failure of the particular service to follow its own procedural regulations or regulations promulgated by the Department of Defense; or (4) the unconstitutionality of the discharge regulation or of its application to the service member.[80] As discussed above, most constitutional challenges to the military's policy of excluding lesbians and gay men have proved unsuccessful where homosexual conduct is involved; challenges are more likely to meet with success where the military has failed to follow its own regulations or has discharged an individual based solely on his or her self-identification as a gay man or lesbian.

What should a military service member do to avoid being discharged for homosexuality?

Perhaps the primary thing to guard against while serving in the military is being a party to one's own undoing: the sad fact is that most servicemen and women charged with homosexuality convict themselves by succumbing to the inducements and threats that confront them at every stage of the process leading to their discharge. If charges are lodged against a service member during her or his military career, the following advice should be considered very carefully:

1. *A service member should not "confess" to homosexual conduct or identify him or herself as a homosexual.* It is rarely in the best interest of a service member to "confess" to charges of being a homosexual and virtually never in his or her interest to admit homosexual conduct. A service member should assume that nothing is off the record and should exercise the right to terminate any interrogation and consult a lawyer before making any written or oral statement that may be used against him or her.

2. *A service member should never attempt to go it alone.* The assistance of a lawyer should be secured as soon as possible if charges have been made or there is reason to believe that an investigation is under way. A military lawyer can be consulted free of charge or the service member may retain private counsel or contact a public interest organization that serves the lesbian and gay community. Furthermore, he or she should not make any statements or cooperate in any way until legal counsel has been consulted.

3. *A service member should make the military play by the rules.* A service member does not completely sacrifice his or her constitutional rights upon entering the military. The service member should take advantage of those rights and of the military rules and regulations that exist for his or her protection. Unless the service member's attorney advises otherwise, the right to an administrative discharge board hearing or to appearance before a board of inquiry should be exercised. A written list of all charges and access to all relevant evidence should be insisted upon. If an adverse discharge does result, a service member should follow through on the right to postseparation review.

4. *A service member should not accept the advice of military authorities regarding the consequences of any of the available options.* From the beginning of the administrative process leading to discharge, the service member will be pressured into "cooperating." The pressure will take many forms. Authorities will often say, for example, that a confession and acceptance of an undesirable discharge will result in more lenient treatment or that the discharge may be upgraded subsequently. The service member should first obtain legal counsel and then identify the options and determine how to proceed.

5. *A service member should not accept a less than honorable discharge as the best option available.* A service member should insist on being given the discharge warranted by his or her service record. Unless the military can prove that the member has engaged in homosexual conduct, he or she should be entitled

to an honorable discharge. Even where evidence of homosexual conduct exists, a good service record warrants an honorable discharge. Otherwise, a general discharge is appropriate. OTH discharges can only be justified when the military can show aggravating circumstances and a relationship between the conduct the service member is accused of and his or her military duties.

NOTES

1. Enlisted Administrative Separations, 32 C.F.R. § 41, app. A, pt. 1, § H.l.a. (1990). This portion of the *Code of Federal Regulations* codifies Department of Defense Directive 1332.14 (promulgated Jan. 28, 1982), which governs enlisted administrative separations for all branches of the service other than Coast Guard. Department of Defense Directive 1332.20 encl. 1(7), encl. 2, (B)(4) (1986) applies virtually identical language to the separation of regular commissioned officers for cause.

Each branch, however, has adopted specific regulations implementing the Department of Defense policy. Though the individual service regulations differ somewhat in wording, they all substantially repeat the Department of Defense policy and, consistent with that policy, require discharge of identified lesbians, gay men, and bisexuals. The individual service regulations pertaining to discharge for homosexuality can be found in the following publications.

U.S. Army

Army Regulation 135–178 (Army National Guard and Army Reserve: Separation of Enlisted Personnel)

Army Regulation 146–1 (Reserve Officers' Training Corps: Senior ROTC Program—Organization, Administration, and Training)

Army Regulation 635–100 (Personnel Separations: Officer Personnel)

Army Regulation 635–120 (Personnel Separations: Officer Resignations and Discharges)

Army Regulation 635–200 (Personnel Separations: Enlisted Personnel)

U.S. Air Force

Air Force Regulation 35–41, vol. III (Separation Procedures for U.S. Air Force Reserve Members)

Air Force Regulation 36–2 (Officer Personnel: Administrative Discharge Procedures—Substandard Performance, Misconduct, Moral or Professional Dereliction, or In the Interest of National Security)

Air Force Regulation 36–12 (Officer Personnel: Administrative Separation of Commissioned Officers)

Air Force Regulation 39–10 (Administrative Separation of Airmen)

U.S. Navy

SECNAVINST 1900.9C (Policy for Members of Naval Service Involved in Homosexual Conduct)

SECNAVINST 1920.4A (Enlisted Administrative Separations, Active and Reserve)

SECNAVINST 1920.6A (Administrative Separations of Officers, Active and Reserve)

NAVMILPERSCOMINS 1910.1C (Personnel Instructions)

MILPERSMAN 3630400 (Separation by Reason of Homosexuality)

U.S. Marine Corps (in addition to Navy Regulations listed above)
Marine Corps Separation and Retirement Manual 1900–16C, 6207 (Officers and Enlisted)

U.S. Coast Guard
Personnel Manual art. 12-B–16 (Discharge for Unsuitability)

Personnel Manual art. 12-B–18 (Discharge for Homosexuality)

Personnel Manual art. 12-B–33 (Discharge Processing).

In addition, homosexuality (defined to include "a person who has committed homosexual acts, or is an admitted homosexual but as to whom there is no evidence that he has engaged in homosexual acts either before or during military service") is a nonwaivable "moral" disqualification from enlistment. *See, e.g.*, Army Regulation No. 601–210 4–17 (Sept. 1, 1982, as amended May 15, 1984).

2. 32 C.F.R. § 41, app. A, pt. 1, § H.1.c. (1990).
3. 32 C.F.R. § 41, app. A, pt. l, § H.1.c.(1)(a)–(e) (1990).
4. 32 C.F.R. § 41, app. A, pt. 1, § H.3.e. (1990). However, if the military believes that the service member is feigning homosexuality to avoid military service, the burden shifts to the service member to prove that he or she really is homosexual or bisexual. *Id.*
5. 32 C.F.R. § 41, app. A, pt. 1, § H.3.f.(4) (1990).
6. 32 C.F.R. § 41, app. A, pt. 1, §§ E.4.a (fraudulent enlistment), G.1 (unsatisfactory performance), I.1 (drug abuse rehabilitation failure),

J.1 (alcohol abuse rehabilitation failure), K.1 (misconduct), and P.1 (reasons established by the military department) (1990).

7. *See* Uniform Code of Military Justice [U.C.M.J.] art. 92, 125, 133, 134, 10 U.S.C.A. §§ 925, 892, 925, 933, 934 (1983); *see also Manual for Courts-Martial, United States 1984*, IV–120, IV 131, para. 90 [hereinafter *Manual for Courts-Martial*].

8. *See* 32 C.F.R. § 41, app. A, pt. 1, § H.3.g.(5) (1990).

9. U.C.M.J. art. 125, 10 U.S.C.A. § 925 (1983).

10. *Manual for Courts-Martial, supra* note 7, at IV–90, para. 51(c).

11. *United States v. Fagg*, No. 29129, slip op. (A.F. Ct. Mil. Rev. Aug. 6, 1991) (reported in National Law Journal, Sept. 30, 1991, at 24, col. 4.).

12. National Law Journal, Sept. 30, 1991, at 24, col. 4.

13. *Manual for Courts-Martial, supra* note 7, at II–144 (Rule 1003), IV–91, para. 51(e)(3). Where aggravating factors, such as the use of force, the absence of consent, or the involvement of a victim under the age of 16 are present, the maximum term of confinement is 20 years. *Id.* at IV–9–91, para. 51(e). Conviction by court-martial for indecent acts, fraternization, or violation of the general articles carries similar penalties depending upon the presence or absence of aggravating circumstances. *See id.* at IV–112, para. 63(e), IV 113, para. 64(e)(2), IV–126, para. 83(e), IV–129–30, para. 87(e), IV–131, para. 63(e).

14. U.C.M.J. art. 133, 134, 10 U.S.C.A. §§ 943, 944 (1983). "Gentleman" is defined to include both male and female officers and midshipmen. *Manual for Courts-Martial, supra* note 7, at IV–108, para. 59(c)(1).

15. U.C.M.J. art. 83, 10 U.S.C.A. § 883 (1983); *Manual for Courts-Martial, supra* note 7, at IV–8, para. 7(e)(1).

16. U.C.M.J. art. 2(a)(4), (5), 10 U.S.C.A. § 802(a)(4), (5) (1983); *see, e.g., Hooper v. United States*, 326 F.2d 982 (Ct. Cl.), *cert. denied*, 377 U.S. 977 (1964). The same is true of reservists while on active or inactive-duty training. U.C.M.J. art. 2(a)(3), (6), 18 U.S.C.A. 802(a)(3), (6) (1983).

17. *See Solario v. United States*, 483 U.S. 435 (1987) (overruling *O'Callahan v. Parker*, 395 U.S. 258 (1969)).

18. Memorandum from Representative Gerry Studds, *reprinted in About Face: Combatting ROTC's Anti-Gay Policy* § E.5 [hereinafter *About Face*].

19. *See, e.g.,* Department of Defense Personnel Security Program Regulation, DOD 5200.2-R–16 (Dec. 1986) (codified at 32 C.F.R. § 154, app. H (1990)); CIA Directive #1/14–14 (April 1986). For a general discussion of the effect of sexual preference on eligibility for security clearances, see ch. 3 of this book.

20. 32 C.F.R. § 41, app. A, pt. 2, § C.2.b. (1990).

21. 32 C.F.R. § 41, app. A, pt. 1, §§ E.4.(c)(4), H.2.a–g (1990).

22. 32 C.F.R. § 41, app. A, pt. 2, § C.3.1 (1990). There are two other kinds of uncharacterized separations that may be applied to administrative discharges, but neither is commonly issued to persons discharged for homosexuality. *See* 32 C.F.R. § 41, app. A, pt. 2, § C.3.b., c. (1990).

23. *See* U.C.M.J. art. 18, 19, 10 U.S.C.A. §§ 818, 819 (1983); *Manual for Courts-Martial, supra* note 7, at II–146 (Rule 1003(b)(10)).

24. These figures are computed from unpublished data contained in Defense Manpower Data Center Report No. DMDC–3436 (Jan. 1991) [hereinafter DMDC Report].

25. *See generally* K. Bourdonnay, *et al.*, *Fighting Back: Lesbian and Gay Draft, Military and Veterans Issues* (1985); D. Addlestone, *et al.*, *Military Discharge Upgrading and Introduction to Veterans Administration Law: A Practice Manual* (1982). For a discussion of difficulties in obtaining security clearances, see ch. 3 of this book.

26. 10 U.S.C.A. §§ 771a(b), 772(c) (1983) (ribbons and service bars); 32 C.F.R. § 578.3(k) (1989) (same); 37 U.S.C.A. § 501(e)(1) (1988) (leave); 32 C.F.R. § 553.17(b) (1989) (Army-operated national cemeteries); 38 C.F.R. §§ 1.620(a), 3.12 (1989) (VA cemeteries).

27. *See* 38 U.S.C. §§ 101(2), 3103(e)(2)(A)(1989). The same applies to officers who resign "for the good of the service." 38 C.F.R. §§ 3.12(c)(3), (e), (g) (1989); *see also* 10 U.S.C.A. §§ 1552, 1553 (1988). Prior to 1980, the VA considered any undesirable discharge (the name formerly used for OTH discharges) received for homosexual acts to be disqualifying for veterans' benefits. *See* 38 C.F.R. § 3.12d (1979); Jones, *The Gravity of Administrative Discharges: A Legal and Empirical Evaluation*, 59 Mil. L. Rev. 1, 11–12 (1973).

28. Veterans-Discharge, Veterans Administration Rules and Regs., *as amended* Jan. 1, 1980, 48 U.S.L.W. 2480 (Jan. 22, 1980) (currently codified at 38 C.F.R. 3.12(d)(5) (1989)).

29. Computed from data contained in DMDC Report, *supra* note 24, and Officer Losses by Service and Interservice Separation Codes (unpublished data provided by Defense Manpower Data Center, Jan. 1991) [hereinafter Officer Loss Report].

30. *See supra* note 1.

31. DMDC Report, *supra* note 24; *see also* T. Sarbin & K. Karols, *Nonconforming Sexual Orientation and Military Suitability* app. B, B–4 (Defense Personnel Security Research Education Center Report No. PERS-TR–89–002, Dec. 1988) [hereinafter PERSEREC Study]. A GAO study indicated that more than half of the discharges for homosexuality during the period 1974 through 1983 were from the Navy. Comptroller-General Decision, *Cost of Department of Defense Homo-*

sexual Exclusion Policy (General Accounting Office 1984) [hereinafter GAO Report].

32. *See* Officer Loss Report, *supra* note 29.
33. DMDC Report, *supra* note 24.
34. *Id.*
35. These computations are based on the figures contained in the DMDC Report, *supra* note 24. *See also* PERSEREC Study, *supra* note 31, at 21–22 & app. B.
36. Gross, *Admiral Says Lesbian Sailors Must Go, Despite Good Work,* Los Angeles Daily Journal, Sept. 10, 1990, § II, at 1, col. 1 (quoting letter from Vice Adm. Joseph S. Donnel to officers in his command).
37. *See* DMDC Report, *supra* note 24.
38. PERSEREC Study, *supra* note 31, at 23 (citing Harry, *Homosexual Men and Women Who Served Their Country,* 10(1–2) Journal of Homosexuality, Fall 1984, at 117, 119).
39. PERSEREC Study, *supra* note 31, at 8, 24; *see also* A. Kinsey, W. Pomeroy, C. Martin, & P. Gebhard, *Sexual Behavior in the Human Female* 474 (1953).
40. PERSEREC Study, *supra* note 31, at 22. The GAO Report indicated that the average service member discharged for homosexuality during the ten-year period encompassing fiscal years 1974 through 1983 had spent three years in the service. The average length of service for all persons discharged during that period was 5.6 years, or 3.9 years if retirement is excluded. GAO Report, *supra* note 31.
41. PERSEREC Study, *supra* note 31, at 25. Even including those who are discovered and discharged for homosexuality, nearly 80 percent of lesbians and gay men complete their military service honorably. *Id.* at 25. Virtually all of the lesbians and gay men who receive less than fully honorable discharges are discharged due to their homosexuality. Harry, *supra* note 38, at 123.
42. GAO Report, *supra* note 31, at enc. 1, p. 5, para. 10, & app.
43. *Report of the Board Appointed to Prepare and Submit Recommendations to the Secretary of the Navy for the Revision of Policies, Procedures and Directives Dealing with Homosexuals* at 5–7 (1957) (unpublished report) [hereinafter the Crittenden Report].
44. PERSEREC Study, *supra* note 31, at 22, 29; *see* M. McDaniel, *Preservice Adjustment of Homosexual and Heterosexual Military Accessions: Implications for Security Clearance Suitability* 21 (Defense Personnel Security Research and Education Center Study No. PERS-TR–89–004 Jan. 1989); *see also* Note, *Developments—Sexual Orientation and the Law,* 102 Harv. L. Rev. 1508, 1560 & n.38 (citing Senate Permanent Subcomm. on Investigations of the Comm. on

Governmental Affairs, *Federal Government's Security Clearance Programs*, S. Hrg. No. 166, 99th Cong., 1st Sess. 171–87, 913–26 (1985)).

45. For a discussion of the military's exclusionary policies toward blacks, see, e.g., Department of the Navy Memorandum, Dec. 24, 1941, *reprinted in About Face, supra* note 18, at § E–7; R. Hope, *Racial Strife in the Military* 26–28 (1974). For a discussion of the military's exclusionary policies toward women, see J. Holm, *Women in the Military* (1982); M. Treadwell, *United States Army in World War II, Special Studies: The Women's Army Corps* (1954); *see also Hearings before Subcomm. 2 of the House Armed Services Comm. on H.R. 9832, 10705, 11267, 11268, 11711, 113729*, 93d Cong., 2d Sess. 29, pt. 5, at 120 (1974) (Serial No. 94–9, May 29, 1974) (quoting Navy's objections to women aboard ships).

46. In *Berg v. Claytor*, 591 F.2d 849 (D.C. Cir. 1978), *rev'g Berg v. Claytor*, 436 F. Supp. 76 (D.D.C. 1977), and in *Matlovich v. Secretary of the Air Force*, 591 F.2d 852 (D.C. Cir. 1978), *rev'g* 414 F. Supp. 690 (D.D.C. 1976), the U.S. Court of Appeals for the District of Columbia Circuit upheld challenges to earlier versions of the discharge regulations. However, a more recent opinion by the same court upheld the constitutionality of the current homosexual discharge regulations. *Dronenberg v. Zech*, 741 F.2d 1388 (D.C. Cir. 1984) (opinion of Bork, J., joined by now-Supreme Court Justice Antonin Scalia). *See also, e.g., Beller v. Middendorf*, 632 F.2d 788 (9th Cir. 1980), *cert. denied*, 452 U. S. 905 (1981), *rev'g Saal v. Middendorf*, 427 F. Supp. 192 (N.D. Cal. 1977), and *aff'g Beller v. Middendorf*, 4 Mil. L. Rep. (Pub. L. Educ. Inst.) 2218 (N.D. Cal. 1976), and *Miller v. Rumsfeld*, 6 Mil. L. Rep. (Pub. L. Educ. Inst.) 3001 (N.D. Cal. 1977). *Cf. United States v. Coronado*, 11 M.J. 522 (A.F.C.M.R. 1981); *Hatheway v. Secretary of the Army*, 641 F.2d 1376 (9th Cir.), *cert. denied*, 454 U.S. 864 (1981); *United States v. Newak*, 15 M.J. 541 (A.F.C.M.R. 1982) (all upholding courts-martial convictions for sodomy).

47. 875 F.2d 699 (9th Cir. 1989) (en banc), *cert. denied*, 111 S. Ct. 384 (1990). An earlier decision of a three-member appellate panel holding the military's ban against lesbians and gay men to be unconstitutional was vacated. *See Watkins v. United States Army*, 847 F.2d 1329 (9th Cir. 1988), *vacated*, 847 F.2d 1362 (9th Cir. 1988) (granting rehearing en banc).

48. 875 F.2d at 701–03, 707–11.

49. *benShalom v. Marsh*, 609 F. Supp. 774 (E.D. Wis. 1988) (*benShalom II*), *rev'd*, 881 F.2d 454 (7th Cir. 1989), *cert. denied*, 110 S. Ct. 1296 (1990); *see also benShalom v. Marsh*, 703 F. Supp. 1372, 1373–74

(E.D. Wis. 1989) (*benShalom III*) (reciting procedural history); *benShalom v. Secretary of the Army*, 489 F. Supp. 964, 972–75 (E.D. Wis. 1980) (*benShalom I*) (holding earlier version of regulations unconstitutional).

50. 881 F.2d at 460–01. For a critique of the court of appeals' ruling in *benShalom III*, see generally Note, *The Seventh Circuit in Ben-Shalom v. Marsh: Equating Speech with Conduct*, 24 Loyola L.A.L. Rev. 421 (1991).

51. *See Pruitt v. Cheney*, 943 F.2d 989 (9th Cir. 1991) (on appeal from order of district court in *Pruitt v. Weinberger*, 659 F. Supp. 625 (C.D. Cal. 1987), dismissing complaint).

52. 943 F.2d at 990–91. In civilian life, Pruitt is the pastor of a Metropolitan Community Church congregation in Long Beach, whose membership consists predominantly of lesbians and gay men.

53. *Id.* at 992–93.

54. *Id.* at 994–95.

55. In *Steffan v. Cheney*, 920 F.2d 74 (D.C. Cir. 1990), a federal appeals court reversed a district court's ruling that would have dismissed the case as a discovery sanction because the discharged midshipman, whose dismissal from the U.S. Naval Academy was based solely on his admission that he was gay, refused to answer questions concerning whether he had engaged in homosexual conduct while in the Navy. When the case returned to the district court, the judge, who referred to Steffan three times on the record as a "homo," granted summary judgment for the Navy, holding that the exclusion of homosexuals was necessary to prevent the spread of AIDS among service members. A new appeal is now pending in the U.S. Court of Appeals for the District of Columbia Circuit. *See also Woodward v. United States*, 871 F.2d 1068, 1974 n.6 (Fed. Cir. 1989), *cert. denied*, 110 S. Ct. 1295 (1990) (avoiding issue of whether regulations would be constitutional if applied in the absence of homosexual conduct); *Matthews v. Marsh*, No. 82–0216P (D. Me. Apr. 3, 1984), *vacated*, 755 F.2d 182, 184 (1st Cir. 1985) (vacating trial court's ruling that homosexuality discharge in the absence of proof of homosexual conduct violates First Amendment, because, while the appeal was pending, discharged reservist admitted having engaged in homosexual conduct).

56. *See generally Fighting Back*, *supra* note 25, at 76–77.

57. *See* Rivera, *Queer Law: Sexual Orientation Law in the Mid-Eighties, Part II*, 11 U. Dayton L. Rev. 275, 301–02 & n.183 (1986) (citing instances in which gay service members seeking treatment for hepatitis and AIDS testing were reported by military doctors); *see also Lauritzen v. Secretary of the Navy*, 546 F. Supp. 1221 (C.D. Cal.

1982) (service member discharged after telling psychiatrist she might have homosexual tendencies), *rev'd sub nom. Lauritzen v. Lehman,* 736 F.2d 550 (9th Cir. 1984).

58. *Manual for Courts-Martial, supra* note 7, at 111–23 (Mil. R. Evid. 503).

59. In *Steffan v. Cheney,* 733 F. Supp. 115, 121 (D.D.C. 1989), a Naval Academy midshipman sought advice concerning rumors of an investigation from military chaplain, who reported midshipman's admissions of homosexuality to commander. See note 55, *supra,* for subsequent procedural history.

60. *See generally Fighting Back, supra* note 25, at 76–77.

61. In one such incident, the well-publicized purge of female sailors aboard the *Norton Sound,* an investigation that began with the allegations of one woman soon spread to include accusations of lesbianism against twenty-four women—one-third of the women assigned to the ship. Rivera, *supra* note 57, at 302–03.

62. Gay and Lesbian Military Freedom Project, *Backgrounder on Homosexuality and the Military,* in *About Face, supra* note 18, at § E–2.

63. *Id.*

64. For a further discussion of the investigative techniques used by the military in ferreting out suspected homosexuals, see generally C. Williams & M. Weinberg, *Homosexuals and the Military* 100–07 (1971).

65. *See generally* U.C.M.J. art. 31, 10 U.S.C. § 831 (1983); *Manual for Courts-Martial, supra* note 7, at III–7 (Rule 305(d)).

66. *See Manual for Courts-Martial, supra* note 7, at III–21 (Rule 501); *see generally* Hayden, *Should There Be a Psychotherapist Privilege in Military Courts-Martial,* 123 Mil. L. Rev. 31 (1989).

67. As described below, the procedure is somewhat different in cases involving officers.

68. All enlisted service members being discharged on grounds of homosexuality have the right to appear before an administrative discharge board. 32 C.F.R. § 41, app. A, pt. 1, § H.3 (1990).

69. 32 C.F.R. § 41, app. A, pt. 3, § C. (1990).

70. 32 C.F.R. § 41, app. A, pt. 3, § C.6 (1990) (as qualified by 32 C.F.R. § 41, app. A, pt. 1, § H.3. (1990)).

71. Probationary officers include regular officers with less than five years' active commissioned service and reserve component officers with less than three years' commissioned service. *See, e.g.,* Army Regulation 635–100, para. 5–30. Generally, probationary officers are given very few due process rights and can be eliminated quickly by the secretary of the service branch on the recommendation of the General Officer Show Cause Authority (GOSCA), after being given an opportunity to

consult with counsel and submit a written response to the charges against them. *See* Tesdahl, *Officer Administrative Eliminations—A System in Disrepair,* Army Lawyer, June 1990, at 4 (Army Pamphlet 27-50-210). However, probationary officers recommended for an OTH discharge are entitled to the full due process rights, including hearing before a board of inquiry, accorded to nonprobationary officers. *Id.*

72. *See* 10 U.S.C.A. §§ 1181–87 (1983 & West Supp. 1990); Department of Defense Directive No. 1332.30 (1986). These provisions apply to the discharge of regular officers in all service branches. The individual service branches have also adopted their own regulations to implement the statute and DOD directive for regular officers, as well as to govern reservists. *See supra* note 3.

73. *See generally* Discharge Review Board (DRB) Procedures and Standards, 32 C.F.R. § 70 (1990). DRBs are also authorized to review discharges imposed by sentence of special, but not general, courts-martial. 32 C.F.R. § 70.3 (1990).

74. Department of Defense Form 293 should be used for this purpose. 32 C.F.R. § 70.8 (a) (1990). Such forms are available at most military installations and regional VA offices. Request for review must be made within 15 years of the date of discharge. 10 U.S.C.A. § 1553(a) (1983); 32 C.F.R. § 70.8 (a) (1990).

75. *See* 10 U.S.C.A. § 1553 (1983 & West Supp. 1990); 32 C.F.R. §§ 70.8 (a)(4), (e), 70.9 (1990).

76. *See* 32 C.F.R. § 70.9 (b)(ii), (c)(1) (1990).

77. *See* 10 U.S.C.A. §§ 1552, 1553 (1983 & West Supp. 1990); *Knehans v. Alexander,* 566 F.2d 312 (D.C. Cir. 1977), *cert. denied,* 435 U.S. 995 (1978). Application for review by the BCMR must be made within three years of the discovery of error or injustice in the service record, although exceptions may be made "in the interest of justice." 10 U.S.C.A. § 1552(b) (1983). DOD Form 149, which may be obtained from any Veterans Administration office, should be used to request review of records by the BCMR.

78. U.C.M.J. art. 66, 10 U.S.C.A. §§ 866(b) 876(b), 876a (1983 & West. Supp. 1990); 28 U.S.C.A. § 1259 (1971).

79. *See* 28 U.S.C.A. § 2241 (1971).

80. *See* Administrative Procedure Act, 5 U.S.C.A. § 701(a) (1977). *See generally* McDaniel, *The Availability and Scope of Judicial Review of Discretionary Military Administrative Decisions,* 108 Mil. L. Rev. 89 (1985).

V

Housing and Public Accommodations

The law still offers lesbians and gay men little protection against discrimination, except in Connecticut, Massachusetts, New Jersey, Wisconsin, and the various cities and counties that have seen fit to add the phrase "sexual orientation" to their civil rights laws. (Hawaii has a gay rights law, but it covers only employment.) Nonetheless, gay people are not totally at the mercy of others in trying to obtain or keep a home or in seeking goods or services. This chapter describes generally the remedies that now exist, in the more advanced jurisdictions and in the rest of the country, in anticipation of the day when federal law will outlaw discrimination against lesbians and gay men throughout the United States.

HOUSING

Can a landlord refuse to rent to or a homeowner decline to sell to a person just because he or she is gay?

In most parts of the country, yes. American law has traditionally invested property owners with enormous discretion. In general, a landlord may rent to anyone he or she chooses—or a homeowner sell to any person—as long as Congress or the state or local legislature has not explicitly limited that discretion. And, so far, most legislatures have declined to exercise their authority in favor of lesbians and gay men.

An infamous decision from New York City illustrates the power of the general rule of laissez-faire. A black, divorced woman sued a landlord over his refusal to rent an apartment to her, claiming triple, illegal discrimination—race, sex, and marital status. The landlord alleged in response that he had turned down her application because she was a lawyer, and lawyers are apt to know and assert their rights. The court believed him and dismissed her complaint. A landlord can act irrationally, the court made clear, provided he does not violate any of the pertinent statutory proscriptions. He may decide "not to rent to bald-headed men because he has been told they give wild parties" or "bar his premises to the lowest strata of society, should he choose, or to the highest, if that be his personal desire."[1]

Yet, if the circumstances are right, a lesbian or gay man may have a claim against the property owner on a ground other than sexual-orientation discrimination. Some places, as just mentioned, have laws that prohibit discrimination on account of a person's marital status.[2] In a case in Washington State, a landlady was held to have violated such a statute in telling two men who were looking for an apartment together that she would rent only to a married couple.[3] In another case in New Jersey, a landlord refused to rent to three gay men because, as the court put it, "he feared that they might later acquire AIDS and thereby endanger his family residing on the premises." The refusal was deemed discrimination on account of a "perceived handicap" and overturned as a violation of the state's handicap discrimination statute.[4] (Chapter 8, "The Rights of People with HIV Disease," includes a more thorough discussion of housing discrimination and handicap discrimination laws.)

Does that mean that a landlord can freely evict a lesbian or gay tenant?

Not necessarily. If the tenant is protected by a written lease, the landlord usually cannot evict him or her without proof that the lease has been violated. Unfortunately, many leases are blatantly one-sided and contain clauses that strictly limit how the tenant may use the apartment and who may share it. For example, leases often restrict occupancy to the person who signed the lease, or to those related "by blood or marriage." If a person has a lease with such a provision and a lover or roommate moves in, the landlord might use the clause to seek to evict *both* the tenant and the roommate.

Not all clauses are enforceable simply because they appear in a lease, however. All states have laws governing the rental of property, and some severely circumscribe a landlord's discretion. New York State has a statute, passed in 1983, that permits every tenant to have at least one other person living in the apartment, regardless of the nature of the relationship between them and regardless of any terms of the lease to the contrary.[5]

So-called rent-control and rent-stabilization laws, where they exist, are especially strict—and advantageous. In a recent case in New York City, a gay man whose lover died of AIDS used a rent-control regulation to keep an apartment from which his landlord had tried to evict him. The man, Miguel Braschi, had lived with his lover, Leslie Blanchard, in the apartment for eleven years, but Braschi's name had never appeared on any lease, and on that basis the landlord began the eviction proceeding. In response, Braschi turned to a rent-control provision stating that a landlord may not dispossess "either the surviving spouse of the deceased tenant or some other member of the deceased tenant's family who has been living with the tenant." He argued that he and Blanchard had been "family" to one another. The New York Court of Appeals, the state's highest court, in a decision of great significance, accepted that argument and ruled in his favor. Three of the court's seven judges explained the decision in this way:

> [T]he term family . . . should not be rigidly restricted to those people who have formalized their relationship by obtaining, for instance, a marriage certificate or an adoption order. The intended protection against sudden eviction should not rest on fictitious legal distinctions or genetic history, but instead should find its foundation in the reality of family life. In the context of eviction, a more realistic, and certainly equally valid, view of a family includes two adult lifetime partners whose relationship is long term and characterized by an emotional and financial commitment and interdependence.[6]

In a subsequent case, the New York courts extended the *Braschi* precedent to rent-stabilized as well as rent-controlled apartments.[7] (In New York the two categories are entirely distinct.)

Whatever the circumstances, whatever the jurisdiction, and whatever the applicable law, a landlord may evict a tenant only after a court has held a hearing and issued a formal order. The tenant is *always* entitled to adequate notice of the hearing, as well as an opportunity to participate. If a landlord threatens eviction or actually serves a notice of eviction, legal advice should be sought immediately.

Which places specifically prohibit housing discrimination against lesbians and gay men?

As already mentioned, four states do: Connecticut, Massachusetts, New Jersey, and Wisconsin. So do many cities, both large and small, and a number of counties. The cities include New York, Los Angeles, Chicago, Philadelphia, Seattle, Portland, San Francisco, San Jose, San Diego, Denver, Minneapolis, St. Paul, Milwaukee, Columbus, Pittsburgh, Atlanta, Boston, Hartford, Baltimore, and Washington, D.C. (See Appendix C.)

Another state, California, has a statute—the Unruh Civil Rights Act—the courts have interpreted to outlaw all forms of arbitary discrimination by landlords, including discrimination against lesbians and gay men.[8]

At this point, federal law prohibits discrimination in housing only on the basis of race, color, religion, sex, or national origin,[9] or on account of "handicap" (including AIDS and HIV infection) or "familial status" (a term intended to protect people with children).[10] Eventually, Congress may see fit to add "sexual orientation" to this list.

Can a lesbian or gay man be denied a mortgage on the basis of sexual orientation?

Yes, except in those places—mentioned above—that have specifically outlawed sexual-orientation discrimination. The personal life of an applicant for a mortgage should be irrelevant to the determination of whether he or she is credit-worthy. But in the past, banks and other lenders, like many employers, have viewed lesbians and gay men as inherently unstable and therefore financially unreliable.

Federal law and many state laws prohibit discrimination in credit on the basis of an applicant's sex or marital status, among other things.[11] These other categories may be of value in some cases, depending on the circumstances.

What special concerns arise for lesbians and gay men who own condominiums or lease co-ops?

Condominiums and cooperative apartments present special problems for lesbians and gay men since they both involve ownership interests held in common with the neighbors, who may not be very friendly or sympathetic.

A condominium is a dwelling—typically, but not necessarily an apartment—that one owns in conjunction with an interest in facilities maintained by all the property owners in the same building or project. A board or members association manages the common areas and makes rules governing life in the building. Although it is also usually run by a board, a cooperative apartment is quite different, at least in theory. The occupant of a "co-op" does not actually own his or her apartment; rather, along with the other tenants in the building, he or she holds stock in the corporation that owns and operates it, and that stock entitles the occupant to a "proprietary lease" to the apartment in question. Co-ops are most common in the Northeast and in Florida.

The law generally allows a condominium or co-op owner at least as much discretion in selecting a buyer as it does an ordinary homeowner. Thus, in most instances, there is little a lesbian or gay man can do to challenge an owner's refusal to sell to him or her, unless there is a statute specifically outlawing housing discrimination on account of sexual orientation.

A lesbian or gay man seeking to sell or transfer, rather than buy, a unit may also encounter difficulties since with most condominiums and co-ops, the board has the right to review the transaction in advance. Often he or she cannot even leave the apartment to a lover under a will without the permission of the board—even if the other person has been living there. An owner preparing a will with such a clause should either seek the board's prospective approval of the arrangement or try to make the lover a joint owner of the apartment.

Can public-housing programs exclude lesbians and gay men from participation?

Lesbians and gay men—at least those who are not parents—are often denied participation in public-housing programs, not because the programs specifically exclude them, but because the government typically gives preference to married couples and people with children. Two women who live together in a loving union may consider themselves "family," but the law, with a few exceptions, sees them only as single, unrelated individuals who happen to occupy the same dwelling. And as single people, they usually fall to the bottom of the eligibility list.[12]

Such preferences are unfair and inhumane, and arguably illegal and unconstitutional. The New York *Braschi* case, described above, indicates that some courts are prepared to extend recognition to gay couples. Precedents like *Braschi* may be used to broaden participation of lesbians and gay men in government benefit programs of all kinds.

How can lesbians and gay men best protect their housing rights?

1. *They should learn the rules that apply in the relevant jurisdiction.* All tenants have rights, under statutes and caselaw, but they vary from state to state and city to city. Tenants groups, among others, are often good sources of information.

2. *They should get a lease and read it carefully.* Among other things to consider is inclusion of other adults in the household on the lease.

3. *They should have a will.* Unless a person has a will, his or her property—including both real and personal property—will pass to blood relatives under the state's intestacy laws.

4. *They should consult a lawyer if faced with discrimination or threatened with eviction.* Knowing one's options and protecting one's interests are well worth the price of an hour's consultation.

PUBLIC ACCOMMODATIONS

What is a "public accommodation"?

A "public accommodation" is an item, service, or benefit offered generally to the public. "Places of public accommodation" include hotels and motels, restaurants, stores, and other businesses that cater to consumers. The definition of the term "public accommodation" can differ from jurisdiction to jurisdiction, and a company or facility subject to the antidiscrimination statute of one state might be exempt from a similar law elsewhere. The issue of what constitutes a public accommodation may seem arcane, but it can determine the life or death of an antidiscrimination claim. In 1990 a newspaper in Green Bay, Wisconsin, successfully evaded a lawsuit brought by two gay organizations whose classified advertisements it had rejected, by convincing an appellate court that newspapers do not offer "accommodations" to the public, as that term is used in the state's civil rights laws. [13]

Under state laws, the offices of doctors, dentists, and other highly trained professionals are often not deemed "places of public accommodation."[14] By contrast, a federal law that protects people with AIDS from discrimination does define physicians' offices as places of public accommodation. (See chapter 8.) State laws also may exclude from this category certain types of companies, like those that sell insurance. (Insurance companies are, in every state, subject to separate regulatory schemes administered by special agencies.[15]) Also exempt from public accommodation statutes are entities, like social clubs, that are truly private in nature. In many places, however, a club or association that calls itself "private" may still be "public" in the eyes of the law if it is relatively unselective in choosing its membership, particularly if it is also large and well known. In 1979 the state of Minnesota filed a complaint against the Jaycees, a national civic organization for young men, alleging a violation of the state's Human Rights Act because the Jaycees refused to admit women as members, and the Supreme Court upheld the constitutionality of the state's attempt to integrate the organization.[16]

Can a store, motel, or restaurant refuse to serve a gay man or lesbian?

In most places, yes. As we have already said, only four states—Connecticut, Massachusetts, New Jersey, and Wisconsin—explicitly outlaw discrimination based on a person's sexual orientation. Many cities and counties also prohibit discrimination against gay people. (See Appendix C.) And under an unusual statute called the Unruh Civil Rights Act, California forbids "business establishments" from engaging in arbitrary discrimination of any kind, including that against lesbians and gay men.[17] But elsewhere in the United States, businesses may deny service to gay people or treat gay people differently simply because they are gay.

Businesses may not, however, discriminate against a person on the basis of "race, color, religion, or national origin"[18] or "disability"[19] since federal law expressly prohibits such discrimination. A bill to add the phrase "sexual orientation" to this list has languished in Congress since 1975. (Note that discrimination on account of "sex" or "gender" is also missing from the current federal list pertinent to "public accommodations.")

What should a person do if refused service in a jurisdiction that outlaws discrimination on account of sexual orientation?

In most of these places, a person may, without a lawyer, file a complaint with a city, county, or state commission. The commission will then notify the establishment of the complaint and begin an investigation. If the investigation indicates there is "probable cause" to believe an act of discrimination took place, the agency will then typically schedule a hearing to look into the matter further. Each agency has its own procedures, however. An attempt to acquaint oneself with them should be made, ideally with the advice and assistance of a lawyer.

Is there recourse of any kind if the discrimination occurred in a place without a law prohibiting discrimination on the basis of sexual orientation?

Possibly. The denial or mistreatment may fall within a category of discrimination prohibited under existing law, such as race or disability. Although federal law does not include the terms "sex" and "marital status," many state and local laws do, and some include additional categories. Moreover, if the discrimination took place in a facility run by the government— federal, state, or local—there might be a constitutional claim under the Fourteenth Amendment's guarantee of "equal protection of the laws."

Can a bar or club prohibit two men or two women from dancing together?

It can, unless the city or state in which it is located outlaws discrimination on account of sexual orientation. Disneyland, the amusement park in Anaheim, California, was sued successfully several years ago under the state's Unruh Civil Rights Act when it tried to stop gay couples from dancing. Later, Disneyland tried to prevent two men from dancing while holding one another, on the claim that the earlier suit had dealt only with "fast dancing." A second lawsuit resulted in a settlement under which the amusement park agreed to let gay couples engage in both kinds of dancing.[20]

NOTES

1. *See Kramarsky v. Stahl Management*, 92 Misc. 2d 1030, 401 N.Y.S.2d 943 (Sup. Ct. N.Y. County 1977).
2. *See, e.g.*, Colo. Rev. Stat. § 24-34-502; N.Y. Exec. Law § 296; Or. Rev. Stat. § 659.033.
3. *See Loveland v. Leslie*, 21 Wash. App. 84, 583 P.2d 664 (Ct. App. 1978).
4. *See Poff v. Caro*, 228 N.J. Super. 370, 549 A.2d 900 (Hudson County 1987).
5. *See* N.Y. Real Prop. Law § 235-f.
6. *See Braschi v. Stahl Associates Co.*, 74 N.Y.2d 201, 544 N.Y.S.2d 784, 543 N.E.2d 49 (1989).
7. *See East 10th St. Assoc. v. Estate of Goldstein*, 552 N.Y.S.2d 257, 154 A.D. 2d 142 (1st Dep't 1990). *See also Rent Stabilization Ass'n v. Higgins*, 562 N.Y.S.2d 962 (A.D. 1st Dep't 1990) (upholding regulation on succession rights to rental apartments adopted by state agency in the wake of *Braschi*). The New York courts have declined so far to extend *Braschi* to areas other than housing; *see, e.g., Estate of Cooper*, 564 N.Y.S.2d 684 (Sur. Ct. Kings County 1990) (gay man's lover cannot be deemed a "surviving spouse" entitled to a share of his intestate estate), and *People v. Suarez*, 148 Misc. 2d 95, 560 N.Y.S.2d 68 (Sup. Ct. N.Y. County 1990) (statement made by a criminal defendant to a woman with whom he lived in a "non-formalized relationship" is not a spousal communication entitled to evidentiary privilege).
8. *See* Cal. Civ. Code § 51, as interpreted by *Hubert v. Williams*, 133 Cal. App. 3d (Supp.) 1, 184 Cal. Rptr. 161 (Super. Ct. 1982).
9. *See* Fair Housing Act of 1968, 42 U.S.C. § 3604.
10. *See* Fair Housing Amendments Act of 1988, 42 U.S.C. § 3604.
11. *See* Equal Credit Opportunity Act of 1975, 15 U.S.C. § 1691.
12. *See, e.g.*, 42 U.S.C. § 1437b(3)("In determining priority for admission to housing under this chapter, the Secretary shall give preference to those single persons who are elderly, handicapped, or displaced before [any other single person].")
13. *See Hatheway v. Gannett Satellite Information Network, Inc.*, 157 Wis. 2d 395, 459 N.W.2d 873 (Ct. App. 1990).
14. *See, e.g., Rice v. Rinaldo*, 119 N.E.2d 657 (Ohio Ct. App. 1951). *Cf. Elstein v. State Dep't of Human Rights*, 161 A.D.2d 1157, 555 N.Y.S.2d 516 (4th Dep't), *appeal denied*, 76 N.Y.2d 710, 563 N.Y.S.2d 61 (1990) (overturning on procedural grounds a ruling that, as a matter of law, a physician's office is not a "place of public accommodation"). *But see Lyons v. Grether*, 218 Va. 630, 239 S.E.2d 103 (1977) and

Leach v. Drummond Medical Group, Inc., 144 Cal. App. 3d 362, 192 Cal. Rptr. 650 (5th Dist. 1983).

15. A number of states now expressly bar insurance companies from discriminating on account of sexual orientation, typically by regulation adopted by the relevant administrative agency. For a review of the statutes and regulations relating to gay people and insurance, see generally Schatz, *The AIDS Insurance Crisis: Underwriting or Overreaching?*, 100 Harv. L. Rev. 1782 (1987).

16. *See Roberts v. United States Jaycees*, 468 U.S. 609 (1984). *See also Curran v. Mount Diablo Council of the Boy Scouts of America*, 147 Cal. App. 3d 712, 195 Cal. Rptr. 325 (2d Dist. 1983), *appeal dismissed*, 468 U.S. 1205 (1984) (the Boy Scouts is a "business establishment" subject to the antidiscrimination provisions of California's Unruh Civil Rights Act).

17. *See* Cal. Civ. Code § 51, as interpreted by *In re Cox*, 3 Cal. 3d 205, 90 Cal. Rptr. 24, 474 P.2d 992 (1970), and *Marina Point, Ltd. v. Wolfson*, 30 Cal. 3d 721, 180 Cal. Rptr. 496, 640 P.2d 115 (1982). *See also Rolon v. Kulwitzky*, 153 Cal. App. 3d 288, 200 Cal. Rptr. 217 (1984) (restaurant may not refuse to serve a lesbian couple under a policy limiting semiprivate booths to heterosexual couples).

18. *See* Civil Rights Act of 1964, 42 U.S.C. § 2000a.

19. *See* Americans with Disabilities Act of 1990, 42 U.S.C. § 12182.

20. See 7 Lambda Update 10 (Winter 1990).

VI
The Lesbian and Gay Family

The notion of what constitutes a family has undergone much change in recent years. While the majority of American households continue to be made up of married couples with or without children, even the so-called traditional family has undergone change due to the rise in the number of households in which both members of the couple work outside the home, the later age at which couples are having children, and the likelihood that most marriages will end in divorce.[1] "The average American marriage does not last a lifetime, but a much more modest 9.6 years."[2] Moreover, many Americans are now living in nontraditional families. Approximately one-fourth of family households today consist of children maintained by a single parent, and nearly a fourth of new births are to unmarried women.[3] Approximately 2.6 million households are maintained by unmarried couples living together, and the number of unmarried cohabiting heterosexual couples increased by more than 500 percent from 1970 to 1989;[4] an additional 2.5 million households consist of other multiple members who were unrelated by blood, marriage, or adoption.[5] In addition, 21.9 million, or 24 percent of all American households, in 1989 consisted of single people living alone.[6] What all of these figures mean is that the majority of Americans will spend more of their lifetimes outside, rather than as part of, married-couple households.[7]

Despite this increasing diversity in American family life, the law still harshly discriminates against unmarried couples and other families in which there has not been a marriage. For lesbians and gay men, marriage is not an option. Thus, among this class of citizens, critically important personal relationships are, as far as the law is concerned, usually treated as though they do not exist.

An elaborate body of laws has developed with respect to the benefits, rights, and privileges of persons who commit themselves to intimate personal relationships that are recognized through marriage. Marital partners have certain advantages in paying their income, gift, and estate taxes. They may inherit from one another without a will; they may own property in tenancy by the entirety; each may recover for the wrongful death of the other; they may adopt children more easily than singles; and they may lawfully have sexual relations. Most of these and many other public benefits are denied to those who elect not to marry or who are not permitted to marry. Employers also often dispense benefits such as insurance, pension survivorship plans, and sick and bereavement leave on the basis of marital status. Private organizations such as airlines, insurance companies, and banks also offer their goods and services on terms that discriminate in favor of married customers.

Many lesbian and gay couples now live together as families and seek to obtain the benefits that society and the government confer on married couples. There is no reason in principle why two gay men or two lesbians should be prevented from entering into a relationship that is deemed, for all purposes, to be a lawful marriage. Nonetheless, the law has consistently refused to recognize same-sex marriages.

This chapter describes the legal barriers to lesbian and gay marriages and the financial disabilities that result for gay men and lesbians because they cannot lawfully marry. It explores alternative means of obtaining some of the financial benefits that are based on marriage. Finally, it discusses the problems of lesbians and gay men who have natural children of their own or who seek to adopt or care for children.

LEGAL RECOGNITION OF LESBIAN AND GAY RELATIONSHIPS

Does any state recognize marriages between same-sex couples?

At present, no state recognizes marriage between people of the same sex. A few states expressly prohibit same-sex marriages.[8] Every state, however, has marriage laws that define what requirements must be met before two people may obtain a marriage license. Such requirements usually specify that the applicants must be of a certain age, not closely related by blood, single, and free from certain types of venereal disease. Some state statutes specifically require that applicants be members of the opposite sex;[9] others contain language referring to "husband

and wife" or "man and woman."[10] Even where the language of
the state's marriage laws is not sex-specific, however, courts
and state officials have interpreted those laws as embodying a
definition of marriage that requires a relationship between a
man and a woman.[11]

**What are the consequences of the states' refusal to recognize
gay marriages?**

When a state refuses to recognize a marriage, neither partner
is entitled—in the absence of an enforceable contract between
the partners—to the financial support of the other, and the
couple may be deprived of other legal benefits that are condi-
tioned upon marriage. These benefits are described more fully
below. Perhaps as important, the refusal to recognize relationships between same-sex partners further entrenches societal
treatment of all lesbians and gay men as second-class citizens.

**What are the risks of obtaining a marriage license from the
state without the state being aware that you intend to enter a
same-sex marriage?**

You may be accused of fraud, although there are no reported
cases. In addition, the attempt may be used as a basis for
discharge from the military.[12]

**What is the significance of a religious ceremony purporting
to join together two people of the same sex?**

Since no state has yet recognized as valid a marriage between
members of the same sex, such ceremonies have no legal significance. In fact they are usually not described as "marriage
ceremonies" but as ceremonies of "holy union." Whatever their
significance to the participants, holy unions do not entitle anyone to the legal benefits of marriage.

**Is it unlawful to perform or to participate in such a cer-
emony?**

Some states have laws forbidding any attempt to join in
marriage persons who have not obtained a license or who otherwise fail to meet the state's legal requirements.[13] However,
there have been no reported cases of prosecutions brought
against persons performing or participating in same-sex holy
unions. Where such ceremonies are purely religious in nature

and do not pretend to convey any legal marital status on the participants, any attempt to bring such a prosecution would be subject to a challenge as a violation of the right to religious free exercise.

Is the fact that states do not recognize such religious ceremonies a violation of the freedom of religion?

No couple has yet sought to obtain legal recognition of a holy union under the doctrine of religious liberty, but it seems unlikely that such a challenge would succeed, given the present legal climate. The United States Supreme Court has held that a state may outlaw polygamous marriages as contrary to public policy, even when the participants in such marriages are acting in response to their religious convictions.[14] This principle has since been extended to other religious rites that are prohibited by law because they offend large segments of the American population.[15]

What are the legal arguments that can be used to challenge a state's refusal to sanction gay marriages?

The constitutional arguments most commonly used are that the refusal is a violation of the First-Amendment right of freedom of association, an abridgment of the constitutional right to privacy, and a denial of the constitutional guarantee of equal protection of the laws.[16]

The First Amendment generally protects the rights of individuals to associate with one another, but the right to marry or to engage in sexual relations has not yet been recognized by the Supreme Court to be protected specifically by the First Amendment.[17]

The Supreme Court has recognized a zone of individual privacy, constitutionally protected against unwarranted governmental intrusion in highly personal decisions relating to marriage and sexuality. Matters so intimate as decisions whether or not to use contraceptives[18] or to have an abortion[19] have been held to be protected. Similarly, the decision of two people to marry and to choose with whom they wish to have consensual sex and an intimate relationship has been held to be protected against needless government interference.[20] However, in light of the Supreme Court's refusal to extend the constitutional right of privacy to include consensual sodomy between two adult gay men, it is unlikely that the federal courts would find that the right to privacy protects the right of lesbian and gay couples to marry.[21]

The most viable argument against the same-sex marriage ban is based upon the Equal Protection Clause of the Fourteenth Amendment. The Supreme Court has overturned laws prohibiting interracial marriages on the ground that the right to marry is a fundamental right and that one's choice of partners may not be restricted based on constitutionally impermissible racial classifications.[22] The same reasoning should apply to prohibitions against same-sex marriages which restrict one's choice of marriage partners on the basis of gender.

Have the courts ever upheld the rights of same-sex couples to obtain marriage licenses?

No. Lesbian and gay couples in several states have unsuccessfully challenged the denial of marriage licenses in state courts.[23] In each case, the court held that the couple did not have a right to obtain a license because the drafters of the applicable legislation contemplated heterosexual marriages only. The United States Supreme Court has not explicitly ruled on this question.

Do other countries recognize same-sex marriages?

Same-sex marriages, or their legal equivalents, are recognized by some foreign countries. Denmark, for example, recognizes "registered partnerships," civil ceremonies that confer upon same-sex couples most of the rights of married heterosexuals, except for the right to adopt or obtain joint custody of children. Sweden and the Netherlands provide similar recognition to same-sex unions.[24]

There are no known cases in which a lesbian or gay couple has attempted to obtain legal recognition in this country of a foreign same-sex marriage. While it is consequently difficult to predict with assurance whether an American court would recognize such a marriage, it appears unlikely that one would do so.[25]

Has any other kind of legal recognition been given to lesbian and gay relationships?

Yes. On the judicial front, the greatest progress has been in the interpretation of laws extending certain benefits to families. In its groundbreaking opinion in *Braschi v. Stahl Associates Co.*,[26] the New York Court of Appeals held that a gay man, who had been living with his lover in a rent-controlled apartment for eleven years before his lover died, was protected under a New York City rent and eviction regulation, which provided that upon the death of a rent control tenant, the landlord could not evict either the surviving spouse or any other member of the deceased tenant's family who had been living with the tenant. The court held:

> We conclude that the term family . . . should not be rigidly restricted to those people who have formalized their relationship by obtaining, for instance, a marriage certificate or an adoption order. The intended protection against sudden eviction should not rest on fictitious legal distinctions or genetic history, but instead should find its foundation in the reality of family life. In the context of eviction, a more realistic, and certainly equally valid, view of a family includes two adult lifetime partners whose relationship is long-term and characterized by an emotional and financial commitment and interdependence.[27]

The court went on to enumerate the factors that should be considered in determining whether a family relationship exists.

> In making this assessment, the lower courts of this State have looked to a number of factors, including the exclusivity and longevity of the relationship, the level of emotional and financial commitment, the manner in which the parties have conducted their everyday lives and held themselves out to society, and the reliance placed upon one another for daily family services. . . . These factors are most helpful, although it should be emphasized that the presence or absence of one or more of them is not dispositive since it is the totality of the relationship as evidenced by the dedication, caring and self-sacrifice of the parties which should, in the final analysis, control.[28]

A New York trial court, relying on the language of *Braschi*, recently upheld the right of the Gay Teachers Association and three same-sex couples to sue the New York City school board for denying domestic partners of unmarried teachers the same health insurance coverage for spouses and other fringe benefits accorded married employees. In one of the first judicial opinions to recognize a legal cause of action for domestic partnership benefits, the court acknowledged the longstanding relationships between each of the individual couples who filed the suit and held that "if, in deciding these motions, this court adhered to the traditional view of legally married, I would be rejecting the reality of family life in this day and age."[29]

In a much earlier case, the California Workers' Compensation Appeals Board found that a gay man was entitled to benefits after the job-related suicide of his lover.[30] Benefits had previously been denied on the ground that because the man's relationship with his lover was "illicit," he could not have been a "good faith member of the decedent's household" as required to receive death benefits. After nearly seven years of litigation, in which the board's originally adverse decision was appealed to the California Court of Appeals,[31] the board found that "the inability to enter a recognized marriage should not control the issue of good faith member of a household" and awarded the benefits.[32]

On other fronts, a number of municipalities—including San Francisco, Los Angeles, West Hollywood, Berkeley, Santa Cruz, and Laguna Beach, California; Seattle, Washington; Minneapolis, Minnesota; Madison, Wisconsin; Takoma Park, Maryland; and Ithaca and New York City, New York—have adopted "domestic partnership" ordinances, executive orders, or municipal policies of varying scope.[33] Other cities are considering similar ordinances, and two states—New York and Illinois—have domestic partnership legislation under consideration.[34] Domestic partnership laws, whatever their vehicle, provide legal recognition for both heterosexual and homosexual unmarried cohabitors. In some instances, such as in San Francisco,[35] domestic partnership ordinances provide legal recognition only, with no attendant public economic benefits. In other cases, domestic partnership laws may grant to registered partners some or all of the economic benefits—typically, sick and bereavement leave and insurance and survivorship benefits for city employees—that are accorded by the municipality to married couples.

A novel approach to legal recognition of lesbian and gay families has been adopted in California, where the secretary of state has agreed to accept registration of "families" as unincorporated nonprofit associations under a portion of the California Corporations Code that is used by such groups as garden clubs, fraternities, and homeowners' associations. In return for a ten-dollar filing fee, a couple or an adult with children may register with the state as "Family of [Doe]" and receive a certificate with the state seal acknowledging the registration of the association. While the registration has no known tax or legal consequences and confers no economic benefits, backers of the registration system hope that the registration will provide a psychological benefit due to the formal acknowledgement of the family's status, as well as assist in documenting hospital visitation and medical emergency approval powers and in receiving bonuses and discounts offered by private entities to families.[36]

Is adoption of one member of the couple by the other a viable alternative to same-sex marriage?

Most states at least theoretically allow the adoption of an adult, as long as the person to be adopted and his or her natural parents (if alive and known) grant their consent. However, as with children, a court must approve the adoption.

Some lesbian and gay couples have attempted to legitimize their family status and secure inheritance rights against possible challenges by relatives by having one member of the couple adopt the other. All of the reported cases dealing with this tactic have arisen in New York. After lower courts in earlier cases divided on the legitimacy of such adoptions, the New York Court of Appeals affirmed a trial court opinion denying the petition for an adult adoption between two gay men, one fifty-seven and the other fifty years old, who had lived together for twenty-five years.[37] The court held that the use of adoption to establish a family relationship between gay sexual partners was "a cynical distortion of the adoption function,"[38] the purpose of which was to create a filial relationship to which "sexual intimacy is utterly repugnant."[39]

Though this decision appeared to sound the death-knell for the use of adult adoptions between lesbian and gay partners, a more recent decision by a New York appellate court appears to breathe new life into the tactic. In *East 53rd Street Associates v. Mann*, the court held that an adoption of one elderly woman by another for the ostensible purpose of ensuring the right of the adopted party to succeed to a rent-controlled apartment was not necessarily fraudulent and that the court would not delve behind the face of an otherwise appropriate adult adoption petition to determine whether something other than a desire for a filial relationship or the establishment of property rights motivated the two women to file the adoption petition.[40]

Even if most courts do eventually accept the legitimacy of adult adoptions between same-sex couples, the step of adopting another adult should be approached with great caution. The financial benefits of adoption are usually minimal. Many benefits generally available to parents apply only if the child is under eighteen or twenty-one, is disabled, or is actually economically dependent on the parent.[41] One court has even indicated that a parent is not entitled to government benefits for an adopted child, regardless of age, if the adoption was made for the purpose of monetary gain.[42]

On the other hand, the disadvantages of adult adoption may be substantial. An adoption is forever; it creates a virtually indissoluble legal link between "parent" and "child." The party who is being adopted may be cut off from any right to inherit from his or her natural parents.[43] Moreover, adoption may impose substantial financial liabilities on both parties. In some states, for example, an adopting parent is responsible for the financial support of the person adopted, at least under circumstances of extreme need; an adopted child may likewise be liable for the financial necessities of the parent.[44] This is not an obligation that can be avoided if the relationship later sours. In addition, in some states, the parties may be guilty of incest if they engage in sexual relations with each other.[45]

In most cases, estate planning tools such as wills, trusts, powers of attorney, and life insurance, together with well-drafted "living together agreements," will prove a far better way to obtain the financial benefits of adult adoption, while avoiding its downside.

PERSONAL FINANCES AND RELATED MATTERS

May a lesbian or gay couple intending to live together enter into a contract setting forth their financial obligations toward each other? Will such an agreement be enforceable?

Traditionally, the law has been reluctant to recognize agreements between two unmarried people that purport to establish a financial relationship similar to that of a married couple, unless the agreements are made in anticipation of marriage. Such agreements have been viewed as undermining marriage as an institution. Indeed, in the eyes of some judges, agreements of this kind are akin to prostitution—establishing a scheme under which one or both partners provide sexual services in return for money or other material benefits.

In 1976 in a famous case involving the actor, Lee Marvin,[46] the California Supreme Court overturned this common-law rule—and made headlines from coast-to-coast—by holding that a property agreement between two unmarried adults who live together and engage in sexual relations is fully enforceable in a court of law (except, as the court put it, "to the extent that the contract is *explicitly* founded on the consideration of meretricious sexual services"). The court went so far as to declare that the agreement need not be written and could be implied from the conduct of the parties. This revolutionary decision, establishing a right to what the popular press has delighted in dubbing "palimony," has since been followed in whole or part by courts in many other states.[47]

The California court's reasoning seems just as applicable to homosexual as to heterosexual couples, and at least two courts in California have issued opinions that appear to bring lesbian and gay couples within the compass of *Marvin*.[48] Other states have indicated some willingness to follow suit.[49] However, the right established in the *Marvin* case is still unsettled and untested, with many courts apparently more willing to find the provision of sexual services an inseparable part of living-together agreements between lesbian and gay couples and therefore declining to enforce such contracts.[50]

The prospect of *Marvin*-type actions presents a twin-edged sword to the lesbian and gay community. On one hand, the possibility that an express or implied contract may later be alleged by a former lover should lead those contemplating long-term relationships to consult a lawyer and place their agreements in writing in order to increase the likelihood that courts will not later find the terms of their agreements tainted by consideration of sexual services and also so that the terms of implied agreements will be less fertile grounds for dispute.

On the other hand, at this point in the law's development, lesbian and gay couples cannot count on their agreements, written or implied, actually being enforced by the courts. The safest course is to undertake protective measures in addition to the agreement—for example, by executing wills, trust instruments, powers of attorney, and any other appropriate documents that express the couple's mutual wishes; by establishing joint ownership of assets the parties wish to hold as a couple; and by doing anything else the partners have determined, in consultation with their lawyer, accountant, banker, or investment counselor, to be appropriate to their circumstances.

May a "living-together agreement" include provisions governing the domestic rights and obligations of each partner?

Many persons entering into marriage have in recent years executed contracts defining their domestic rights and obligations toward each other. Such contracts may include provisions regarding such matters as dishwashing, cooking, cleaning, and childcare. It is doubtful that such provisions are intended to be, or would be, enforceable in the courts. Instead, they are presumably intended merely to set forth, for the private guidance of the parties, the outlines of their mutual obligations. Lesbian and gay couples, if they wish to do so, could lawfully create similar guidelines for themselves. However, for the reasons described above, it is a good idea to keep descriptions that may bear upon sexual intimacies separate from any financial agreements the couple may wish to see enforced in court.

May a lesbian or gay couple enter into joint financial obligations to third parties?

Yes, provided the third party is also willing to enter into such an agreement. Although many banks, credit card companies, insurance companies, landlords, and other creditors refuse to enter into agreements with unmarried couples, such agreements actually benefit the creditor. Many unmarried persons living together sign leases obligating both of them to pay the rent and assume other obligations of their leases. Many unmarried persons, whether living together or not, sign notes at banks obligating both of them to pay the amounts due under loans. Such obligations are termed *joint* and *several*, which means the creditor may, at its election, sue either or both of the parties and collect the full amount from either of them. It does not necessarily mean that if the creditor sues one party and collects the whole amount the other debtor will escape all liability. Depending on the understanding between them, the debtor who has been required to pay the creditor may have a right to obtain from the other debtor all or a portion of the amount involved.

If a lesbian or gay couple is living together, will one be liable for the debts of the other?

Not unless the one who did not incur the debt has affirmatively undertaken to be responsible for its payment.

Under the laws of most states, a married partner (traditionally, the husband only) must assume liability for "necessaries" (food, clothing, and so forth) purchased by the other (traditionally, the wife). In addition, when one partner customarily buys items from a particular shop and the other regularly pays the bills, the shop may be justified in assuming that one acts as agent for the other and that his or her purchases are made on the credit of the other. In such situations, a husband or wife may be liable for anything the other purchases.[51] However, when unmarried people are involved, unless one has expressly or implicitly indicated to a third party that the other acts as agent, the person who did not incur the debt would not be liable. An undertaking to pay debts incurred by one's partner is created under some domestic partnership ordinances, which provide that couples registering as domestic partners assume a legally enforceable responsibility for basic living expenses.[52]

May a lesbian or gay couple own property together?

Certainly. Many persons not married to each other are co-owners of property. There are essentially three forms of co-ownership of property: (1) tenancy in common; (2) joint tenancy with the right of survivorship; and (3) tenancy by the entirety, which is available only to married couples. A tenancy in common means that two or more persons own undivided interests in the same property. The co-owners may allocate their interests in the property equally or in any proportion they choose. If one of the co-owners dies, that owner's estate receives his or her share of the property, and it is passed on according to the terms of the deceased owner's will or, if there is no will, to his or her blood relatives according to the state's intestacy laws. A joint tenancy with the right of survivorship means that two or more persons own undivided interests in the same property and that upon the death of one of the owners, her share passes to the surviving owners. The most common illustration is the joint bank account, which customarily is registered in the form "A or B, payable to either or survivor." While the parties to a joint account are both living, each is entitled to share equally in the account, but either is empowered to dispose of any or all of the funds in the account; upon the death of either party, the survivor is entitled to the entire account.

While the option of joint ownership of property is always available, it is not always wise. First, unlike married couples, lesbian and gay couples do not have divorce courts available to them when they separate. If one of two or more tenants in common or joint tenants with the right of survivorship is unhappy with the situation and wishes to terminate the co-ownership, she may bring an action in court to partition the property. The court will direct the property to be sold, and the proceeds divided among the co-owners in accordance with their respective interests. Unless a legally enforceable written contract dictates otherwise, courts are likely to split co-owned property down the middle if one of the parties brings a partition action, even if that was not the initial intention of the parties when the property was acquired.

Second, unlike married couples, who may make unlimited gifts to one another during their marriage and in their wills, lesbian and gay couples may be liable for gift tax on any transfer in excess of $10,000 in a single tax year. When two members of a couple who are not contributing equally to the payments on a piece of property place title in both names, or when the name of a lover is placed on a piece of property that was previously owned solely by one member of the couple, the titling of the property may be treated as a gift. Given the rapid appreciation of real property in many areas, drastic federal and state tax consequences may ensue. Often these problems are undiscovered until one of the members of the couple dies and estate tax returns must be prepared; then the survivor may be left with an unexpected tax bill, plus interest and penalties from the time of the original transfer.

Finally, minor differences in language, varying from state to state, may make the difference between whether title to the property is viewed as a tenancy in common or as a joint tenancy. It is not unheard of for a surviving member of a couple who thought property was held with her lover as joint tenants, to be evicted when title is found to be a tenancy in common, with the deceased lover's share passing instead to her estate.

For all of these reasons, lesbian and gay couples should exercise care in taking title to property as joint tenants or tenants in common and should consult an attorney or tax advisor where appropriate.

What is community property, and may a lesbian or gay couple hold property as community property?

Community property is a system of ownership derived from Spanish law and now used in number of states, including Texas, California, Washington, Arizona, Louisiana, Nevada, New Mexico, and Idaho. Under the law of community property, income earned by either married party during the marriage is deemed to be held in "community," and each party owns half. Likewise, all debts incurred during the marriage are shared equally. Property earned and debts incurred prior to the marriage, and property acquired during the marriage by gift, bequest, devise, or inheritance is not part of the "community" and is the "separate" property of the spouse earning or receiving it.[53]

Since community property applies only to married couples, a lesbian or gay couple living together will not be governed by it. However, those couples who desire to do so may create financial arrangements similar to community property by means of a written living-together agreement.

Do lesbian and gay couples living together have any legal obligation to support each other?

In general, unmarried persons living together have no legal obligation to support each other. Such an arrangement may be created, however, in the form of a *Marvin*-style living-together agreement. Moreover, under some domestic partnership legislation, couples who register as domestic partners may assume a responsibility of mutual support. For example, in Berkeley, Santa Cruz, and West Hollywood, all in California, domestic partners must certify that they are "responsible for [each other's] welfare." The domestic partnership law recently adopted by San Francisco voters imposes a mutual responsibility for "basic living expenses" and "basic food and shelter." The duty to provide for these expenses can be enforced by any party to whom these expenses are owed.[54]

Is there any way a lesbian or gay man can ensure that financial and other important decisions will be made by her or his partner in the event of illness or incapacity?

In many states, the answer is "yes." A power of attorney is a legal document in which one person confers upon another the power to make decisions and take certain actions on behalf of the person executing the power of attorney. A power of attorney can be "special," that is, limited to a particular decision or act, such as selling a home or a car. There are also "general" powers of attorney that authorize the person named in the document to take virtually any action that the party conferring the power of attorney could take, other than making a will.

Normally, a power of attorney becomes void if the person executing the power dies or becomes mentally incompetent. A number of states, recognizing that a period of incompetency is precisely the time at which a person would want to have a previously identified person empowered to make decisions in his or her stead, have created what are known as "durable" powers of attorney. A durable power of attorney will continue in force even after the person making it becomes mentally incapacitated. Indeed, in some states a durable power of attorney can be drafted so that it only comes into effect in the event the party making it becomes mentally incapacitated. A durable power of attorney can convey not only the power to engage in financial transactions, but also the power to make decisions concerning the medical treatment and living situation of the party who executed the power of attorney—including whether to remove life support or withhold resuscitation if the patient has no chance of recovery. California has a power of attorney specifically for health care decisions.

Some states also allow an individual to name in advance a conservator—*i.e.*, a person designated to assume control of the affairs of an individual who has been declared mentally incompetent. A court is not required to appoint the conservator named by the incompetent party but will usually defer to the wishes expressed by the party when mentally competent. Another legal document recognized by many states is a living will. A living will does not appoint another person to make decisions for the party making the will but does express the party's wishes concerning the termination of life support in the event recovery is impossible. While a living will may not always be legally enforceable, most courts will give considerable weight to the expression of a party's wishes, and, in some states, the living will may be the only form of expression of the party's wishes that will be legally enforced.

A power of attorney is a very powerful document because the party executing the power is legally bound by the actions taken by the agent appointed in the power, even if he or she later disapproves of the agent's actions. Accordingly, care should be taken in deciding what powers should be granted in a power of attorney and in assuring oneself of the faithfulness and good judgment of the party to whom a power of attorney is granted. The same is true in appointing a conservator. On the other hand, creating a power of attorney or naming a conservator while one is in good health may be an important means of exercising control of one's personal and financial affairs in the event of an unexpected tragedy. One may name anyone, including a lesbian or gay lover, as an agent in a power of attorney or as a conservator. However, where no power of attorney or nomination of conservator has been made by a party while competent, courts will usually be unsympathetic to the claims of a lesbian or gay lover or friend and will most often appoint a parent or sibling to take control of the affairs of a mentally incapacitated person.

Do lesbian and gay couples have rights of inheritance from each other?

No. If a person dies without a will, her property is distributed in accordance with the intestate statutes of the state in which she was domiciled (a permanent resident) at the time of death. Such statutes commonly provide that the decedent's estate is distributed to her surviving spouse or descendants in varying shares. If there is no surviving spouse or descendant, the estate is usually distributed to the parents of the deceased; or if they are not living, to the brothers and sisters of the deceased; or, if none are living, to nephews and nieces of the deceased, and so on to more distant relatives. If none of the deceased's relatives are alive, her property will be forfeited to the state.[55]

May lesbians or gay men living together name each other as beneficiaries in their wills?
Yes.

Would the will be subject to challenge by blood relations?
Every will is subject to challenge by persons who would stand to gain if the will is invalidated. This includes not only blood relatives, who would share in the estate if there were no will, but also any person who may have been named in the final or any previous will. In general, wills are subject to challenge on the following grounds: (1) improper execution; (2) lack of mental competency of the testator; (3) undue influence; and (4) fraud.

The most likely ground on which blood relatives might contest such a will would be that the testator (the person making the will) had been unduly influenced in the preparation and execution of the will. Undue influence has been defined as physical coercion, such as threats of physical harm, or duress (any form of influence so potent as to overpower the will of the testator and subject it to the will and control of another).[56] Ordinarily, undue influence is not found to exist merely because there is a relationship of affection or friendship between the parties.[57] To the contrary, when the beneficiary is a "natural object" of the testator's affection, such a relationship is usually a circumstance favorable to sustaining a will.[58] A person is entitled to dispose of his property by will in any manner that is not illegal or contrary to public policy,[59] and nothing is more natural than to bequeath one's property to one for whom one has an emotional fondness. That a person is said to have ingratiated himself or herself with another in order to encourage a bequest is not cause for upsetting a will.[60]

Nonetheless, despite these general rules, undue influence is ultimately a question of fact to be decided by a judge or jury. While some wills made by lesbian and gay testators in favor of their lovers or gay charities have been upheld against attacks by disappointed relatives,[61] homophobic judges and juries may consider such dispositions "unnatural."[62] As a result, at least one study has suggested that wills and trusts executed by gay and lesbian testators leaving property to their lovers or life partners are more likely than those of heterosexual testators to be successfully challenged by relatives on grounds of undue influence.[63]

What may be done to avoid any possible challenge to such a will?

First and foremost, lesbians and gay men should not attempt to write and execute a will on their own except in cases of emergency when consultation with an attorney is impossible. The technicalities of executing a will and the law involving the validity of holographic, or handwritten, wills vary from state to state. A slight error in a do-it-yourself or form will may result in the entire will being invalidated.

In addition, every possible step should be taken to provide evidence that the will is the independent choice of the testator. Here again, consulting an attorney who has no business or other relationship with the proposed beneficiary may prove helpful. The person making the will should explain the situation fully to the attorney. At a minimum, the testator should acquaint the lawyer with the extent of his or her assets and the identity of any relatives excluded from the will. The reason for this is that one of the prerequisites for establishing competence to make a will is that the testator knew the extent of the estate and the "natural objects of his or her bounty." The testator should ask the attorney to make a memorandum of such information. If the testator was formerly involved in a heterosexual marriage, this fact should be discussed. If there has never been a final divorce decree, the testator's former spouse may take a portion of the testator's estate, notwithstanding any contrary provisions of of a will. A divorce or separation agreement may require certain provisions to be made in a will. In some states, children, unless expressly mentioned in the will, may be considered forgotten and may be permitted to take a share of the estate.

If a lesbian or gay relationship is of long standing, the parties might consider drawing up new wills periodically without destroying the prior versions. The repetition will itself provide evidence of the testator's seriousness of purpose, and those interested in contesting the will may be deterred by the fact that even if they are successful in contesting the last will, they will also have to contest each of the earlier versions. There are a number of estate planning strategies that may be discussed with an attorney in the event that a will contest is likely. For instance, videotaping the execution of the will, executing the will outside the presence of the intended beneficiaries, leaving at least some token bequests to biological relatives, inserting disinheritance clauses in the will to discourage potential challengers, and appointing as an executor a person who is not a beneficiary of the will but is willing to fight to uphold the testator's intent are all possiblities. In addition, a testator who considers a will contest probable should leave sufficient life insurance in the names of her or his intended beneficiaries to enable them to manage in the event of a prolonged probate.

If a lesbian or gay man fails to provide for a lover by will, does the survivor have any recourse against the deceased's estate?

No. Unlike a marital spouse who may take an "elective share" of the estate if not provided for in a will, an unmarried person has no rights against the estate of his or her partner unless an obligation to provide for the survivor was created by contract or court order.

May a gay man or lesbian recover damages for the wrongful death or negligent injury of his or her same-sex partner?

Almost every state has provided by statute that a surviving spouse or other family member may recover damages for the wrongful death of a husband, wife, or child; in essence, the family member is allowed to recover for the loss of the victim's company, as well as economic support. In many states, a spouse or family member may also recover damages for emotional distress incurred when witnessing the accidental death or injury of a victim. Although a handful of courts have extended this right to unmarried heterosexual partners,[64] no such right has been recognized for a lesbian or gay partner of the victim.[65]

May a gay man or lesbian purchase life insurance on his or her own life and name a lover as beneficiary?

Yes. There are no legal restrictions on the purchase of life insurance by a gay man or lesbian on his or her own life and none on the persons whom he or she may designate as beneficiaries.

However, some life insurance plans offered by employers restrict beneficiaries to specified family members and some insurance companies are reluctant to issue policies to those who wish to name as beneficiaries persons with whom the insureds have "meretricious" relationships. Moreover, since the onset of the AIDS crisis, some insurers have refused to issue policies to any male who seeks to name another adult male as a beneficiary. In some instances, such underwriting practices on the part of employers and insurance companies may be successfully challenged if they violate state employment, marital status, or insurance laws. An alternative solution is to purchase a policy naming the insured's estate as beneficiary, reserve the right to change the beneficiary, and thereafter change the beneficiary.

May a lesbian or gay man purchase insurance on the life of her or his partner, naming herself or himself as the beneficiary?

In order to purchase life insurance, the applicant must have an insurable interest in the life of the person to be insured.[66] In New York, for example, the term "insurable interest" means (a) in the case of persons related closely by blood or law, a substantial interest engendered by love and affection; and (b) in the case of other persons, a lawful and substantial economic interest in having the life, health, or bodily safety of the insured continue.[67] The statutes of other states are generally comparable. The rule is obviously intended to avoid inducements for homicide and to prevent unlawful wagering contracts.

Any question of insurable interest may be avoided by having the insured purchase the insurance on her or his own life, designating the lover as beneficiary. The insured may, if he or she chooses, then assign ownership of the policy to the beneficiary. In this way, although the beneficiary may be forbidden to purchase the policy, he or she may ultimately obtain ownership.

Will the next of kin of the insured person have a right to contest the beneficiary designation in the same manner as they could contest a will?

No. Insurance policies are governed by the law of contracts and not by the laws pertaining to wills. An insurance policy is a contract between the insured and the company, whereby the company agrees to pay a third party the proceeds of the policy upon the death of the insured. Only in unusual circumstances, for example, where a divorce or settlement agreement from a prior marriage requires the insured to name his or her former spouse or children as beneficiary and the insured has failed to do so, will a disappointed relative be able to successfully challenge a beneficiary designation.

Are automobile insurance rates and homeowner's insurance rates higher for unmarried people?

Yes. Many automobile insurers and home insurers use marital status as a premium-rating and underwriting criterion. Unmarried people are often looked upon as poor risks by insurers because they are viewed as relatively unstable, pleasure oriented, and rootless in comparison to married people. Many insurers refuse to sell homeowners' or tenants' insurance to unmarried people living alone or together and may also refuse to sell automobile insurance to unmarried persons under a specified age. Even when companies do insure them, the rates for unmarried people are often higher.[68]

What can be done about such discriminatory practices?

Automobile and homeowner insurers are private companies and, like other private parties (including, among others, landlords, auto clubs, banks, credit card companies, health clubs, and airlines), cannot be forced by the courts to treat all citizens evenhandedly unless some statute or administrative regulation requires it. Many states have laws on the books prohibiting marital status discrimination in employment, housing, government benefits, and public accommodations.[69] However, most states have done little to enforce their laws to protect unmarried people, whether heterosexual or homosexual, against discriminatory treatment based on marital status in insurance or any other area. Some states specifically forbid insurance carriers from discriminating on the basis of sexual orientation[70] or marital status,[71] but even in those states, carriers may usually impose unequal rates if they can show some actuarial basis for them. California recently issued emergency regulations that prohibit automobile insurers from using marital status as a basis for rate discrimination; two insurance companies immediately filed suit to block the new regulations, which were stayed pending the outcome of the litigation.[72]

In contrast, some states have proven responsive when insurance discrimination takes the form of outright refusals by insurance companies to issue joint policies to lesbian and gay couples. In several recent cases, insurance companies have reversed their previous refusals to write policies after lesbian and gay couples have filed lawsuits or complained to state insurance regulators.[73]

May one lesbian or gay man name another as a beneficiary of pension proceeds that are payable upon death?

There is no legal impediment to such a designation; however, whether such a designation can be made depends upon the terms of the plan. Pension plans are essentially insurance agreements for the payment of money upon retirement or death. The terms of pension plans are usually dictated by the employer and vary widely. It is not uncommon for such plans to provide an automatic survivorship benefit for the employee's spouse or to restrict the choice of beneficiaries to the employee's family members. The plan may or may not permit the employee to designate another survivor beneficiary.

Are unmarried people living together eligible for family rates in nongovernmental medical insurance plans such as Blue Cross and Blue Shield?

Generally, no. "Families" are usually defined in such plans as married people and their children. However, a number of municipalities and a few private employers now offer coverage to "domestic partners" of their employees.[74] The expansion of such domestic partnership benefits is an issue of great economic significance to lesbians and gay men since as much as 40 percent of a worker's total compensation package now consists of fringe benefits, such as health insurance and various forms of paid leave.[75]

What is the difference in federal income tax treatment between married persons and unmarried people living together and sharing expenses?

Under present tax laws, married people have several significant advantages over unmarried people. For example, while the tax rates for unmarried people (whether living together or not) and married people are the same, married people are allowed a greater amount of joint income before they shift to a higher rate bracket or become ineligible for certain deductions. The greatest difference in income tax treatment between married and unmarried people is that married couples may file a joint return, thereby pooling their income, deductions, credits, gains, and losses. This is a significant advantage when one member of the couple earns substantially more or has much larger allowable deductions than the other. These benefits are denied unmarried people who, no matter how long they have lived together, must file separate returns.

Do unmarried persons suffer any disadvantages under federal estate and gift tax laws?

Yes. That portion of a decedent's estate that passes to a surviving spouse is not subject to any estate tax at all.[76] This is referred to as the "marital deduction" and is not available to unmarried people.

The federal gift-tax scheme, like the estate-tax scheme, includes a marital deduction for transfers to spouses. Under the gift-tax marital deduction, a wife may give her husband (or a husband his wife) a gift of any size, totally tax free.[77]

Moreover, under the Internal Revenue Code, a person may make a gift of up to $10,000 to anyone else in any one year without having to pay gift tax.[78] The code also provides that a spouse may allow half of any gift made by the other spouse to be deemed a gift of the consenting spouse.[79] Thus, a husband may give $20,000 and, if the wife consents, each will be deemed to have made a gift of $10,000, and neither will have to pay gift tax.

These advantages are not available to unmarried individuals. Nevertheless, there are various ways in which unmarried persons may minimize the adverse tax consequences of making gifts or leaving their estates to their loved ones. One should consult an attorney or tax advisor before making a will or any substantial lifetime transfer.

Are there tax disadvantages under state law for unmarried persons?

The law of each state is different, but most states have provisions similar to the federal statutes described above with similar consequences for unmarried people.

Are there other governmental benefits available to married people but denied to unmarried people who are living together and sharing expenses?

Yes. Many government programs, such as social security, veterans' benefits, and some disability insurance, provide payments that are larger for married recipients or that involve benefits that may be paid not only to the individual qualifying for the benefit but also to his or her surviving spouse or children in the event of the primary beneficiary's death or disability. Such benefits are not available to unmarried partners of the principal beneficiary.[80]

May lesbian and gay couples who otherwise qualify participate in welfare, food stamp, and Aid to Families with Dependent Children (AFDC) programs?

Although there are no reported cases addressing precisely this issue, the answer would appear to be "yes."[81] The food stamp program now provides that any "household" that satisfies the financial criteria may qualify to receive food stamps.[82] The pertinent statute originally provided that a household could qualify only if all members of the household were related by blood or marriage. The limitation was evidently intended to discourage alternative lifestyles, such as unmarried cohabitation and the communes of the late sixties. The Supreme Court of the United States held in *United States Department of Agriculture v. Moreno*[83] that the limitation was impermissible because it was unrelated to the purpose for which the law was adopted—to provide food at a relatively low cost for needy persons. Marital status is not necessarily related to need. Although the Court found that unrelated persons may elect to live together and pool their resources, it did not find that all discrimination on the basis of marital status is unconstitutional.

Similarly, there is no reason why a lesbian or gay parent who has custody of a child should be excluded from participating in the AFDC program on the basis of the parent's homosexuality.[84] The statute provides for participation by individuals who live in the same house with, and are interested and concerned with the welfare of, an otherwise eligible child or relative.[85] While some courts have suggested that one of the purposes of the AFDC program is to preserve a "conventional family structure,"[86] the primary goal of the program is clearly to provide needy children with the basic necessities of life,[87] a goal that would be frustrated if a child were rendered ineligible by the sexual preference of its parent.

It is important to note that, unlike the food stamp program, in which eligibility is determined on the basis of the household's income, eligibility for AFDC is based on the income available to support the child. In determining need for AFDC, the state may not assume that a person who is not legally bound to support a child is in fact doing so. It must have proof that the person in question is actually contributing to the household or participating in the benefits.[88]

CHILD CUSTODY AND VISITATION RIGHTS

Until recently, and with good reason, few lesbian and gay parents—even those already separated or divorced—were willing to reveal their homosexuality for fear they would jeopardize their rights as parents. Traditionally, American courts, and child welfare agencies as well, have been totally unsympathetic to lesbian and gay parents, accepting without question historic prejudices against lesbians and gay men and insupportable theories about what happens to children who grow up in homosexual households.

Since 1970 the prospects for lesbian and gay parents have improved considerably. In a significant number of recent cases, judges faced with custody issues involving a lesbian or gay parent have shown an openmindedness that was almost completely absent twenty years ago.

This section is concerned basically with two rights—the right to custody and the right to visitation. The right to custody is simply the right to live with and care for a child. For biological parents, this right arises automatically at the birth of a child and continues until the child comes of age or leaves home, unless events intervene that lead a court to order a termination of custody.

The right to visitation is the right of a parent who does not have custody of his or her child to see the child for brief periods of time, one night a week, perhaps, or weekends or holidays. The precise times of visitation are generally set forth in a court order, although they may be determined by a separation agreement between the parents or in another document.

When might challenges to child custody arise?

Custody battles tend to arise in one of three settings: (1) a dispute between the child's parents; (2) a dispute between one or both of the child's biological parents and a person who is not a biological parent; and (3) an attempt by the state to terminate parental rights, temporarily or permanently, due to the unfitness of the parent.

Custody questions are most likely to arise in connection with a divorce or a separation prior to a divorce. Every divorce must be officially granted by order of a court. Customarily, when couples divorce, the court decides which parent will have custody of the children and what the visitation rights of the other parent will be.

A parent may confront challenges to custody even after it has been awarded. Often the remarriage of the noncustodial parent triggers a suit seeking a change of custody. If one parent discovers the homosexuality of the other after the divorce and custody are granted, he or she may go back to the court and seek custody of children on the basis of the other's homosexuality.

No custody order is truly final. Courts are generally given wide discretion to protect the children brought before them, and they have continuing authority until the children leave the jurisdiction or reach majority. If a court believes it would be best to remove custody from a parent, it may do so at any time. Moreover, custody questions may be reopened in any state in which the children reside. If, for example, the original custody order was issued in New York, and the mother thereafter moves to Arizona with her child, any interested persons wishing to challenge her custody on the basis of "changed circumstances" may do so in the Arizona courts. The Arizona court is not bound by the New York order, but it is unlikely to alter the order if there are no new circumstances that were unknown to the New York court at the time the order was issued.

What should a parent do if custody rights are challenged?

A lawyer's help should be sought immediately. A parent is entitled to a hearing to determine custody of his or her children.

If the parent cannot afford a lawyer, some courts will appoint one, or the parent can consult a local legal-aid society, community legal-services office, or other law group that provides free or inexpensive legal services. It is important to be certain that the lawyer is sympathetic to the rights of lesbian and gay parents to have custody of their children. A local lesbian and gay rights organization can be contacted for the names of lawyers who have handled such cases before or are sympathetic to the issue. It is important for the parent to be open with the attorney about his or her sexual preference in order to explore the lawyer's feelings about the lesbian or gay parent's right to custody and also so that the lawyer will be prepared to defend this right.

What is the law governing custody and visitation?

The standard for determining questions of custody and visitation in a divorce or separation proceeding is the "best interests" of the child. Obviously, this standard gives a judge extraordinary latitude; virtually anything deemed relevant to the child's welfare, including a parent's sexuality, can be taken into consideration. The flexibility of the "best interests" standard permits a narrowminded or unsophisticated judge to indulge prejudices about unorthodox behavior.

The standard is somewhat stricter in neglect proceedings. A neglect proceeding occurs when the state brings legal action against a parent alleging that a child has been abused or neglected and should be placed in the custody of the state or of a third party. Such proceedings generally arise only when the family has come to the attention of a state social worker, usually because the parent has been receiving public assistance or has a criminal record. In neglect proceedings, the state must show by clear and convincing evidence that the parent is an unfit custodian and that the child has suffered or will suffer harm as a result.[89]

Whatever the appropriate standard, it is clear that any parent whose custody has been challenged is entitled under the U.S. Constitution to a full and fair hearing of the allegations against him or her.[90]

Have the courts upheld the right of lesbian and gay parents to custody of their children?

In recent years, while homosexuality undoubtedly remains

an impediment to child custody, there has been a growing trend toward acceptance of custody rights for lesbian and gay parents. One scholar has suggested that much of the resistance to lesbian and gay parental rights is now concentrated in the central and southern regions of the United States, while the courts on the east and west coasts have grown more accepting of lesbian and gay parents.[91]

Some states have created virtually irrebuttable presumptions against granting custody to lesbian or gay parents.[92] Others require lesbian and gay parents to prove their sexual orientation will not harm the child.[93] However, many other states have rejected any per se rule forbidding custody by lesbian and gay parents and require the party opposing custody to prove the lesbian or gay parent's sexual orientation will harm the child.[94]

The following excerpt from a 1976 Ohio trial court opinion illustrates how antigay prejudice has been used against parents.

> There is no question in the court's mind, of course, that society as a whole disapproves of sexual aberration of any kind, particularly homosexualism [*sic*], and that is a very ancient disapproval. You read in the Old Testament of Sodom and Gomorrah. . . . An overwhelming majority of the people in this country strongly disapprove of homosexualism, regard it as a very wide aberration from what they do approve as indicated by various cant appellations they give to it, such as "Queer," "Faggot," and so forth, so there can be no question in the court's mind that the conduct revealed here is against the mores of our present day society, even this society that grows more permissive.[95]

The judge in this case concluded that the mother was unfit because she had "boldly and brazenly se[t] up in the home where the children are to be reared, the lesbian practices which have been current there, clearly to the neglect of supervision of the children."[96]

More than twenty years later, such rank prejudice is still sometimes reflected in such cases as that in which a Missouri appellate court affirmed the grant of custody to a heterosexual father based soley on the mother's lesbianism. This arrangement was found to advance the "best interests of the child," even though the mother provided the child with his own room in a well-kept house, enrolled him in preschool, had a steady job as a nurse, and otherwise cared for the child's welfare. The father, to whom custody was awarded, "ha[d] a limited education, an income of $6500 and live[d] in basically a one-room cabin containing a toilet surrounded by a curtain [where] the child [slept] in a fold-up cot by a woodstove and play[ed] in an area littered with Busch beer cans . . . ," while the father occupied his time leering at "girly magazines."[97]

In contrast, a Massachusetts appellate court in 1980 reversed a trial court's decision that had withdrawn custody from a lesbian mother. The appellate court found no support in the record for the trial judge's holding that the mother's lesbianism "'creates an element of instability that would adversely [a]ffect the welfare of the children.'"[98] Citing the lack of evidence that "'children who are raised with a loving couple of the same sex are any more disturbed, unhealthy, [or] maladjusted than children raised with a loving couple of mixed sex,'" the court went on to hold that "[t]he State may not deprive parents of custody of their children 'simply because their households fail to meet the ideals approved by the community . . . [or] simply because the parents embrace ideologies or pursue life-styles at odds with the average.'"[99]

For substantially the same reasons, the Alaska Supreme Court, in a 1985 opinion, reversed a trial court's decision removing custody from a lesbian mother and awarding it to the child's father and his new wife. The supreme court observed:

> In marked contrast to the wealth of testimony that Mother is a lesbian, there is no suggestion that this has or is likely to affect the child adversely. The record contains evidence showing that the child's development to date has been excellent, that Mother has not neglected him, and that there is no increased likelihood that a male child raised by a lesbian would be homosexual. Simply put, it is impermissible to rely on any real or imagined social stigma attaching to Mother's status as a lesbian.[100]

Similarly, in 1988, the New Mexico Supreme Court reversed a trial court that ordered that, despite the contrary recommendations of the state department of social services and the child's guardian *ad litem*, a child who had been removed from her parents' custody due to abuse and neglect should be institutionalized by the state, rather than being placed in the care of her gay older brother. The supreme court held that "[d]isapproval of morals or other personal characteristics cannot be used to determine the fitness of a person to care for a child. . . . We believe the sexual orientation of a proposed custodian, standing alone, is not enough to support a conclusion that the person cannot provide a proper environment."[101]

If a lesbian or gay parent is not awarded custody, is he or she entitled to visitation?

The best interests standard also applies to visitation, but most courts presume that some form of continuing contact between parent and child is in the best interests of the child.[102] Although some courts have denied visitation in order to "protect" the child from the parent's homosexual behavior or lifestyle,[103] most courts have been liberal in awarding some visitation rights to gay and lesbian noncustodial parents, even if certain conditions are imposed.[104]

May a court require a parent to refrain from lesbian or gay relationships as a condition of receiving custody or visitation rights?

In many instances in which custody is awarded to a lesbian or gay parent, substantial restrictions are imposed. For example, in one Kentucky case, a lesbian mother was awarded custody of her children but was required to maintain a home separate from her life partner, to refrain from allowing her children contact with lesbians and gay men, and to use only heterosexual babysitters.[105] However, a New York appellate court struck down similar restrictions imposed upon a gay father's visitation with his daughter. The New York court held that the restrictions served "no real purpose other than as a punitive measure against the father."[106]

May a person other than a natural parent challenge a lesbian or gay parent's right to custody?

In a handful of cases, grandparents, aunts and uncles, other relatives, and even the state have successfully challenged a lesbian or gay parent's right to custody.[107] Generally speaking, the law will award custody to the natural parent unless that parent is proven unfit or other compelling reasons for a different arrangement are shown.[108] While some courts may consider a parent's homosexuality as a negative factor, sexual preference by itself is usually insufficient basis to declare a parent unfit.[109]

May a lesbian or gay man who has separated from a same-sex relationship obtain custody or visitation rights with respect to a child that she or he has helped to raise?

The answer, for the most part, has been no. The Uniform Marriage and Divorce Act, adopted by a number of states, disallows custody actions by third parties when the child is in the custody of its natural parent.[110] While other states allow "any person including but not limited to a foster parent, stepparent, grandparent . . . who has established emotional ties creating a child-parent relationship with a child" to seek visitation or custody rights,[111] there are no reported cases in which such rights have been granted to a lesbian or gay nonbiological parent in preference to the biological parent.

Even when couples have provided for visitation rights in a written agreement, courts have been reluctant to allow former same-sex partners standing to sue for custody or visitation.[112] Nonetheless, lesbian and gay couples should solidify their agreements concerning child custody, visitation, and support in writing when they first contemplate raising a child together. While a court may or may not enforce a written agreement, without one, the party who is not the biological or adoptive parent of the child will have a far more difficult time of proving his or her role as the child's psychological parent and enforcing whatever oral understanding existed between the parties.

For similar reasons, lesbian and gay coparents should provide for the guardianship of their children in their wills. While courts are not obliged to honor the wishes of the deceased parent, such a provision will improve the likelihood that the surviving coparent will retain custody of the couple's children. In at least one case, custody has been awarded to a lesbian coparent following the death of her lover, the child's biological mother, in preference to the child's blood relatives.[113]

How can a gay or lesbian parent prove to a court that he or she is a proper custodian?

It is generally useful in custody cases to have both the children and parents examined by a qualified psychiatrist or psychologist. If possible, this should be done with the consent of the court prior to the hearing. The psychiatrist may be able to testify at the hearing that the parent is a stable and good parent and that the children will not be adversely affected by exposure to a homosexual parent or the parent's lover.

A common question doctors are asked at custody hearings is whether it is likely the child will become a homosexual if he or she continues to live or visit with the lesbian or gay parent (which the court ordinarily concludes is a negative result, given society's disapproval). Doctors are also commonly asked whether the child is overly anxious about the parent's homosexuality—that is, embarrassed or distressed by it. Sometimes doctors are even asked whether there is any likelihood that the child will be molested by either the parent or the parent's gay or lesbian friends. A gay or lesbian parent facing such a hearing should be examined, if possible, by a doctor who has actually done research in the field of homosexuality and who is sympathetic to the problems of lesbian and gay parents. Local gay and lesbian organizations often keep lists of such doctors.

Will a gay or lesbian parent be compelled to testify about the details of his or her sexual activities?
In custody cases, the court is entitled to have information regarding all aspects of the parents' behavior in order to ascertain whether such behavior is in the best interests of the child. Despite the latitude given courts in collecting such information, a person may not be compelled to provide detailed information regarding her or his sexual activities. First, if sodomy is a crime in the state of residence, the parent may be able to refuse to answer any questions about her or his sexual activity on the ground that it might prove incriminating. Second, the constitutional right of privacy limits inquiries into private sexual activities, unless there is a compelling state interest in obtaining the information. A parent should not be forced to answer such questions unless the state or the challenging person first shows how those activities may affect the welfare of the child.

What are the constitutional arguments that can be asserted so that lesbian and gay parents can gain custody of their children?
If a state applies an irrebuttable presumption against custody on the part of lesbian and gay parents, regardless of the merits

of the individual case, the parent may argue that he or she has been denied due process.[114] On the other hand, if a court's decision as to which of two qualified biological parents should be granted custody of a child has been based on a fair hearing and consideration of the evidence, there is little opportunity for constitutional challenge.

If a parent has been denied custody in favor of a third party or has been denied visitation rights or has been declared unfit by the state and had his or her parental rights terminated on the basis of his or her sexual preference, there are several constitutional arguments that can be raised. The rights of parents to have and raise children has been deemed by the Supreme Court to be "essential to the orderly pursuit of happiness by free men,"[115] "one of the basic civil rights of man,"[116] and "far more precious . . . than property rights."[117] The only legitimate justification the state may have for interfering with the parent-child relationship is to protect the welfare of the child. If the state attempts to remove a child from the home because of parental conduct, it must prove by clear and convincing evidence that the conduct renders the parent so unfit as to endanger the child's welfare.[118] It may be further argued that a denial of custody to a gay parent infringes the constitutional guarantee of equal protection.

ADOPTION AND FOSTER CARE

May a lesbian or gay man adopt a child?

The laws of many states permit an unmarried person to be an adoptive parent. However, two states—Florida and New Hampshire—have enacted legislation prohibiting lesbians and gay men from adopting.[119] The Florida statue was recently declared unconstitutional by a state trial court.[120] Even where there is no law prohibiting such adoptions, adoption of children by lesbians or gay men remains controversial. A court must first find that the best interests of the child will be served by the adoption. Some courts have vehemently rejected the notion that adoption by a lesbian or gay parent could ever serve the child's best interests. For example, an Ohio trial court ruled that "[i]t is not the business of the government to encourage homosexuality. . . . The so-called 'gay lifestyle' is patently incompatible with the manifest spirit, purpose and goals of adoption. Homosexuality negates procreation."[121] Although this decision was reversed on appeal, other courts have demonstrated similar, if less strident, hostility to the notion of lesbian and gay adoptive parents.[122]

Nevertheless, "anecdotal reports suggest that adoptions and foster care by gay men and lesbians are not uncommon."[123] Most adoptions take place under the auspices of public or private placement agencies. Some placement agencies may be unaware of a prospective adoptive parent's sexual preference; others may believe that a gay or lesbian applicant will be a good parent.[124] Where the agency is unopposed to the placement, it is less likely to be challenged by the court.

If the question of fitness arises, the prospective parent should insist that a hearing be held on the question. Expert psychiatric testimony should be obtained, and a psychiatric evaluation of the child should be made to determine whether the homosexuality of the potential parent would have any adverse effect on the child.

In contrast to the Ohio opinion noted above, a New York court permitted a gay man to retain permanent custody of a thirteen-year-old boy he had adopted a year previously, even though he had subsequently declared his sexual preference publicly and was living with another man. The judge reportedly stated:

> I saw no reason why this adoption should not be permanent. I'm not just trying to get into new avenues. I'm just trying to deal with this one matter before me. I assume some people will be critical, but look at it this way: the man doesn't beat his son, and when you look at all the cases of child abuse you get from so-called straights, you grasp for words.[125]

May a lesbian or gay couple adopt a child jointly?

Most instances of lesbian and gay adoptions appear to involve adoption by a single parent. Lesbian and gay couples seeking to adopt will often place the application in one name only in order to avoid calling attention to their relationship. Such arrangements make it more difficult for the nonadoptive parent to perform such tasks as registering the child for school or consenting to medical treatment. Powers of attorney granting the nonadoptive parent the right to make such decisions may alleviate these problems if they are accepted by the other parties involved (schools, doctors, hospitals, and others may, but are not obliged to, honor the power of attorney). However, no legal document short of an adoption order can at this time adequately address the nonadoptive parent's vulnerability to loss of custody and visitation should the relationship between the parents dissolve. For these reasons, as well as for the sense of emotional closeness to the child a joint adoption may afford, some lesbian and gay parents may attempt to adopt jointly or to have the nonbiological parent adopt her lover's child.

Even states that do not prohibit adoptions by lesbian and gay parents may have no mechanism for joint or coparent adoptions by same-sex couples. In most states, adoption serves to extinguish the parental rights of both biological parents.[126] Stepparent adoptions, an exception to this rule, allow an adopting parent to step into the shoes of a biological parent, but are often limited to married couples in which the adopting stepparent assumes the place of the biological parent of the same gender.[127] Nevertheless, courts in California, Alaska, and Oregon have allowed lesbians and gay men to adopt the children of their same-sex partners as coparents without terminating the partner's parental rights,[128] and at least two California courts have allowed lesbian and gay couples to adopt children jointly.[129]

May a lesbian or gay man qualify as a foster parent?

As in the case of adoptions, some states have adopted laws prohibiting the placement of foster children in the custody of lesbians and gay men.[130] In general, state agencies have been more reluctant to place children with gay males than with lesbians.[131] Nevertheless, in a number of states, both lesbians and gay men have been permitted to become foster parents to lesbian or gay adolescents. Some lesbian and gay organizations have been working with child welfare and placement agencies to promote such arrangements.

NOTES

1. "Current patterns suggest that more than half of all marriages contracted during the 1970's will end in divorce, about double the ratio of

the 1950's." Wetzel, *American Families: 75 years of Change*, Monthly Labor Review, March 1990, at 4, 9. The divorce rate since the mid-1970s is approximately twice the average for the period between 1950 and 1965 and approximately three times that of the 1920s and 1930s. *Id.*

2. Hunter, *Marriage, Law and Gender: A Feminist Inquiry*, 1 J of Law & Sexuality 1, 19 (1991); Bureau of the Census, U.S. Dep't of Commerce, Current Population Reports, Population Characteristics Series P–20, No. 445, *Marital Status and Living Arrangements: March, 1989*, at 1 (1990).

3. Wetzel, *supra* note 1, at 11.

4. *Id.* at 12; London, *Cohabitation, Marriage, Marital Dissolution and Remarriage: United States, 1988*, in 193 Advance Data from Vital and Health Statistics of the National Center for Health Statistics 1 (Jan. 4, 1991) [hereinafter cited as "London"].

5. Wetzel, *supra* note 1, at 11–12.

6. *Id.* at 11.

7. Hunter, *supra* note 2, at 19.

8. *See, e.g.*, Md. Fam. Law Code Ann. § 2–201 (1984) ("Only a marriage between a man and a woman is valid in this State"); Tex. Fam. Code Ann. § 1.01 (1989) (providing that "[a] license may not be issued for the marriage of persons of the same sex"); Utah Code Ann. § 30–1–2 (1990) (marriage between persons of the same sex void).

9. *See, e.g.*, Cal. Civ. Code § 4100 (Deering 1991) (defining marriage as "a personal relation arising out of a civil contract between a man and a woman"); La. Civ. Code Ann. art. 86 (West 1990) (same); Minn. Stat. § 517.01 (1990) (same); Mont. Code Ann. § 40-1-103 (1990) (same); Del. Code Ann. § 101 (1990) (defining marriage as "civil status of one man and one woman legally united for life"); Ohio Rev. Code Ann. § 3101.01 (Baldwin 1991) (male persons and female persons of requisite age may be joined in marriage).

10. *See, e.g.*, Colo. Rev. Stat. § 14-2-104 (1990); Ill. Rev. Stat. ch. 40, para. 201 (1989); Ga. Code Ann. § 19-3-40 (1990); Hawaii Rev. Stat. §§ 572-1, 572-13 (1990); Mich. Comp. L. § 551.101 (1990); Miss. Code Ann. § 91-1-7 (1990); N.H. Rev. Stat. Ann. 460:2-a (1989); N.M. Stat. Ann. § 40-2-1 (1990); N.C. Gen. Stat. § 51-1 (1990); 43 Okla. Stat. § 214 (1990); W. Va. Code § 48-1-126 (1990).

11. *See, e.g.*, *Baker v. Nelson*, 291 Minn. 310, 311–12, 191 N.W.2d 185–86 (1971) (denying marriage license to gay male couple), *appeal dismissed*, 409 U.S. 810 (1972); *Anonymous v. Anonymous*, 67 Misc. 2d 982, 325 N.Y.S.2d 499 (N.Y. Sup. Ct. 1971)(granting dissolution petition of woman who entered into marriage believing her partner was male); *Jones v. Hallahan*, 501 S.W.2d 588 (Ky. Ct. App. 1973);

Singer v. Hara, 11 Wash. App. 247, 259, 522 P.2d 1187, 1195 (rejecting notion of same-sex marriage as antithetical to purpose of marriage), *review denied,* 84 Wash. App. 247, 522 P.2d 1187 (1974); *Irwin v. Upardu,* No. 78-D-97925 (Ohio Ct. App., 8th Dist., June 26, 1980) (declining to recognize a "divorce" action by two women alleging a common-law marriage on ground that marriage is, by definition, a heterosexual relationship) (*discussed in* Rivera, *Queer Law: Sexual Orientation Law in the Mid-Eighties, Part II,* 11 U. Dayton L. Rev. 275, 324 & n.340 (1986) [hereinafter *Queer Law*]); *DeSanto v. Barnsley,* 328 Pa. Super. 181, 476 A.2d 952 (1984) (declining to recognize gay common-law marriage); *see also Adams v. Howerton,* 486 F. Supp. 1119, 1122–23 (C.D. Cal. 1980) (finding that federal immigration law did not intend to recognize same-sex marriages even though plaintiffs had obtained licenses through a Colorado county clerk), *aff'd,* 673 F.2d 1036 (9th Cir.), *cert. denied,* 458 U.S. 1111 (1982); *Connecticut Defines "Marriage" to Exclude Same Sex Couples,* 6 Fam. L. Rep. (BNA) 2737 (Sept. 12, 1980) (opinion letter from Connecticut Attorney General to Department of Health Services).

12. *See* ch. 4 of this volume.

13. *See, e.g.,* Miss. Code Ann. § 93-1-13 (1990); N.C. Gen. Stat. 51-6 (1990).

14. *Reynolds v. United States,* 98 U.S. 244 (1879).

15. *Employment Div., Dep't of Human Resources of Oregon v. Smith,* 494 U.S. 872 (1990).

16. *See generally* Rivera, *Our Straight-Laced Judges: The Legal Position of Homosexual Persons in the United States,* 30 Hastings L.J. 799, 874–78 (1979); Note, *The Legality of Homosexual Marriage,* 82 Yale L.J. 573 (1973); Comment, *Homosexuals' Right to Marry: A Constitutional Test and a Legislative Solution,* 128 U. Pa. L. Rev. 193 (1979).

17. The First Amendment, as construed by the Supreme Court, includes a number of other rights, among them the right to engage in free and private associations. *Williams v. Rhodes,* 393 U.S. 23 (1968); *NAACP v. Alabama,* 357 U.S. 449 (1958). Most right of association cases to date have dealt with association for political purposes, although in *Griswold v. Connecticut,* 381 U.S. 479, 484 (1965), Justice Douglas referred to marriage as an "association."

18. *Griswold v. Connecticut,* 381 U.S. 479 (1965); *Eisenstadt v. Baird,* 405 U.S. 438 (1972).

19. *Roe v. Wade,* 410 U.S. 113 (1973).

20. *See Skinner v. Oklahoma,* 316 U.S. 535 (1942); *Loving v. Virginia,* 388 U.S. 1 (1967); *Zablocki v. Redhail,* 434 U.S. 374 (1978); *see generally* Barnett, *Sexual Freedom and the Constitution* (1973).

21. *Bowers v. Hardwick,* 478 U.S. 1039 (1986).

22. *Loving v. Virginia*, 388 U.S. 1 (1967); *see also Zablocki v. Redhail*, 434 U.S. 374 (1978).

23. *See, e.g., Baker v. Nelson*, 291 Minn. 310, 191 N.W.2d 185 (1971), *appeal dismissed*, 409 U.S. 810 (1972); *Jones v. Hallahan*, 501 S.W.2d 588 (Ky Ct. App. 1973); *Singer v. Hara*, 11 Wash. App. 247, 522 P.2d 1187 (1974).

24. *See Domestic Partnership: Issues and Legislation* § 1, at 8 (Lambda Legal Defense and Educ. Fund, Inc., Family Relationships Project, 1990) [hereinafter *Domestic Partnership*].

25. A state may refuse to recognize foreign marriages or other contracts that would violate its own public policy. However, the mere fact that the marriage or contract could not have been entered into in the state in which recognition is sought does not necessarily mean that the foreign marriage or contract is void as against public policy.

26. *Braschi v. Stahl Associates, Co.*, 74 N.Y.2d 201, 543 N.E.2d 49, 544 N.Y.S.2d 784 (1989).

27. *Braschi*, 544 N.Y.S.2d at 788–89; *accord East 10th St. Associates v. Goldstein*, 154 A.D.2d 142, 552 N.Y.S.2d 257 (1990) (extending *Braschi* definition of family to evictions from rent-stabilized apartments despite statutory language limiting "family members" to enumerated marital or blood relations).

28. *Id.* at 790.

29. *Gay Teachers Association v. Board of Educ. of the City School Dist. of New York*, No. 43069/88, slip op. at 3, 7–9 (N.Y. Sup. Ct. Aug. 16, 1991).

30. *Donovan*, No. 73 LA 385–107, slip op. at 9 (Cal. Workers' Comp. App. Bd. Nov. 3, 1983) (opinion and notice of intention).

31. *Donovan v. Workers' Compensation Appeals Board*, 138 Cal. App. 3d 323, 187 Cal. Rptr. 869 (1982).

32. *Donovan*, No. 73 LA 385–107, slip op. at 2 (Cal. Workers' Comp. App. Bd. Dec. 3, 1983) (opinion and decision after remittitur).

33. *See Domestic Partnership, supra* note 24, at 1–3, pt. 1, at 1–10.

34. *Id.*

35. Los Angeles Times, Feb. 15, 1991, at A3.

36. Los Angeles Times, Dec. 3, 1990, at A3.

37. *In re Robert Paul P.*, 63 N.Y.2d 233, 471 N.E.2d 424, 481 N.Y.S.2d 651 (1984).

38. *Id.* at 238, 471 N.E.2d at 427, 481 N.Y.S.2d at 655.

39. *Id.* at 236, 471 N.E.2d at 425, 481 N.Y.S.2d at 653.

40. 121 A.D.2d 289, 292, 503 N.Y.S.2d 752, 754–55 (1986), *aff'd*, 70 N.Y.2d 660, 512 N.E.2d 541, 518 N.Y.S.2d 958 (1987).

41. For example, the federal income tax exemption of $2,000 for each dependent is available for a child who is nineteen or over only if the

child is a full-time student or earned less than $2,000 during the year.
26 U.S.C.A. § 151(c)(1), (d)(1) (West. Supp. 1991).

42. *Craig v. Gardner*, 299 F. Supp. 247 (N.D. Tex. 1969), *rev'd on other grounds sub nom. Craig v. Finch*, 425 F.2d 1005 (5th Cir. 1970).

43. *See, e.g.*, N.Y. Dom. Rel. Law § 117(b) (McKinney 1988).

44. *See, e.g.*, La. Civ. Code Ann. art. 229 (West Supp. 1991).

45. *See, e.g.*, N.C. Gen. Stat. § 14–178 (1990); 18 Pa. Cons. Stat. Ann. § 4302 (1989).

46. *Marvin v. Marvin*, 18 Cal. 3d 660, 557 P.2d 106, 134 Cal. Rptr. 815 (1976).

47. *See, e.g.*, *Levar v. Elkins*, 604 P.2d 602 (Alaska 1980); *Mason v. Rostad*, 476 A.2d 662 (D.C. 1984); *Glasgo v. Glasgo*, 410 N.E.2d 1325 (Ind. Ct. App. 1980); *Heistand v. Heistand*, 384 Mass. 20, 423 N.E.2d 313 (1981); *Carlson v. Olson*, 3 Fam. L. Rptr. (BNA) 2467 (Minn. 1977); *Brooks v. Kunz*, 637 S.W.2d 135 (Mo. Ct. App. 1982); *Dominguez v. Cruz*, 95 N.M. 1, 617 P.2d 1322 (N.M. Ct. App. 1980); *Morone v. Morone*, 50 N.Y.2d 481, 413 N.E.2d 1154, 429 N.Y.S.2d 592 (1980); *Beal v. Beal*, 4 Fam. L. Rptr. (BNA) 2464 (Or. 1978); *In re Estate of Steffes*, 95 Wis. 2d 490, 290 N.W.2d 697 (1980); *see also In re Eriksen*, 337 N.W.2d 671 (Minn. 1983) (recognizing constructive trust in inheritance setting based on cohabitation); *In re Estate of Thornton*, 81 Wash. 2d 72, 499 P.2d 864 (1972) (recognizing implied partnership based on cohabitation in inheritance setting). *But see, e.g.*, *Rehak v. Mathis*, 239 Ga. 541, 238 S.E.2d 81 (1977); *Hewitt v. Hewitt*, 77 Ill. 2d 49, 394 N.E.2d 1204 (1979); *Roach v. Buttons*, 6 Fam. L. Rep. (BNA) 2355 (Tenn. Ch. Ct. Feb. 19, 1980), all refusing to adopt the *Marvin* approach. *See generally* Note, *Developments—Sexual Orientation and the Law*, 102 Harv. L. Rev. 1508, 1624–26 (1989) [hereinafter *Developments in the Law*].

48. *Whorton v. Dillingham*, 202 Cal. App. 3d 447, 248 Cal. Rptr. 405 (1988) (enforcing oral agreement between gay couple as severable from portion of the agreement regarding provision of sexual services); *Richardson v. Conley*, 4 Fam. L. Rep. (BNA) 2532 (Cal. Super. Ct. June 27, 1978) (awarding $100 per month support payments to one member of a lesbian couple, based on couple's written union agreement). Another California case, decided after *Richardson* but before *Whorton*, declined to extend *Marvin* to a same-sex couple because it found that the provision of illicit sexual services was an inseparable part of the consideration for the couple's agreement. *Jones v. Daly*, 122 Cal. App. 3d 500, 176 Cal. Rptr. 130 (1981).

49. In *Cox v. Elwing*, 432 A.2d 736 (D.C. App. 1981), an appellate court vacated a lower court's dismissal of a suit brought by a gay man who alleged that his lover had expressly promised to support him until he

became employed after leaving his job to follow his lover to a new geographic area. The case was remanded for further factual findings. *See* Rivera, *Queer Law, supra* note 11, at 374–75. An Arkansas court, while not enforcing an express contract, used its equitable powers to find a constructive trust over property acquired in a homosexual relationship, holding that "a court of equity should not deny relief to a person merely because he is a homosexual." *Bramlett v. Selman*, 268 Ark. 457, 465, 597 S.W.2d 80, 85 (1980).

50. *See, e.g., Jones v. Daly*, 122 Cal. App. 3d 500, 176 Cal. Rptr. 130 (1981) (affirming dismissal of complaint because rendition of sexual services was an inseparable part of the consideration for the contract between gay couple); *Barnett v. King*, No. C365232 (Cal. Super. Ct., Los Angeles County, Dec. 22, 1982) (dismissing for failure to state a cause of action Barnett's suit against Billy Jean King for enforcement of alleged express oral contract for King to support Barnett in exchange for sexual and emotional intimacies); *Thornton v. Liberace*, No. C428492 (Cal. Super. Ct., Los Angeles County, Oct. 14, 1985) (dismissing *Marvin* portion of action against Liberace by alleged male lover because alleged contract was for sexual services). *See generally* Rivera, *Queer Law, supra* note 11, at 374–77.

51. *See, e.g., Wanamaker v. Weaver*, 176 N.Y. 75, 68 N.E. 135 (1903).

52. Hunter, *supra* note 2, at 28 n.71.

53. *See, e.g.*, Ariz. Rev. Stat. Ann. §§ 14-1201, 25-211 (1989).

54. Hunter, *supra* note 2, at 27–28 & nn.70–71.

55. *See, e.g.*, New York Est., Powers & Trusts Law § 4–1.1 (1990).

56. *See, e.g., Marx v. McLynn*, 88 N.Y. 358, 370–72 (1882).

57. *See, e.g., Matter of Brand*, 185 App. Div. 134, 173 N.Y.S. 169 (3d Dep't), *aff'd*, 227 N.Y. 630, 125 N.E. 169 (1918); *Matter of Dunn*, 184 App. Div. 386, 171 N.Y.S. 1056 (3d Dep't 1918).

58. *See, e.g., Matter of Fleischmann's Will*, 176 App. Div. 785, 163 N.Y.S. 426 (2d Dep't 1917).

59. *In re Estate of McBride*, No. 251 (Pa. C.P. Ct., Orphan's Ct. Div., Erie County, Sept. 20, 1984).

60. *See, e.g., Matter of Brand*, 185 App. Div. 134, 173 N.Y.S. 169 (3d Dep't), *aff'd*, 227 N.Y. 630, 125 N.E. 169 (1918).

61. *See, e.g., In re Spaulding's Estate*, 83 Cal. App. 2d 15, 187 P.2d 889 (1947); *In re Estate of McBride*, No. 251 (Pa. C.P. Ct., Orphan's Div., Erie County, Sept. 20, 1984).

62. *See, e.g., Matter of Kaufmann*, 20 A.D. 2d 464, 247 N.Y.S. 2d 664 (1st Dep't 1964), *aff'd*, 15 N.Y. 2d 825, 257 N.Y.S. 2d 941, 205 N.E. 2d 864 (1965).

63. *See generally* Sherman, *Undue Influence and the Homosexual Testator*, 42 U. Pitt. L. Rev. 225, 227, 267 (1981).

64. *See, e.g., Bulloch v. United States*, 487 F. Supp. 1078, 1088 (D.N.J. 1980); *Ledger v. Tippit*, 164 Cal. App. 3d 625, 210 Cal. Rptr. 814 (1985), *overruled, Elden v. Dheldon*, 46 Cal. 3d 267, 758 P.2d 582, 250 Cal. Rptr. 254 (1988).

65. *See, e.g., Coon v. Joseph*, 192 Cal. App. 3d 1269, 237 Cal. Rptr. 873 (1987).

66. *Cross v. National Fire Ins. Co.*, 132 N.Y. 133, 30 N.E. 390 (1892).

67. New York Ins. Law § 3205(a)(1) (McKinney 1985).

68. *See* Los Angeles City Consumer Task Force on Marital Status Discrimination, *Final Report, Unmarried Adults: A New Majority Seeks Consumer Protection* 29–35 & Supp. 81–105, 136, 138, 149–51, 193–94, 201–10, 214–18, (1990); Los Angeles City Task Force on Family Diversity, *Final Report, Task Force on the Changing Family* 40–42, 82 (1988).

69. *See, e.g.*, Alaska Stat. §§ 18.80.210, 18.80.220, 18.80.240 (1990); Ark. Stat. Ann. § 4-87-104 (1990); Cal. Gov't Code §§ 12920, 12921 (Deerings 1991); Conn. Gen. Stat. § 46a-60 (1989); Fla. Stat. §§ 760.05, 760.10 (1989); Ind. Code Ann. § 20-6.1-6-11 (Burns 1990); Md. Ann. Code art. 49B, § 20 (1989); N.J. Stat. Ann. § 10:5-9.1 (West 1990); N.Y. CLS Exec. § 296 (1990); Or. Rev. Stat. § 30.670 (1989); Va. Code Ann. § 2.1-716 (1990); West Va. Code § 33-17A-6 (1990).

70. *See, e.g.*, D.C. Code Ann. § 35-223(b)(1) (1988 & Michie Supp. 1990).

71. *See, e.g.*, Ariz. Rev. Stat. Ann. § 20-1104 (1989); Cal. Ins. Code §§ 280–87, 10110.1 (1991); New York Ins. Law § 3205 (1990).

72. *See* Los Angeles City Consumer Task Force on Marital Status Discrimination, *supra* note 68, at 33 & Supp. 82–105.

73. Rivera, *Queer Law, supra* note 11, at 390–91; Los Angeles City Consumer Task Force on Marital Status Discrimination, *supra* note 68, at 29–32.

74. *Domestic Partnership, supra* note 24, at pt. 1, 2–4, 11–13.

75. *Id.*

76. 26 U.S.C.A. § 2056(a) (West Supp. 1991).

77. 26 U.S.C.A. § 2523(a) (West Supp. 1991).

78. 26 U.S.C.A. § 2503(b) (West Supp. 1991).

79. 26 U.S.C.A. § 2513 (1989).

80. See generally *The Catalogue of Federal Domestic Assistance* (Office of Management and Budget, Washington, D.C.) for a guide to what federal benefits are available. The catalogue is updated regularly.

81. *Cf. King v. Smith*, 392 U.S. 309 (1968) (overturning an Alabama regulation denying AFDC payments to children whose mother "cohabits" with a man).

82. 7 U.S.C.A. § 2012(i), 2014 (1988 & West Supp. 1990).

83. 413 U.S. 528 (1973).

84. 42 U.S.C.A. §§ 602, 606 (1983 & West Supp. 1990).

85. 42 U.S.C.A. § 606(b) (West Supp. 1990).

86. *See, e.g., Boucher v. Minter*, 349 F. Supp. 1240 (D. Mass. 1972).

87. *See, e.g., Gardenia v. Norton*, 425 F. Supp. 922 (D. Conn. 1976).

88. *See Lewis v. Martin*, 397 U.S. 552 (1970).

89. For an excellent and comprehensive discussion of the law surrounding custody and visitation rights for lesbian and gay parents, see Rivera, *Queer Law, supra* note 11, at 327–71; *see also Developments in the Law, supra* note 47, at 1629–48.

90. *See Stanley v. Illinois*, 405 U.S. 645 (1972).

91. Rivera, *Queer Law, supra* note 11, at 335.

92. *See, e.g., Roe v. Roe*, 228 Va. 722, 723–24, 324 S.E.2d 691, 693–94 (1985); *N.K.M. v. L.E.M.*, 606 S.W.2d 179, 186 (Mo. Ct. App. 1980).

93. *See, e.g., Constant A. v. Paul C.A.*, 344 Pa. Super. 49, 58, 496 A.2d 1, 5 (1985).

94. *See Developments in the Law, supra* note 47, at 1631 & n.15 (citing cases from ten states, including Alaska, California, Indiana, Massachusetts, New Jersey, New York, South Carolina, Vermont, Washington, and West Virginia).

95. *Towend v. Towend*, No. 639 (Ohio Ct. App., Portage County, Sept. 00, 1976) (LEXIS, States library, Pa. file).

96. *Id.*

97. *G.A. v. D.A.*, 745 S.W.2d 726, 727–28 (Mo. Ct. App. 1987); *id.* at 729 (Lowenstein, J., dissenting).

98. *Bezio v. Patenaude*, 381 Mass. 563, 569, 410 N.E.2d 1207, 1211 (1980).

99. *Id.* at 579, 410 N.E.2d at 1215–16.

100. *S.N.E. v. R.L.B.*, 699 P.2d 875, 879 (Alaska 1985).

101. *In the Matter of Jacinta M.*, 107 N.M. 769, 772, 764 P.2d 1327, 1330 (1988).

102. *See, e.g., Conkel v. Conkel*, 31 Ohio App. 3d 169, 170–71, 509 N.E.2d 983, 985 (1987) (child has an interest in continued bond with noncustodial parent); *see generally Developments in the Law, supra* note 47, at 1632–33.

103. *See, e.g., Roberts v. Roberts*, 22 Ohio App. 3d 127, 129, 489 N.E.2d 1067, 1070 (1985).

104. *See, e.g., Miller v. Hawkins*, 549 So. 2d 102 (Ala. Civ. App. 1989) (awarding allegedly bisexual or lesbian mother right to visit son at least twice a weak for not less than one hour in home of child's father or maternal grandmother but prohibiting unsupervised overnight visits in mother's home); *In re Marriage of Birdsall*, 243 Cal. Rptr. 287, 197 Cal. App. 3d 1024 (1988) (reversing restraint imposed by trial court prohibiting gay father's overnight visits with son in the

presence of any other known homosexual); *Stewart v. Stewart*, 521 N.E.2d 956 (Ind. Ct. App. 1988) (reversing trial court order terminating father's visitation rights due to HIV infection); *Irish v. Irish*, 102 Mich. App. 75, 300 N.W.2d 739 (1980) (affirming trial court's restriction on lesbian mother's overnight visitation if mother's lover was present); *J.P. v. P.W.*, No. 15937, 15981, slip op. (Mo. App. May 5, 1989) (affirming trial court's restriction of gay father's visitation to exclude presence of father's lover or any other male with whom the father resides).

105. *Gerde v. Butler*, No. 80-CI–2230 (Ky. Cir. Ct., Kenton County, Sept. 30, 1981).

106. *Gottlieb v. Gottlieb*, 108 A.D.2d 120, 488 N.Y.S.2d 180, 182 (1985).

107. *See, e.g., Chaffin v. Frye*, 45 Cal. App. 3d 39, 119 Cal. Rptr. 22 (1975); *Roberts v. Roberts*, 25 N.C. App. 198, 212 S.E.2d 410 (1975); *In the Interest of Holt*, 102 Idaho 44, 625 P.2d 398 (1981).

108. *Gerald & Margaret D. v. Peggy R.*, No. C–9104, Petition No. 9-12-143-CV (Del. Fam. Ct. Nov. 17, 1980) (LEXIS, States library, Del. file); *Bezio v. Patenaude*, 381 Mass. 563, 576, 410 N.E.2d 1207, 1214 (1980); *Albright v. Commonwealth ex rel. Fetters*, 491 Pa. 320, 323, 421 A.2d 157, 158 (1980); *People v. Brown*, 49 Mich. App. 358, 212 N.W.2d 55 (1973).

109. *See Developments in the Law, supra* note 47, at 1634–35.

110. Unif. Marriage & Divorce Act § 401(d)(2), 9A U.L.A. at 550 (1987).

111. *See, e.g.,* 1989 Or. Rev. Stat. § 109.19[1].

112. *See, e.g., In re Alison D. v. Virginia M.*, 155 A.D.2d 11, 552 N.Y.S.2d 321 (1990), *aff'd*, 77 N.Y.2d 651, 572 N.E.2d 27, 569 N.Y.S.2d 586 (1991); *Nancy S. v. Michele G.*, 228 Cal. App. 3d 831, 279 Cal. Rptr. 212 (1st Dist. 1991).

113. *In re Hatzopoulos*, 4 Fam. L. Rptr. (BNA) 2075 (Col. Juv. Ct., Denver Cty., 1977).

114. *Stanley v. Illinois*, 405 U.S. 645 (1972) (invalidating law that presumed without a hearing that unwed fathers were unfit).

115. *Meyer v. Nebraska*, 262 U.S. 390, 399 (1923).

116. *Skinner v. Oklahoma*, 316 U.S. 535, 541 (1942).

117. *May v. Anderson*, 345 U.S. 528, 533 (1953).

118. *Santosky v. Kramer*, 455 U.S. 745 (1982); *see also Washburn v. Washburn*, 49 Cal. App. 2d 581, 588, 122 P.2d 96, 100 (1942).

119. *See, e.g.,* Fla. Stat. § 63.042(3) (1989); N.H. Rev. Stat. Ann. §§ 170-B:4, 170-F:6 (1989).

120. *Seebol v. Farie*, No. 90-923-CA-18, slip op. (Fla. Cir. Ct. Mar. 15, 1991).

121. *In re Adoption of Charles B.*, 1988 Ohio App. LEXIS 4435, No. CA–3382 (Oct. 28, 1988), *rev'd*, 50 Ohio St. 3d 88, 552 N.E.2d 884 (1990).

122. *In re Adoption of Charles B.*, 50 Ohio St. 3d 88, 552 N.E.2d 884 (1990); *see In re Appeal in Pima County Juvenile Action B–10489*, 151 Ariz. 335, 340, 727 P.2d 830, 835 (Ct. App. 1986).

123. *Developments in the Law, supra* note 47, at 1643.

124. *Id.* at 1643–44.

125. New York Times, June 21, 1979, B1.

126. *See, e.g.*, N.Y. Dom. Rel. Law § 117(a) (McKinney 1988).

127. *See, e.g.*, Va. Code Ann. § 63.1–233 (1987).

128. *In re Adoption Petition of N.*, No. 18086 (Cal. Super. Ct., San Francisco County, Mar. 11, 1986); *In re Adoption of a Minor Child*, No. 1-JU-86-73 (Alaska Super. Ct. Feb. 6, 1987); *In re Adoption of M.M.S.A.*, No. D-8503-61930 (Or. Cir. Ct., Multnomah County, Sept. 4, 1985).

129. Ricketts & Achtenberg, *The Adoptive and Foster Gay and Lesbian Parent*, in *Gay and Lesbian Parents* 98 (F. Bozett ed. 1987) (citing No. 17350 (Cal. Super. Ct., Alameda County, Apr. 8, 1986), and No. 17945 (Cal. Super. Ct., San Francisco County, Feb. 24, 1986)).

130. *See, e.g.*, N.H. Rev. Stat. Ann. § 161:2 (1989); N.D. Admin. Code § 75-03-14-04(1) (1984) (allowing placement of foster children only in homes of married couples); *see also* Mass. Regs. Code tit. 110, § 7.103(3)(a) (1986) (placing lesbians and gay men in bottom priority level for receiving foster placements).

131. New York Times, Nov. 27, 1979, B2. *Cf. Big Brothers, Inc. v. Minneapolis Comm'n on Civil Rights*, 284 N.W. 2d 823 (Minn. 1979) (nonprofit corporation providing services to boys without fathers may require adult volunteers to disclose sexual orientation and may communicate that information to boys' families, even though city has an antidiscrimination ordinance covering gay people).

VII

The Criminal Law

One evening in 1982, a police officer in Atlanta gained entry to the home of a gay man by the name of Michael Hardwick, watched secretly while Hardwick made love to another man in his own bedroom, and then arrested both men for violating Georgia's sodomy statute—a law providing for up to twenty years in prison. The district attorney ultimately chose not to prosecute either Hardwick or his partner, but Hardwick refused to put the matter to rest. He brought a lawsuit against the state for invalidation of the sodomy statute, asserting that it violated his constitutional right to privacy.

Michael Hardwick's lawsuit had fateful consequences. It eventually reached the United States Supreme Court, and, in a decision with reverberations for every lesbian and gay man in the country, the Court, by a narrow margin of five to four, upheld Georgia's sodomy law and, by implication, every other similar statute, as least insofar as those statutes apply to gay people.[1]

Consensual sodomy statutes form the cornerstone of the oppression of lesbians and gay men. While they do not make homosexuality itself a crime[2] and while they are enforced only infrequently, they convey the sense that gay people are inherently criminal and provide an official justification for prejudice and mistreatment in every realm of existence, public and private, from housing and employment to parenthood and domestic partnership. Thus in *Bowers v. Hardwick* the Supreme Court did much more than merely enunciate constitutional doctrine. The Court, in essence and effect, endorsed and thereby perpetuated the conditions that have tormented lesbians and gay men throughout the history of the United States.

This chapter addresses the subject of consensual sodomy statutes and related laws, with the hope of putting the decision in *Bowers v. Hardwick* in its proper perspective. Indeed, despite *Hardwick*, the long-term trends are encouraging; since 1962, half of the states have abolished their consensual sodomy statutes, in most instances voluntarily by act of the state legislature. The chapter will also describe the growth in violence

against lesbians and gay men and the law's response—or lack
of it.

What exactly do consensual sodomy statutes prohibit?

The statutes vary from state to state and rely on different
terms—"consensual sodomy" and "deviate sexual intercourse"
in some states and "buggery" and "crime against nature" in
others—but in general they outlaw oral sex and anal sex. In
most states, the prohibition applies not only to homosexual
couples, but heterosexual couples as well. Indeed, of the twenty-five states that still retain consensual sodomy statutes, only
eight limit their statutes to same-sex couples: Arkansas, Kansas,
Kentucky, Missouri, Montana, Nevada, Tennessee, and
Texas.[3] (Appendix A is a state-by-state compilation of consensual sodomy statutes and related laws.)

The statute books of some states go considerably beyond oral
and anal sex. Maryland, for example, has not only a sodomy
statute, but also laws that prohibit "lewdness" and "unnatural
or perverted sexual practices."[4] Michigan outlaws "gross lewdness" and "gross indecency."[5] Oklahoma has a criminal statute
entitled "grossly outraging public decency," a term defined as
the commission of any act "that openly outrages public decency
or is injurious to public morals."[6] Statutes of this sort may
be constitutionally vulnerable because of their vagueness and
breadth, at least if they are applied to conduct other than oral
or anal sex, sex with minors, or sex in public.[7]

Every state has laws that criminalize sex with minors, sex
committed with force or without the consent of the other person, sex in a public place and sex for money (except Nevada,
which gives counties the option of permitting prostitution).

Which states still have sodomy statutes?

At the time this is written, exactly half the states and the
District of Columbia still have consensual sodomy statutes:
Alabama, Arizona, Arkansas, Florida, Georgia, Idaho, Kansas,
Kentucky, Louisiana, Maryland, Massachusetts, Michigan,
Minnesota, Mississippi, Missouri, Montana, Nevada, North
Carolina, Oklahoma, Rhode Island, South Carolina, Tennes-
see, Texas, Utah, and Virginia. (See Appendix A for details on
each state.) But the statutes may be unenforceable in at least
four of those states. In 1974, the Supreme Judicial Court of

Massachusetts ruled that a statute criminalizing "unnatural and lascivious acts" could not constitutionally be applied to private, consensual conduct by adults, implying that it would similarly interpret the state's sodomy statute.[8] And, more recently, lower-court judges in Kentucky, Michigan, and Texas have issued rulings declaring their state's consensual sodomy statutes unconstitutional under their *state* constitutions.[9] (The Supreme Court's decision in *Bowers v. Hardwick* has essentially foreclosed any possibility of such a ruling under the federal constitution.)

Which states have eliminated their consensual sodomy statutes, and how did they do it?

The twenty-five states that have fully eliminated their sodomy statutes are Alaska, California, Colorado, Connecticut, Delaware, Hawaii, Illinois, Indiana, Iowa, Maine, Nebraska, New Hampshire, New Jersey, New Mexico, New York, North Dakota, Ohio, Oregon, Pennsylvania, South Dakota, Vermont, Washington, West Virginia, Wisconsin, and Wyoming. Astonishingly, all but two of these states acted through their state legislatures. However, in virtually no state did the legislature consider explicitly and separately whether or not to retain consensual sodomy as a crime; in most instances, the repeal came as part of a general recodification of criminal statutes, and the fact that the omnibus reform left out sodomy was hardly noticed or commented upon.[10] The first state to act was Illinois in 1961. The most recent to eliminate its sodomy statute was Wisconsin in 1983. The two exceptions are New York and Pennnsylvania. Sodomy laws still appear in the statute books of those states, but the states' highest courts have ruled the laws unconstitutional and therefore unenforceable.[11]

In light of the fact that until 1961 every state in the union had a consensual sodomy statute, the abolition of those laws in twenty-five states constitutes nothing short of a legal revolution. The pace of reform has slowed considerably, though. No state has repealed its sodomy statute since 1983. Moreover, the states remaining in the "unreformed" column tend to be politically conservative and resistant to change. (The list includes, for example, the entire South.)

How did the Supreme Court justify its ruling in *Bowers v. Hardwick*?

The Court relied essentially on two arguments: history and popular opinion. "Proscriptions against [homosexual sodomy] have ancient roots," wrote Justice Byron White in the opinion for the five justices in the majority. He then paid homage to, in his words, "the presumed belief of a majority of the electorate in Georgia that homosexual sodomy is immoral and unacceptable." He added: "The law . . . is constantly based on notions of morality, and if all laws representing essentially moral choices are to be invalidated under the Due Process Clause [of the Fourteenth Amendment], the courts will be very busy indeed."[12]

The most interesting and telling aspect of the Court's opinion is what it failed to say. Nowhere did Justice White offer a principled distinction between *Hardwick* and the Supreme Court's earlier cases extending the constitutional right to privacy to procreation, contraception, and abortion, even though other courts, including the court of appeals in the *Hardwick* case itself, had interpreted those precedents as leading to a contrary result.[13] The opinion makes clear that Justice White and his four colleagues refused to accord any degree of gravity to Michael Hardwick's claims; at one point, Justice White belittled the arguments made on Hardwick's behalf by calling them "at best, facetious."

Justice Blackmun, writing for the four dissenting members of the Court, sharply and passionately disputed this characterization of the case. He accused the majority of betraying "the values most deeply rooted in our Nation's history" and asserted his objection to the idea that "either the length of time a majority has held its convictions or the passions with which it defends them can withdraw legislation from this Court's scrutiny." He also articulated a resounding defense of the value of recognizing sexual diversity.

> Only the most willful blindness could obscure the fact that sexual intimacy is a "sensitive, key relationship of human existence, central to family life, community welfare, and the development of human personality." . . . The fact that individuals define themselves in a significant way

through intimate sexual relationships with others suggests, in a Nation as diverse as ours, that there may be many "right" ways of conducting those relationships, and that much of the richness of a relationship will come from the freedom an individual has to *choose* the form and nature of these intensely personal bonds.[14]

The only solace offered by *Bowers v. Hardwick* is the scorn and ridicule accorded it by editorial writers, cartoonists, and other commentators, including most legal scholars.[15] And one justice in the majority—Justice Lewis Powell—conceded after his retirement that he had "made a mistake."[16]

How does *Bowers v. Hardwick* bear on the movement to repeal or eliminate sodomy statutes?

A ruling in favor of Michael Hardwick would probably have meant the invalidation, in one blow, of all the remaining sodomy statutes. The contrary, however, is not true: the ruling against him does not revive the sodomy statutes already discarded by the states, or otherwise reverse the movement to abolish those laws. It simply makes further progress more arduous. In essence, it renders futile any future judicial challenges to a sodomy statute under the *federal* constitution.[17]

Nonetheless, as we have already said, trial-court judges in three states—Kentucky, Michigan, and Texas—have, since *Bowers v. Hardwick*, declared their sodomy statutes unconstitutional under their *state* constitutions. (The Supreme Court plays no role in the interpretation of state constitutional provisions and thus will have no chance to examine these decisions, regardless of how they develop at the state level.) These bold rulings furnish the best proof that *Hardwick* will not be the final word on sodomy statutes.

As we have already made clear, no state has repealed its sodomy statute since *Hardwick*. Nor, happily, has any state resurrected its sodomy statute.

Under what other kinds of criminal statutes are lesbians and gay men especially vulnerable?

Two kinds in particular: solicitation statutes and loitering statutes. These laws may exist even in states that have repealed their sodomy statutes.[18] (See Appendix A.)

What are solicitation statutes?

Solicitation statutes prohibit the solicitation of—that is, the invitation, request, or offer to perform—an illegal or improper act. Michigan's solicitation law, for example, makes criminal the "accosting, soliciting, or inviting another person in public to do a lewd or immoral act."[19] An arrest for solicitation is possible in any state that has retained its sodomy statute regardless of whether that state has a specific "solicitation" law like Michigan's since in every state, soliciting another person to engage in criminal activity, regardless of its nature, is a crime by itself.

Most states that have abolished consensual sodomy as a crime no longer make solicitation of sodomy a crime. In some of those states, the courts have narrowed or actually overturned solicitation statutes as unconstitutional.[20]

What are loitering statutes?

Loitering statutes—sometimes called vagrancy or disorderly conduct statutes—criminalize being or remaining in a public place for no apparent purpose or an illegal or improper purpose. Such statutes may be subject to constitutional attack to the extent they outlaw merely being in public without a purpose or explanation.[21] Some states have loitering statutes specifically aimed at gay people; Delaware's loitering law, for instance, prohibits "remaining in a public place for the purpose of engaging or soliciting another person to engage in sexual intercourse or deviate sexual intercourse."[22]

The police in many cities and states still use loitering and solicitation statutes to harass lesbians and gay men and to patrol gay bars, cruising grounds, and other places where gay people gather. In some places, the police rely on these statutes to justify entrapment schemes.

What should a person do if arrested for an offense?

A person should not resist arrest (resisting arrest is itself a crime) but should not volunteer any information or admit to any conduct to either the arresting officer or any other police official. An arrestee is not required to furnish anything other than name and address and should refuse to discuss the case further until he or she has had a chance to talk to a lawyer.

Is it ever advisable to plead guilty to a lesser offense?
The question of whether to "cop a plea"—that is, to plead guilty to a less serious crime to avoid a trial and the possibility of a harsher conviction and sentence—should only be resolved after both the defendant and a lawyer have carefully examined all the facts, including the possible effect on employment.

The issue often comes down to proof: what evidence will be presented and what and who will be believed? Even if a person is innocent, there is a possibility that the witnesses against him or her will lie and sound credible to the judge or jury.

What are the factors to be considered in such a decision?
The first consideration is the criminal record that would be established by a conviction on the original charge and the effect such a record would have on an individual's future, as compared to the record that would be created by a plea to the lesser offense and then the likelihood of a conviction on the original charge. Other factors include whether the individual already has a criminal record and how the judge would view that record at sentencing, what various penalties are possible on each charge, what publicity might ensue from a trial and what effect that publicity would have, and how much time and money a full defense would entail.

If the individual holds an occupational license from the state—as do all teachers, lawyers, and many other professionals—the effect on that license should be weighed. In many states, being convicted of a felony (and sodomy is still a felony in some states) will lead automatically to the suspension or revocation of an occupational license. An individual may also lose an occupational license if the conviction is viewed by the licensing authority as involving "moral turpitude." (See chapter 2, "Employment.")

If a person decides to contest the charge and plead not guilty, should he or she ask for a jury trial?
It depends. The personal attitudes of the judge likely to try the case should be considered and then compared to the probable reactions of people in the community from which the jury will be drawn. If a jury trial is requested, the lawyer should examine all the prospective jurors during the voir dire proceedings to determine their views on gay people and homo-

sexuality. Jurors who reveal prejudices should be challenged for cause.

Can the victim of an undercover police operation allege entrapment?

Such a defense is unlikely to succeed. The Supreme Court has limited severely the defense of entrapment. In essence, it must be shown not only that the police set a trap but also that the targeted individual lacks the "predisposition" to commit crimes of the sort of which he or she is accused.[23]

If the defendant prevails and the charges are dismissed, can he or she have the arrest removed from his or her record?

Many states now have laws that let defendants obtain their fingerprints and photographs if they are acquitted or the charges against them are dismissed. Many also have laws that permit arrest records to be expunged or sealed. A motion to the same effect might be successful even in a state without such a statute.

What should a person do if someone tries to blackmail him or her on the basis of being gay?

The frequency of such threats, as well as the damage they can do, seem to be diminishing as lesbians and gay men become more visible and outspoken. Nonetheless the victim of blackmail should discuss the matter immediately with a lawyer, especially in an area without civil-rights protections for gay people. Simply giving in to the demands almost never allows an advantage since the demands typically continue and may even multiply. The victim of an attempt to blackmail should stall until he or she can receive help. Blackmail is a form of extortion and therefore a crime. It deserves punishment.

How prevalent is violence against lesbians and gay men simply because they are gay?

Shockingly, violence against gay people seems to be growing. A report issued in 1987 under the sponsorship of the National Institute of Justice concluded that "homosexuals are probably the most frequent victims" of hate-motivated violence in the United States.[24] The National Gay and Lesbian Task Force reviewed the crime statistics for six American cities for the year

1990 and found an average rise in reported incidents against lesbians and gay men of 42 percent over 1989.[25]

The increase is probably attributable in part to the growing visibility and activism of gay people, in part to fear and ignorance of AIDS, and in part to better documentation. Moreover, there is evidence that crimes motivated by hate are more common generally, regardless of group or category.[26]

Has the law responded to this increase in hate-motivated crimes against lesbians and gay men?

To a very limited extent. Virtually every state has by now enacted some form of legislation to address bias-related violence, but as of this writing, only fourteen of them extend to lesbians and gay men.[27] (See Appendix C.) These laws are generally of three kinds: enhanced penalties for crimes motivated by hatred or bias; authorization of special civil suits for damages or injunctive relief; or direction to government agencies to gather statistics on hate-motivated activity.[28]

In 1990 Congress passed the Hate Crime Statistics Act, which authorized the Department of Justice to collect data regularly on crimes motivated by the victim's "race, religion, sexual orientation or ethnicity."[29] While limited on its face to record-keeping, the law does constitute an official declaration by the federal government that violence against lesbians and gay men is worthy of attention. It also contains the first use in a federal statute of the term "sexual orientation."

The National Gay and Lesbian Task Force declared in its 1990 report, "Despite a very large body of evidence to show that lesbians and gay men face an epidemic of bigotry and violence, they are often intentionally excluded from hate crime measures." It further stated: "Although some leaders in government, law enforcement, and religion actively support efforts to oppose violence and discrimination based on sexual orientation, they frequently encounter fierce resistance from those seeking to deny lesbian and gay people the same protections accorded to other groups in our society. The continued denial of such protections is a legal and moral disgrace that must be challenged and overcome."[30]

What are the rights of the victim of a hate-motivated crime?

They vary from state to state. A victim may, depending on where he or she lives, have a right to compensation from the government for losses, including lost wages; to restitution from the perpetrator; to a civil suit for damages; and to some degree of involvement in the criminal prosecution of the defendant. In any case, the advice and help of a victim assistance agency should be sought. Every state and many cities have such agencies. Some cities now have, in addition, nonprofit organizations for lesbians and gay men who are victims of crime.[31]

The crime should also be reported to the National Hate Crimes Hotline at 1–800–347-HATE, as well as to the police. In 1990, in the first six months of the hotline's operation, eight percent of the calls it received related to sexual orientation.

May a defendant who attacked a lesbian or gay man offer a defense of "homosexual panic"?

Defendants in several recent cases have tried to escape or lessen their culpability by claiming they "panicked" in response to the defendant's sexual orientation. Their lawyers have asserted that "homosexual panic" is a form of insanity or evidence of diminished mental capacity. Most courts have rejected such a defense.[32]

NOTES

1. *See Bowers v. Hardwick,* 478 U.S. 186 (1986).
2. A statute making homosexuality itself a crime would almost certainly violate the constitutional proscription against "cruel and unusual punishment" and perhaps other constitutional provisions as well. *See generally Robinson v. California,* 370 U.S. 660 (1962) (invalidating a California statute making it a crime to be "addicted to the use of narcotics"). No state has ever made homosexuality itself a crime.
3. As noted later in this chapter, the sodomy statutes in Kentucky and Texas are of uncertain enforceability at the time of this writing since lower courts in both states have declared them unconstitutional under their state constitutions.
4. *See* Md. Ann. Code art. 27, §§ 27-15 & 27-554.
5. *See* Mich. Comp. Laws §§ 750.335, 750.338, & 750.338a.
6. *See* Okla. Stat. tit. 21, § 22.
7. *See, e.g., Commonwealth v. Balthazar,* 366 Mass. 298, 318 N.E.2d 478 (1974) (statute prohibiting "unnatural and lascivious acts" held not applicable to private, consensual adult behavior); *Revere v. Aucella,*

369 Mass. 138, 338 N.E.2d 816, *appeal dismissed,* 429 U.S. 877 (1975) (statute prohibiting "open and gross lewdness" held vague and overbroad). *Cf. District of Columbia v. Garcia,* 335 A.2d 217 (D.C. Ct. App. 1975)(District of Columbia ordinance outlawing "lewd, obscene and indecent sexual proposals" interpreted to cover only invitations to commit sodomy, indecent exposure, or sexual acts with minors). *But see State v. Walsh,* 713 S.W.2d 508 (Mo. 1986) (upholding a conviction under Missouri's sodomy statute for the mere "touch[ing]" of an undercover officer's "genitalia through his clothing"; the accusatory instrument alleged that "such conduct was a substantial step toward the commission" of the crime of sodomy).

8. *See Commonwealth v. Balthazar, supra* note 7.
9. *See Commonwealth v. Wasson,* No. 86-XX-048 (Fayette County Cir. Ct. 1989) (appeal pending); *Michigan Org. for Human Rights v. Kelley,* No. 88-815820 CZ (Wayne County Cir. Ct. July 9, 1990)(no appeal taken); and *Morales v. State,* No. 461, 898 (Travis County Dist Ct., Mar. 15, 1991) (appeal pending). *See generally Gay Groups Turn to State Courts to Win Rights,* New York Times, Dec. 21, 1990, at B6.
10. In 1955 the prestigious American Law Institute considered a new version of its Model Penal Code that, for the first time, omitted consensual sodomy as a crime. *See* Model Penal Code, § 213.2 (Tentative Draft No. 4, 1955), at 276–91. The Institute later formally accepted the recommendation that the Code exclude any such offense. *See* Model Penal Code, § 213.2 (Official Draft, 1962). The state legislatures that voted subsequently to eliminate their sodomy statutes were, by and large, following the recommendations of the American Law Institute.
11. *See People v. Onofre,* 51 N.Y.2d 476, 434 N.Y.S.2d 947, 415 N.E.2d 936 (1980), *cert. denied,* 451 U.S. 987 (1981) (New York's consensual sodomy statute violates the federal constitution's right to privacy and guarantee of equal protection); and *Commonwealth v. Bonadio,* 490 Pa. 91, 415 A.2d 47 (1980) (Pennsylvania's "deviate sexual intercourse" statute exceeds the state's police power and also violates equal protection principles).
12. *See Bowers v. Hardwick, supra* note 1.
13. *See Hardwick v. Bowers,* 760 F.2d 1202 (11th Cir. 1985) ("The activity [Hardwick] hopes to engage in is quintessentially private and lies at the heart of an intimate association beyond the proper reach of state regulation."). *See also People v. Onofre, supra* note 11.
14. *See Bowers v. Hardwick, supra* note 1, at 199 (Blackmun, J., dissenting). Justice Blackmun was joined in dissent by Justices Brennan, Marshall, and Stevens.

15. Critical commentaries in the popular press include Kilpatrick, *Sodomy Ruling Strays from Good Sense*, Washington Post, July , 1986; Goodman, *Don't Ignore Court's Footnote Trap*, The Tennessean, July 4, 1986, at 15A; Brest, *Supreme Court Proscribes a View of Privacy*, Los Angeles Times, July 13, 1986; and T.R.B., *The Purpose of Privacy*, The New Republic, July 1986, at 4. Legal commentaries include Conkle, *The Second Death of Substantive Due Process*, 62 Ind. L.J. 215 (1986–87); Richards, *Constitutional Legitimacy and Constitutional Privacy*, 61 N.Y.U.L. Rev. 800 (1986); *The Supreme Court, 1985 Term—Leading Cases*, 100 Harv. L. Rev. 100, 210–20; Stoddard, *Bowers v. Hardwick: Precedent by Personal Predilection*, 54 U. Chi. L. Rev. 648 (1987); L. Tribe & M. Dorf, *On Reading the Constitution* (1991); and L. Tribe, *American Constitutional Law*, 1422–35 (2d ed. 1988).

16. *See Powell Regrets Backing Sodomy Law*, Washington Post, Oct. 26, 1990, at A3.

17. As a formal matter, the Supreme Court only ruled on one specific aspect of the constitutionality of sodomy statutes: whether they violate the federal right to privacy first articulated by the Court in *Griswold v. Connecticut*, 381 U.S. 479 (1965). It is theoretically possible that a sodomy statute would be constitutional under the right to privacy but unconstitutional under another constitutional guarantee, like the equal protection clause of the Fourteenth Amendment or the cruel and unusual punishment clause of the Eighth Amendment. *See* Sunstein, *Sexual Orientation and the Constitution: A Note on the Relationship Between Due Process and Equal Protection*, 55 U. Chi. L. Rev. 1161 (1988). However, several federal appellate courts have crudely and misguidedly interpreted *Bowers v. Hardwick* to undercut, in essence, the possibility of a successful equal protection challenge. *See, e.g., Padula v. Webster*, 822 F.2d 97 (D.C. Cir. 1987) ("It would be quite anomolous, on its face, to declare status defined by conduct that states may constitutionally criminalize as deserving of strict scrutiny under the equal protection clause."); *ben-Shalom v. Marsh*, 881 F.2d 454 (7th Cir. 1989) ("Although the Court analyzed the constitutionality of the statute on a due process rather than an equal protection basis, *Hardwick* nevertheless impacts on the scrutiny aspects under an equal protection analysis."); and *High Tech Gays v. Defense Indus. Sec. Clearance Office*, 895 F.2d 563 (9th Cir. 1990) ("[B]y the *Hardwick* majority holding that the Constitution confers no fundamental right upon homosexuals to engage in sodomy, and because homosexual conduct can thus be criminalized, homosexuals cannot constitute a suspect or quasi-suspect class entitled to greater than rational basis

review for equal protection purposes."). Moreover, at the very least, *Hardwick* demonstrates that the Supreme Court is not now receptive to constitutional attacks on sodomy statutes.

18. *See, e.g.*, Del. Code Ann. tit. 11, § 1321 (loitering); and Wis. Stat. Ann. § 947.02 (vagrancy).

19. *See* Mich. Comp. Laws § 750.448.

20. *See, e.g., Pryor v. Municipal Court,* 25 Cal. 3d 238, 158 Cal. Rptr. 330, 599 P.2d 636 (1979) (California's "disorderly conduct" statute must be limited to acts or solicitations in public involving "touching of the genitals, buttocks, or female breast, for purposes of sexual arousal, gratification, annoyance or offense"); *State v. Phipps,* 58 Ohio St. 2d 271, 389 N.E.2d 1128 (1979) (Ohio "importuning" statute is limited to cover only "fighting words"—"words that by their very utterance inflict injury or tend to incite an immediate breach of the peace"); *State v. Tusek,* 52 Or. App. 997, 630 P.2d 892 (1981)(Oregon statute outlawing solicitation to engage in "deviate sexual intercourse" violates the First Amendment); *People v. Uplinger,* 58 N.Y.2d 936, 447 N.E.2d 62, 460 N.Y.S.2d 514 (1983), *cert. denied,* 467 U.S. 246 (1984)(New York statute outlawing loitering for the purpose of engaging in "deviate sexual intercourse" is unenforceable in light of earlier judicial decision invalidating the state's consensual sodomy statute).

21. *See, e.g., People v. Berck,* 32 N.Y.2d 567, 347 N.Y.S.2d 33, 300 N.E.2d 411 (1973).

22. *See* Del. Code Ann. tit. 11, § 1321.

23. *See generally Sherman v. U.S.,* 356 U.S. 369 (1958).

24. *See Open Season on Gays,* Time, Mar. 7, 1988. The study also concluded that the "criminal-justice system—like the rest of society—has not recognized the seriousness" of the problem.

25. *See Anti-Gay/Lesbian Violence, Victimization & Defamation in 1990,* published by the NGLTF Policy Institute, 1991, at 1. The six cities and their individual percentages of increase are Chicago, 11%; Los Angeles, 20%; San Francisco, 29%; New York City, 65%; Boston, 75%; and Minneapolis/St. Paul, 133%.

26. *See generally* G. Herek & K. Bernill, *Hate Crimes: Confronting Violence Against Lesbians and Gay Men* (1991).

27. *See generally Hate Crimes Statutes Abound,* The National Law Journal, May 21, 1990.

28. *See, e.g.,* Vt. Stat. Ann. tit. 13, §§ 1454–57 (providing, among other things, for enhanced penalties for any crime "maliciously motivated by the victim's actual or perceived race, color, religion, national origin, sex, ancestry, age, service in the armed forces of the United States, handicap . . . or sexual orientation"); and Ca. Penal Code § 422.6

(providing, among other things, for imprisonment of up to six months or a fine of up to $5,000 or both, for any act of force or threat of force that "wilfully injure[s], intimidate[s] or interfere[s] with, oppress[es] or threaten[s] any other person in the free exercise or enjoyment of any right or privilege secured to him or her by the Constitution of the United States because of the other person's race, color, religion, ancestry, national origin, or sexual orientation").

29. *See* Hate Crime Statistics Act, Pub. L. No. 101–275, 104 Stat. 140 (1990). The act contains the following proviso, which, although it has uncertain legal significance, without a doubt constitutes a political affront to gay people: "Nothing in this Act shall be construed, nor shall any funds appropriated to carry out the purpose of the Act be used, to promote or encourage homosexuality."

30. *Anti-Gay/Lesbian Violence, supra* note 25, at 25–26.

31. *See generally* J. Stark & H. Goldstein, *The Rights of Crime Victims* (ACLU Handbook) (1985).

32. *See, e.g., Commonwealth v. Carr*, No. CC–385–88 (Pa. Ct. of C.P., Adams County, Apr. 3, 1989), cited in 1988 Lesbian/Gay Law Notes 64.

VIII
The Rights of People with HIV Disease

In many ways, AIDS shaped the decade of the 1980s for the lesbian and gay community. Acquired immune deficiency syndrome especially dominated the concerns of gay men, among whom this new and terrifying virus first appeared. Because it was a fatal and sexually transmissible disease associated with a stigmatized minority, AIDS engendered widespread public panic. The impulse to exclude those with the disease led to firings, evictions, denials of government benefits, refusals to treat, loss of insurance, and sometimes banishment from families.

Civil rights advocates, together with public health officials who sought rational policies to try to control the spread of the virus, fought back. A series of lawsuits, beginning with the cases of children with AIDS who were kept out of school, established that many courts were willing to force government agencies and others to make policy based on objective medical evidence, not hysteria. Hundreds of bills were introduced in state legislatures and in Congress to enact public health laws to deal with the disease; some established new laws for the confidentiality of medical records and prohibited tests to detect the virus that causes AIDS unless done with the patient's informed consent.

As the 1990s began, the medical normalization of AIDS—now called "HIV disease" to indicate the full spectrum of disease beginning with an asymptomatic stage after the initial infection and gradually advancing into the final and fatal stage of AIDS—was underway. Spurred by the demands of activists, medical researchers developed drugs to slow the progressive deterioration of the body's immune system caused by the virus and to fight off some of the opportunistic diseases that commonly manifest themselves through the weakened immune system. Securing access to those treatments became a primary goal of AIDS activists.

The social response to AIDS, however, lagged behind the advances in science. Although much of the initial panic over the risk of uninfected persons "catching" the disease diminished with greater public information, incidents of discrimination continued to increase.[1] As the expense of treatments grew and as health care budgets tightened, public debate shifted from fear of contagion to fear of cost. The demographics of HIV patients varied dramatically in different regions of the United States and the world; in the New York-New Jersey area, for example, the epidemic became even more widespread among intravenous drug users than among gay men. Race- and class-linked bias merged with antigay prejudice as obstacles to equal treatment for persons with this disease.

In short, the fight against medically unjustified discrimination and the fight for full and equal access to lifegiving treatment continue to shape the legal issues for people with HIV disease. This chapter addresses some of the most frequently raised questions about AIDS and the law; the list of resource organizations in the back of the book can help in locating a lawyer who can provide more details in response to specific situations.

EMPLOYMENT DISCRIMINATION

In general, what kinds of laws protect HIV-infected people against discrimination?

Both state and federal laws prohibit medically unjustified discrimination against persons with disabilities. All of the federal laws that cover disability discrimination include HIV disease as a disability and thus prohibit that form of discrimination as well. Most states have antidiscrimination laws as well, and most of these have been invoked to protect people with HIV disease. The state laws tend to provide less powerful remedies than the federal laws.

The primary federal law that protects people with HIV disease is the Americans with Disabilities Act (the ADA). The ADA was enacted in 1990; its provisions start to actually take effect (so that a person can file a lawsuit under it) in 1992.[2] A free brochure on what the ADA means for people living with AIDS and HIV disease is available from the ACLU AIDS Project, at the address listed in Appendix D. The ADA is by far the most comprehensive law protecting people with HIV disease against discrimination, and its enactment was a breakthrough for civil rights principles.

How do these laws protect against employment discrimination?

The ADA prohibits employment discrimination by most employers, public or private. The law is structured to take effect in two stages. Beginning in 1992 employers with twenty-five or more employees will be covered; in 1994 employers with fifteen or more employees will be covered. Employers with fewer than fifteen workers are not covered.

Another federal law, Section 504 of the Rehabilitation Act,[3] prohibits employment discrimination by the federal government and by all entities that receive federal funds; this includes all private businesses that have federal contracts. Section 504 has been used since the beginning of the AIDS epidemic to stop employers from firing people with HIV disease.

In addition, a number of states have laws that protect against job discrimination based on handicap, including HIV disease. The ACLU and other groups can provide information on state handicap discrimination laws.

Can job applicants be required under the ADA or Section 504 to take an HIV test before an employer offers them a job?

Job applicants can be required to undergo a medical examination, including an HIV test, if two critically important conditions are met. First, an employer must offer the applicant the job, conditional on results of the exam, *before* the examination. That ensures that the employer cannot later claim there was another reason for not hiring the applicant if the HIV test is positive; if the offer is withdrawn, the employer then has to prove that not being HIV-infected is a legitimate qualification for the job. Second, the employer must require all applicants to take medical examinations; particular individuals cannot be singled out for testing.[4]

Can an employer require an HIV test as a condition of continued employment?

An employer may not require an HIV test of an individual already employed unless the employer can prove the test is necessary for the job.[5]

Can a person be fired or hired because the employer fears that HIV can be transmitted to coworkers or others?

No, a mere fear of contagiousness cannot justify a discriminatory action. The Supreme Court ruled on this very question in 1987, in a case involving a school teacher with tuberculosis. The Court held that one major purpose of the federal law against disability discrimination was to protect individuals from myths and stereotypes—including a fear of contagion that is not justified by objective knowledge about a disease.[6]

Of course, if the fear is justified—if there really is a risk of transmission—the employer would be justified in taking action. In the same 1987 case, the Supreme Court adopted the prevailing standard: a person who poses "a significant risk" of transmission will not be qualified for a job, unless use of reasonable accommodations (such as protective gloves or other devices) will eliminate the risk.[7] The "significant risk" standard has now been formally adopted by Congress as part of the ADA and Section 504.[8] Because HIV cannot be transmitted by normal workplace conduct, however, there is virtually no situation in which discrimination based on a risk of harm would be permitted.

Does the law prohibit discrimination against persons who are suspected of having the disease?
Yes. Both the ADA and Section 504 cover persons who are "regarded" as having a disability.[9] Several court decisions have interpreted this provision to apply to people who are believed, but not known, to be infected with HIV. (Not all of the state laws include this category of protection.)

Does the ADA protect friends, family, and care-givers of HIV-infected people?
Yes, the ADA covers persons who associate with HIV-infected persons, including those who live with, care for, or provide services to those with HIV disease.[10]

Can an employer claim that HIV-infected people are likely to cost the company more in insurance premiums?
Under the ADA, that is not a valid reason to fire or refuse to hire someone.[11]

Does the ADA require that an employer's health insurance policy has to cover HIV-related expenses?
That depends on the specific situation. The ADA specifically

allows employers to offer health insurance policies that include limited coverage for certain expenses, as long as certain conditions are met. Limitations on coverage must be based on legitimate actuarial principles or a bona fide classification of risks. A health insurance plan may not deny all coverage to a person with a disability, or charge a different rate for the same coverage because of an individual's disability, independent of actuarial classification. Although limitations or caps may be placed on reimbursement for a specific procedure or the types of procedures or drugs covered, that limitation must apply to all persons with or without disabilities.[12]

The law concerning health insurance benefits is extremely complex. In addition to the ADA, there are other federal laws and some state laws that may apply, depending in part on whether the employer is self-insured or purchases group coverage from an insurance company. For answers to questions on this topic, an attorney experienced in insurance law should be consulted.

Can an employer refuse to hire a person with asymptomatic HIV disease because he or she might get sick in the future?

No. An employer is not allowed to use the fact that a person might become too sick to work in the future as an excuse for not hiring or for firing him or her.[13]

What if an employee is already so ill that she or he cannot continue to work?

That's different. Under both the ADA and Section 504, discrimination is prohibited only against *qualified* persons with a disability. To be qualified, a person must be able to perform all the essential functions of the job, despite the HIV disease. This includes being well enough to go to work and to perform the job properly.

Can an employee be fired if symptoms cause her or him occasionally to have to leave work early because of fatigue or to receive treatment?

Under both the ADA and Section 504, an employer must make reasonable accommodations for workers with disabilities. If the employee can perform the essential functions of the job but needs help in overcoming the impact of the disability, the law places a duty on the employer to make accommodations that do not cause an undue hardship (in expense or management) for the business. Establishing a flexible work schedule or allowing time off for treatment could qualify as reasonable accommodations.

What are the rules for healthcare workers with HIV disease?

In 1985 the Centers for Disease Control, the agency of the federal government responsible for public health measures, published a series of guidelines for healthcare workers (HCWs) with HIV infection.[14] Under these guidelines, HIV testing is not recommended as an infection-control measure for three reasons: first, the risk of transmission from provider to patient is extremely low; second, the surest method of preventing the slight risk of transmission that does exist is by the use of what are called "universal precautions" such as gloves; and third, HIV tests cannot detect the presence of the virus in the first weeks or months after exposure, and therefore can be inaccurate. Healthcare experts were sensitive to the fear that use of testing would lead to the attitude that precautions such as gloving could be safely ignored or enforced only episodically. In this way, allowing testing can create a sense of false security and actually result in less, rather than more, safety for the patient.

Despite these guidelines, some hospitals required HIV testing of employees. The outcome of court cases was mixed. The New York State Division of Human Rights ruled that firing a hospital pharmacist who was HIV-infected was illegal under that state's law.[15] A federal appeals court, however, allowed a hospital to require an HIV test of a nurse who had exhibited symptoms of infection.[16]

In 1991 the state of the law became even murkier. Intense publicity surrounding the transmission of HIV that occurred in one dental office in Florida led the Centers for Disease Control to publish new recommendations in July, 1991, concerning this issue.[17] The new recommendations contain these statements:

- "Infected HCWs who adhere to universal precautions and who do not perform invasive procedures pose *no risk* for transmitting HIV or HBV [hepatitis virus] to patients." (emphasis added)

- "Currently available data provide no basis for recommendations to restrict the practice of HCWs infected with HIV or HBV who perform invasive procedures not identified as exposure-prone," provided that the workers comply with what are known as "universal precautions" for infection control (such as using gloves and complying with standards for sterilization and disinfection).
- "HCWs who perform exposure-prone procedures should know their HIV antibody status . . . HCWs who are infected with HIV . . . should not perform exposure-prone procedures unless they have sought counsel from an expert review panel and been advised under what circumstances, if any, they may continue to perform these procedures. Such circumstances should include notifying prospective patients of the HCW's seropositivity before they undergo exposure-prone invasive procedures."

These new recommendations were immediately attacked for multiple reasons. First, there appeared to be no basis for the sudden change in previous guidelines that had not endorsed restrictions on practice by infected HCWs in any context, other than as an overreaction to the sympathetic but unique case of the dental patients in Florida. Second, there were no data to support the proposed restrictions; in all instances involving follow-up studies of the patients of an infected HCW except the dentist in Florida, there had never been a reported case of doctor-to-patient HIV transmission. Any projections of possible risk of transmission were thus entirely speculative. Third, at the time it issued these recommendations, the CDC did not define which invasive procedures were "exposure-prone." Until there is a clear definition, the recommendations cannot be rationally implemented. Fourth, the proposed restrictions appeared to violate the legal principle that entities could not discriminate against a person whose disability was a communicable disease unless there was objective medical evidence of a "significant risk" of transmitting the disease.[18] In sum, the new recommendations appeared to have been driven by public emotion rather than by science.

It seems likely that the standards for employment of HIV-infected healthcare workers will remain a controversial and highly contested issue, no doubt engendering a substantial amount of future litigation.

What can be done to enforce employment rights and discourage discrimination?

Under the ADA, a person who has been fired, not hired, or not promoted because of discrimination can file a complaint in either of two ways. A lawsuit can be filed in court, or a complaint can be filed with the Equal Employment Opportunity Commission. The same choice—either a lawsuit or an agency complaint (but with a different agency)—is available under Section 504. The list of organizations in Appendix D can help in finding a lawyer to consult.

HOUSING DISCRIMINATION

Is there a federal law that prohibits housing discrimination against people with HIV disease?

Yes. The Fair Housing Act was amended in 1988 to add disability to its list of characteristics on which bases discrimination is prohibited (these include race, sex, religion, and national origin).[19] The regulations implementing the new law specify that HIV infection is one of the conditions included within the meaning of disability or handicap.[20] The act outlaws discrimination in the sale, rental, or financing of virtually all housing in the United States; only buildings with four or less units where the landlord lives on the premises may be excluded from coverage under the act.

Does it cover lovers or roommates of HIV patients?

Yes. It is unlawful to threaten, intimidate, or interfere with persons in the enjoyment of their dwelling because of their handicap or because of the handicap of their visitors or associates.[21]

How can rights be enforced under the Fair Housing Act?

A lawsuit can be filed in court, or a complaint can be filed with the federal Department of Housing and Urban Development. An agency complaint can be filed by calling the nearest HUD office and asking for assistance.

CONFIDENTIALITY

Are there laws protecting the confidentiality of medical records pertaining to HIV-related condition(s)?

The confidentiality of most medical records is controlled by state law. Nearly every state has enacted some form of confidentiality law specifically concerning HIV-related medical records. Each law is detailed and covers a number of exceptions to confidentiality, as well as protections for confidentiality. There is no single nationwide standard. Questions about the coverage of a particular state's law can be answered by consulting a lawyer.

If an individual tests HIV positive, will his or her name be reported to the state health department?

That depends on where the test is conducted. In about half the states, there is no reporting of names; in the other states, names of persons who test positive are reported to the state health department. There are special anonymous test sites in some states; in a few states, names are reported from doctors' offices but not from other locations authorized to offer anonymous testing. If these options are not available, one could consider traveling to a state that does allow anonymous testing.

Can testing for HIV be done without the knowledge and consent of the subject?

In most states, that is against the law in most or all situations. A person who learns after the fact that his or her blood was tested for HIV without consent may want to consider filing a lawsuit, a charge of discrimination with a government agency, a formal complaint against the healthcare provider with a licensing authority, or all three. Surreptitious testing is a violation of the patient's right to insist that informed consent precede any procedure that carries serious ramifications, social and psychological as well as physical.

There are exceptions, however. In some states, mandatory testing is authorized by law for certain groups of persons, especially prisoners. Additionally, all states except California allow insurance companies to require an HIV test when persons apply for an individual (rather than a group) policy. Thus, despite the right to consent to or to refuse an HIV test in that situation, the insurance company can make consent a condition of selling the policy.

Are there situations where the law allows a breach of confidentiality?

Yes. Again, state laws vary enormously in their details. One common exception allowed by state laws is to warn an unsuspecting third party, someone with whom an HIV-infected person has had sexual relations or has shared needles. Persons who wish to notify these third parties themselves should inform the doctor or agency that they will do so. Another exception may arise if a healthcare worker has a needlestick accident involving an HIV-infected person's blood; some states allow that healthcare worker to be informed of the person's HIV status if there was sufficient blood exposure involved in the accident to create the risk of HIV transmission. In both cases, however, the person being warned should be informed only that a possible exposure has occurred; the HIV-infected person's identity can remain confidential, at least theoretically.

ACCESS TO HEALTH CARE

Can a healthcare provider discriminate against a person with HIV disease?

No. As with employment-related law, there are three possible sources of a legal right against discrimination by a healthcare provider: the ADA, Section 504, and state antidiscrimination laws. Also similarly, by far the most powerful protection lies in the ADA, which defines providers of healthcare services to fall within the category of "public accommodations," entities that are forbidden to discriminate on the basis of disability.[22]

What kinds of healthcare providers are covered under the ADA?

The ADA includes a variety of providers: doctors, dentists, hospitals, nursing homes, ambulance companies, paramedic services, and other healthcare providers are all considered "public accommodations" under the ADA.

Will the public accommodations provisions of the ADA (like the employment provisions) also take effect in stages?

Yes. For most providers, the effective date is January 1992. For providers with twenty-five or fewer employees and gross receipts of $1 million or less, the effective date is July 1992. For providers with ten or fewer employees and receipts of $500,000 or less, suits can be filed beginning in January 1993.

Which providers are covered by Section 504?

Section 504 covers healthcare institutions and individual physicians that receive federal financial assistance. Federal financial assistance includes grants, loans, contracts, and, most significantly, receipt of Medicaid or Medicare payments.[23]

Are state laws useful?

Some are. Unfortunately, most state laws that prohibit disability discrimination by public accommodations do not explicitly include physicians' offices within the definition of that term. Therefore, a great deal of litigation has occurred simply in order to establish that a doctor's or dentist's office even falls within the purview of the law.

There are a few state laws that clearly apply to HIV patients, however. California's state antidiscrimination law does include medical offices within the scope of public accommodations.[24] A Wisconsin statute prohibits healthcare providers from refusing to treat HIV patients or providing them with substandard care.[25] An Iowa law prohibits care facilities from denying admission to persons based on their disease or condition unless the facility is unable to provide the treatment needed.[26] Finally, a Maryland statute prohibits professionals licensed by the state from refusing care or discriminating against an individual with respect to services for which the license was issued.[27]

GOVERNMENT BENEFITS

If a person with HIV disease lacks private health insurance, can she or he qualify for government benefits to help pay for medical care?

Perhaps, although there are a maze of programs that persons with HIV disease (or any other serious illness) must navigate.

The program that persons with HIV disease have utilized most frequently is Medicaid, which has both financial and degree-of-disability requirements for eligibility.

How does Medicaid work?

To qualify, an individual must have income and assets below the levels set for eligibility in that state; because Medicaid is a joint federal-state program, the financial guidelines vary from state to state. Additionally, an individual must be a disabled person as determined by the Social Security Administration or fall within certain special categories.[28] If one meets the disability test, one qualifies for both Medicaid and SSI (Social Security Income) disability payments in most states. A person with a documented diagnosis of AIDS is considered automatically disabled, but persons with mild or no symptoms and even persons with AIDS-related complex (ARC), who have more serious symptoms, have had difficulty establishing eligibility.[29]

Does Medicaid cover the full range of expenses?

If one can qualify for it, Medicaid does cover hospital care, skilled and intermediate nursing facilities, and physician services. But there are many inadequacies in the program. Reimbursement rates are so low that many physicians decline to accept Medicaid patients. Although prescription drugs are covered, some states limit the number of refills, the total quantity of each prescription, or the total cost of the drug that will be reimbursed.[30] Home healthcare and personal care attendants are covered in only a few states.

Can a person with HIV disease qualify for Medicare?

Eligibility for Medicare is very different and much more difficult to achieve than for Medicaid. Medicare eligibility for persons younger than sixty-five is based solely on disability status; financial status is irrelevant, but the disabled person must have an on-the-books work history (usually of five years or more) sufficient to establish eligibility for the SSDI (Social Security Disability Income) program. SSDI uses the same strict criteria for disability status as the SSI program, which have been impossible to meet without a diagnosis of AIDS or, in some cases, ARC. In addition, after disability has been determined (a five-month period), there is a twenty-four-month waiting period. So, for a total of twenty-nine months, even a person with full-blown AIDS cannot qualify for Medicare.

The primary advantage of Medicare is that it reimburses at higher levels, enabling patients to have a greater choice of physicians and hospitals.

Are there alternatives to these programs for the person being forced to leave her or his job, with its health benefits, because of illness?

Options should definitely be investigated for converting the group health insurance plan offered through the employer (if one was offered). Most departing employees have a right to stay on that plan and be covered at group, rather than individual, rates by paying the group rate themselves. When leaving a job because of a disability, a person can retain coverage in this way for twenty-nine months, the full waiting period for Medicare.[31] In some states, if a person cannot afford these payments, the Medicaid agency may elect to pay them, as a way of conserving Medicaid funds.

FAMILY LAW

How can partners who are not married ensure that they will be treated as spouses would in the case of illness?

At present, no state allows a gay or lesbian couple to marry. In part because of AIDS and the attention it has directed to gay men who have had to face the death of a partner, hospitals and other agencies have become more sensitive to the kind of family ties that exist in such relationships. The most important protections are legal documents that will give the greatest force to a person's or a couple's intentions: a will, a durable power of attorney, and a living will. A power of attorney allows someone to act on another's behalf; a living will enables a person to decide in advance about the kinds of medical efforts to be made on his or her behalf in the event of incapacity. In both documents, an individual can designate the person(s) who should be accorded visitation privileges and decision-making authority. A lawyer should be consulted for help in these matters; free legal advice is often available through local AIDS service organizations.

Is there a legal duty on the part of an HIV-infected person to inform his or her partner that he or she has HIV disease?

Aside from ethical obligations, the law establishes that a person can be liable for money damages in a personal injury suit for knowing transmission of an infectious disease. In some states it can be considered a crime for HIV-infected persons who know they are infected to have intercourse if their partners are not informed, regardless of whether transmission occurs. A person who has engaged in sexual conduct that could transmit HIV—knowing the possibility of transmission—should consult an attorney for advice. A person who has just learned he or she is HIV-infected and has not been using condoms, dental dams, or other safe sex devices can notify his or her partners that they may be infected and may want to be tested, or he or she can ask that a health department office notify them without revealing his or her name. A lawyer or a local AIDS service provider should be consulted about what procedures are established in the appropriate state. In any case, the practice of safe sex should begin immediately! Legal liability—either for money damages or for prosecution—begins only if a person fails to practice safer sex *after* learning that he or she is HIV-infected.

Can an HIV-infected parent be denied custody of or visitation with his or her children because of the disease?

No court would be justified in so ruling. So far, courts encountering such cases have been unanimous in holding that an HIV-infected parent cannot be denied custody or visitation on that basis.[32]

NOTES

1. ACLU AIDS Project, *Epidemic of Fear* (1990).
2. 42 U.S.C. § 12101 (Dec. 1990 Supp.).
3. 29 U.S.C. § 794 (1982).
4. 42 U.S.C. § 12112(c)(3).
5. *Id.*
6. *School Board of Nassau County v. Arline*, 480 U.S. 273, 282–86 (1987).
7. *Id.* at 287 n.16.

8. 42 U.S.C. §§ 12111(3), 12113(b); 29 U.S.C. § 706(8)(D) (1985 and Supp.).

9. 42 U.S.C. § 12102(2)(c); 29 U.S.C. § 706(8)(B).

10. 42 U.S.C. § 12112(b)(4).

11. H.R. Rep. No. 485 (Committee on the Judiciary), 101st Cong., 2d Sess. 71, *reprinted in* 1990 U.S. Code Cong. and Admin. News 445, 494.

12. H.R. Rep. No. 485, at 38, 71; 1990 U.S. Code Cong. and Admin. News 460–61, 494.

13. H.R. Rep. No. 485, at 34; 1990 U.S. Code Cong. and Admin. News 456.

14. United States Centers for Disease Control [CDC], *Recommendations for Preventing Transmission of Infection with HTLV III/LAV in the Workplace,* 34 Morbidity and Mortality Weekly Report [MMWR] 45 (Nov. 15, 1985); CDC, *Recommendations for Preventing Transmission of Infection with HTLV III/LAV During Invasive Procedures,* 35 MMWR 221 (Apr. 11, 1986); CDC, *Recommendations for Prevention of HIV Transmission in Health-Care Settings,* 36 MMWR (Supp. 2S) (Aug. 21, 1987); CDC, *Update: Universal Precautions for Prevention of Transmission of HIV, HBV, and Other Bloodbourne Pathogens in Health Care Settings,* 37 MMWR 377 (June 24, 1988).

15. *Doe v. Westchester County Medical Center,* NY Div. of Human Rights (Dec. 12, 1990), reported in AIDS Litigation Rptr. 5555 (Dec. 28, 1990).

16. *Leckelt v. Board of Hosp. Comm'rs,* 909 F.2d 820 (5th Cir. 1990).

17. U.S. Centers for Disease Control, *Recommendations for Preventing Transmission of Human Immunodeficiency Virus and Hepatitis-B Virus to Patients During Exposure-Prone Invasive Procedures,* 40 Mortality and Morbidity Weekly Report, No. RR–8, July 12, 1991.

18. An excellent discussion of these issues can be found in Barnes, Rango, Burke, and Chiarello, *The HIV-Infected Health Care Professional: Employment Policies and Public Health,* 18 Law, Medicine & Health Care 311 (1990).

19. 42 U.S.C. § 3601 *et seq.* (1982 and Supp. 1991).

20. 54 Fed. Reg. 32345 (Jan. 23, 1989). *See Baxter v. City of Belleville,* 720 F. Supp. 720 (S.D. Ill. 1989).

21. § 100.400(c)(1)–(2) of the regulations, 54 Fed. Reg. 3291 (Jan. 23, 1989).

22. 42 U.S.C. § 1218(7)(f).

23. 45 C.F.R. § 84.3(h) (1988); *United States v. Baylor University Medical Center,* 736 F.2d 1039 (5th Cir. 1984), *cert. denied,* 469 U.S. 1189 (1984).

24. Cal. Civ. Code §§ 51ff.

25. Wis. Stat. Ann. § 146.024 (West Supp. 1991).
26. Iowa Code Ann. § 135C.23 (West Supp. 1991).
27. Md. S.B. 719 Ch. 789 (1989) (codified in various sections of the Health Occupations Code).
28. If not disabled, one may meet the categorical qualifications (i.e., the nonfinancial) test by being a member of a family receiving Aid to Families with Dependent Children (AFDC), a pregnant woman, a child under 7, or an adult over 65. Some states also deem persons between the ages of 7 and 21 categorically eligible for Medicaid.
29. *See* T.P. McCormack, *The AIDS Benefits Handbook* (1990).
30. Intergovernmental Health Policy Project, *Intergovernmental AIDS Reports* 5 Mar.–Apr. 1990.
31. This option is often referred to as "COBRA" because it was first enacted as part of the Consolidated Omnibus Budget Reconciliation Act of 1985. The extension of the continuation period to twenty-nine months in cases of disability was added in 1989.
32. *See, e.g., Stewart v. Stewart,* 521 N.E.2d 956 (Ind. Ct. App. 1988); *Doe v. Roe,* 139 Misc. 2d 209, 526 N.Y.S.2d 718 (N.Y. Sup. Ct. 1988).

Appendix A
Criminal Statutes Relating to Consensual Homosexual Acts Between Adults

ALABAMA

Indecent Exposure (13A-6-68)

Purposeful exposure of one's genitals in a public place or on the private premises of another person, intending sexual arousal or gratification under circumstances likely to cause affront or alarm.

—Class A misdemeanor, 1 year and/or $2,000.

Loitering (13A-11-9)

Remaining or wandering in a public place for the purpose of engaging, or soliciting another person to engage, in a sex act involving the sex organs of one person and the mouth or anus of another.

—Violation, 30 days and/or $200.

Public Lewdness (13A-12-130)

Reckless exposure of anus or genitals or commission of any lewd act in a public place.

—Class C misdemeanor, 3 months and/or $500.

_____

The authors gratefully acknowledge the able assistance of Jay Ward Brown, a student at New York University School of Law, in the preparation of these appendixes.

This table does not include statutes that prohibit sexual acts or the solicitation of sexual acts for money. Nor does it include statutes prohibiting, in general, obscene language or gestures that give offense. The table does include criminal statutes specifically directed at persons with HIV, but the reader is cautioned that many states criminalize behavior involving the spread of sexually transmitted diseases broadly defined, and those more general statutes are not listed here.

All statutory citations are to the relevant state criminal code. In some states, for some crimes, repeat offenders are subject to higher penalties.

Unless otherwise noted, sentences and fines are the maximum penalty prescribed by statute.

Registration of Sex Offenders (13A-11-200)
Individual convicted of sexual misconduct or indecent exposure required to register with sheriff in county of legal residence.
—Felony, not less than 1 year nor more than 5 years and/or $1,000.

Sexual Misconduct (13A-6-65)
Any sex act between persons not married involving the sex organs of one person and the mouth or anus of the other. Consent is not a defense.
—Class A misdemeanor, 1 year and/or $2,000.

ALASKA

DECRIMINALIZED:
Private consensual adult homosexual acts. 1978 Alaska Sess. Laws § 21 ch. 166 (eff. Jan. 1, 1980).

Disorderly Conduct (11.61.110)
Intentional exposure of buttock [sic] or anus with reckless disregard for possible offensive or insulting effect on another.
—Class B misdemeanor, 10 days and/or $1,000.

Indecent Exposure (11.41.460)
Intentional exposure of genitals with reckless disregard for offensive, insulting, or frightening effect on another.
—Class B misdemeanor, 90 days and/or $1,000.

ARIZONA

Crime Against Nature (13-1411)
Anal intercourse.
—Class 3 misdemeanor, 30 days and/or $500.
—Oral penetration not included. *State v. Potts*, 75 Ariz. 211, 254 P.2d 1023 (1953).

Indecent Exposure (13-1402)
>Exposure of genitals, anus or female breast to another person with recklessness as to offensive or alarming effect.
>—Class 1 misdemeanor, 6 months and/or $2,500.

Lewd and Lascivious Acts (13-1412)
>Commission of any lewd or lascivious act, including sodomy and fellatio, with another in an unnatural manner.
>—Class 3 misdemeanor, 30 days and/or $500.

Loitering (13-2905)
>In a public place, soliciting another in an offensive or disturbing manner to engage in any sexual offense.
>—Class 3 misdemeanor, 30 days and/or $500.

Public Sexual Indecency (13-1403)
>Direct or indirect fondling of any part of the genitals, anus or female breast, or oral contact with another person's sex organs, or sexual intercourse with another, in the presence of another person with recklessness as to offensive or alarming effect.
>—Class 1 misdemeanor, 6 months and/or $2,500.

Registration of Sex Offenders (13-3821)
>Individual convicted of sexual offense required to register with sheriff of any county in which individual intends to reside for more than 30 days.
>—Class 6 felony, mandatory 18 months and/or $150,000.

ARKANSAS

Exposing Another Person to HIV (5-14-123)
>An act of anal or vaginal intercourse, cunnilingus or fellatio, by a person with AIDS or who tests positive for HIV, without informing the other person of the presence of HIV.
>—Class A felony, not less than 6 months nor more than 30 years and/or not to exceed $15,000.

Indecent Exposure (5-14-112)

Exposure of one's sex organs in a public place or in circumstances likely to cause affront or alarm, with intent to arouse or gratify.

Class A misdemeanor, 1 year and/or $1,000.

Loitering (5-71-213)

Lingering or remaining in a public place for the purpose of engaging or soliciting someone to engage in anal or oral penetration by penis, or anal or vaginal penetration by any other object.

—Class C misdemeanor, 30 days and/or $100.

Public Sexual Indecency (5-14-111)

Engaging in sexual intercourse, any sex act involving the mouth or anus of one person and the penis of another, or any act of sexual contact, in a public place.

—Class A misdemeanor, 1 year and/or $1,000.

Sodomy (5-14-122)

Performing any act of sexual gratification involving oral or anal penetration by the penis of a person of the same sex, or vaginal or anal penetration by any body member of a person of the same sex.

—Class A misdemeanor, 1 year and/or $1,000.

CALIFORNIA

DECRIMINALIZED:

Private consensual adult homosexual acts. 1975 Cal. Stat., ch. 71 § 7 (eff. July 1, 1976).

Disorderly Conduct (647)

Soliciting or engaging in lewd or dissolute conduct in a public place, or loitering about in a public toilet for the purpose of soliciting or engaging in any lewd, lascivious, or unlawful act.

—Misdemeanor, 6 months and/or $500.

—Interpreted to cover only public conduct involving touching of the genitals, buttocks, or female breast for purposes of arousal, gratification, annoyance, or offense. *Pryor v. Municipal Court*, 25 Cal. 3d 238, 158 Cal. Rptr. 330, 599 P.2d 636 (1979).

Lewd or Obscene Conduct (314)
Willful exposure of one's genitals in any public place or where others are present to be offended or annoyed.
—Misdemeanor, 6 months and/or $500.

Outraging Public Decency (650.5)
Commission of an act which openly outrages public decency.
—Misdemeanor, 6 months and/or $500.

Registration of Sex Offenders (290)
Individual convicted of disorderly conduct must register with local chief of police.
—Misdemeanor, 6 months and/or $500.

COLORADO

DECRIMINALIZED:
Private consensual adult homosexual acts. 1971 Colo. Sess. Laws, ch. 121 § 1 (eff. Jan. 1, 1972).

Indecent Exposure (18-7-302)
Exposure of one's genitals to any person under circumstances likely to cause affront or alarm.
—Class 2 misdemeanor, sentence not less than 3 months nor more than 1 year and/or not less than $250 nor more than $1,000.

Loitering (18-9-112)
Lingering, remaining, or wandering in a public place for the purpose of engaging in, or soliciting, any deviate sexual intercourse.
—Class 1 petty offense, 6 months and/or $500.
—Held unconstitutional. *People v. Gibson*, 184 Colo. 444, 521 P.2d 774 (1974).

Public Indecency (18-7-301)
> Performance of oral or anal sex, lewd exposure of one's body for sexual arousal, or lewd fondling of another person in a public place.
> —Class 1 petty offense, 6 months and/or $500.

CONNECTICUT

DECRIMINALIZED:
> Private consensual adult homosexual acts. 1969 Conn. Pub. Act 828, § 214 (eff. Nov. 1, 1971).

Public Indecency (53A-186)
> Performance of anal or oral sex, lewd exposure of one's body for sexual arousal, or lewd fondling or caressing of another's body in a public place.
> —Class B misdemeanor, 6 months and/or $1,000.

DELAWARE

DECRIMINALIZED:
> Private consensual adult homosexual acts. 58 Del. Laws, ch. 497, § 1 (eff. Apr. 1, 1973).

Indecent Exposure (11-764)
> Exposure of genitals or buttocks to another person under circumstances likely to cause affront or alarm.
> —Unclassified misdemeanor, 30 days and/or $500.

Lewdness (11-1341)
> Performance of lewd act in public place.
> —Class B misdemeanor, 6 months and/or $1,000.

Loitering (11-1321)
> Remaining in a public place for the purpose of engaging or soliciting another person to engage in sexual intercourse or deviate sexual intercourse.
> —Violation, $300.

Sexual Harassment (11-763)
>Suggesting, soliciting, requesting or otherwise attempting to induce another person to have sex knowing that such advance is likely to cause annoyance, offense or alarm.
>—Unclassified misdemeanor, 30 days and/or $500.

DISTRICT OF COLUMBIA

Inviting for Purposes of Prostitution (22-2701)
>Inviting or addressing any person for purposes of prostitution or any other immoral or lewd purpose.
>—Misdemeanor, 90 days and/or $300.

Lewdness (22-1112)
>Exposing one's body in an obscene or indecent manner, making a lewd, obscene, or indecent sexual proposal, or committing a lewd, obscene or indecent act.
>—Misdemeanor, 90 days and/or $300.

Sodomy (22-3502)
>Performing any sex act involving the mouth or anus of one person and the sex organs of another.
>—Felony, 10 years and/or $1,000.
>—Repealed by District in Sexual Assault Reform Act of 1981 but reinstated by one-house veto of Congress. *See United States v. Langley*, 112 W.L.R. 801 (Super. Ct. 1982).

FLORIDA

Exposure of Sexual Organs (800.03)
>Exposure of one's sex organs in any public or private place except in a place specifically set apart for that purpose.
>—First degree misdemeanor, 1 year and/or $1,000.

Lewd and Lascivious Behavior (798.02)
>Open and gross lewdness and lascivious behavior.
>—Second degree misdemeanor, 60 days and/or $500.

Prostitution (796.07)
   Engaging in sexual activity for hire, or in any indecent or obscene act, or to solicit for such acts.
   —Second degree misdemeanor, 60 days and/or $500.

Transmission of HIV (384.24)
   Sexual intercourse by person with HIV without informing partner and obtaining consent.
   —First degree misdemeanor, 1 year and/or $1,000.

Unnatural and Lascivious Act (800.02)
   Commission of any unnatural sex act.
      —Second degree misdemeanor, 60 days and/or $500.
      —Interpreted in dictum to include oral and anal sex. *Franklin v. State*, 257 So. 2d 21 (Fla. 1971).

GEORGIA

Public Indecency (10-0-0)
   Performing sexual intercourse, lewdly exposing one's sex organs, lewdly appearing in a state of partial or complete nudity, or lewdly caressing the body of another person, in a public place.
   —Misdemeanor, 1 year and/or $1,000.

Reckless Conduct by HIV Infected Persons (16-5-60)
   Engaging in sexual intercourse or any sexual act involving the sex organs of one person and the mouth or anus of another when the actor knows he or she is infected with HIV, without first disclosing the HIV status.
   —Felony, 10 years.

Sodomy (16-6-2)
   Any sex act involving the mouth or anus of one person, and the sex organs of another.
      —Felony, sentence not less than 1 year nor more than 20 years.
      —Upheld as to homosexuals on grounds that there is no fundamental federal constitutional right to "en-

gage in sodomy." *Bowers v. Hardwick,* 478 U.S. 186 (1986).

Solicitation of Sodomy (16-6-15)
Soliciting any person to perform or submit to an act of sodomy.
—Misdemeanor, 1 year and/or $1,000.

HAWAII

DECRIMINALIZED:
Private consensual adult homosexual acts. 1972 Haw. Sess. Laws, Act 9, § 1 (eff. Jan. 1, 1973).

Indecent Exposure (707-738)
Exposure of one's genitals to another person under circumstances likely to cause affront or alarm.
—Petty misdemeanor, 30 days and/or $500.

Open Lewdness (712-1217)
Commission of any lewd act in a public place under circumstances likely to cause affront or alarm.
—Petty misdemeanor, 30 days and/or $500.

IDAHO

Crime Against Nature (18-6605)
Performance of sodomy, fellatio, or any other unnatural copulation.
—Felony, 5 years.

Public Display of Offensive Sexual Material (18-4105)
Exhibition or display in public of genitals or pubic area, or actual or simulated sex act.
—Misdemeanor, 6 months and/or $300.

Transfer of Body Fluid Which May Contain HIV Virus (39-608)

Engaging in any sexual act which might involve transfer of body fluids by person who has any manifestation of HIV Infection.

—Felony, 15 years and/or $5,000.

ILLINOIS

DECRIMINALIZED:

Private consensual adult homosexual acts. 1961 Ill. Laws 1983, § 11-2 (eff. Jan. 1, 1962).

Public Indecency (38-11-9)

Performance of anal or oral sex, lewd exposure of one's body for sexual arousal, or lewd fondling or caressing of another's body, in a public place.

—Class A misdemeanor, 1 year and/or $1,000.

INDIANA

DECRIMINALIZED:

Private consensual adult homosexual acts. 1976 Ind. Acts Pub. L. No. 148, § 124 (eff. July 1, 1977).

Public Indecency (35-45-4-1)

Intentional performance of sexual intercourse, or sexual act involving the mouth or anus of one person and the sex organs of another, or nudity, or fondling one's own genitals, or those of another in a public place.

—Class A misdemeanor, 1 year and/or $5,000.

IOWA

DECRIMINALIZED:

Private consensual adult homosexual acts. 1976 Iowa Acts, ch. 1245, § 520 (eff. Jan. 1, 1978).

Indecent Exposure (709.9)

Exposure of genitals or pubes to another, or commission of a sex act in front of another knowing that the act is offensive to the viewer.

—Serious misdemeanor, 1 year and/or $1,000.

KANSAS

Lewd and Lascivious Behavior (21-3508)

Commission of any sex act with reasonable anticipation of being viewed by another, or exposure of one's sex organs for sexual arousal to another who has not consented.

—Class B misdemeanor, 6 months and/or $1,000.

Sodomy (21-3505)

Oral or anal copulation between persons of the same sex.

—Class B misdemeanor, 6 months and/or $1,000.

—Interpreted to require penetration, hence cunnilingus not proscribed by section. *State v. Crawford*, 247 Kan. 223, 795 P. 2d 401 (1990).

Vagrancy (21-4108)

Loitering on the streets or in a public place intending to solicit someone for immoral purposes.

—Class C misdemeanor, 1 month and/or $500.

KENTUCKY

Indecent Exposure (510.150)

Intentional exposure of one's genitals under circumstances likely to cause affront or alarm.

—Class B misdemeanor, 90 days and/or $250.

Sodomy (510.100)

Oral or anal sex with a person of the same sex. Consent is not a defense.

—Class A misdemeanor, 1 year and/or $500.

—Held unconstitutional under state constitution.

Com. v. Wasson, No. 86-XX-048 (Fayette Cir. Ct. 1989) (appeal pending).

LOUISIANA

Crime against Nature (14.89)
Any unnatural copulation, including oral and anal sex.
—Felony, 5 years and/or $2,000.

Obscenity (14.106)
Intentional public exposure of genitals, pubic hair, anus, vulva, or female breast to arouse sexual desire, or in a way which appeals to prurient interests, or is patently offensive.
—Misdemeanor, sentence not less than 6 months nor more than 3 years and/or not less than $1,000 nor more than $2,500.

MAINE

DECRIMINALIZED:
Private consensual adult homosexual acts. 1975 Me. Acts, ch. 499, § 5 (eff. May 1, 1976).

Public Indecency (17-A-854)
Engaging in any sex act in a public place or exposing one's genitals in circumstances likely to cause affront or alarm in either a public place or a private place which may be viewed from elsewhere.
—Class E crime, 6 months and/or $500.

MARYLAND

Exposure of Other Individuals to HIV (HG 18-601.1)
Knowing or attempted transmission of HIV.
—Misdemeanor, 3 years and/or $2,500.

Lewdness (27-15)
  Engaging in, permitting others to engage in, or soliciting any unnatural sexual practice.
  —Misdemeanor, 1 year and/or $500.

Sodomy (27-553)
  Sodomy. [No further statutory explanation given.]
  —Felony, 10 years.

Unnatural or Perverted Sexual Practices (27-554)
  Commission of oral or any other unnatural sex act. Consent is not a defense.
  —Felony, 10 years and/or $1,000.

MASSACHUSETTS

Crime Against Nature (272-34)
  Anal intercourse.
  —Felony, 20 years.

Disorderly Conduct (272-53)
  Exposure of one's genitals to another.
  —Misdemeanor, 6 months and/or $200.

Open and Gross Lewdness (272-16)
  Open and gross lewdness and lascivious behavior, so as to produce alarm or shock.
  —Felony, 3 years and/or $300.
  —Interpreted to apply primarily to acts performed in front of children. *Com. v. Frita*, 391 Mass. 394, 461 N.E. 2d 820 (1984).

Resorting to Restaurant or Tavern for Immoral Purposes (272-26)
  Entering a restaurant or bar for the purpose of soliciting another to engage in immoral conduct, or, as an owner, permitting others to do so.
  —Misdemeanor, not less than $25 nor more than $500 and/or sentence not to exceed 1 year.

Unnatural and Lascivious Acts (272-35)
> Performance of oral sex, or oral-anal contact or other sexual
> acts which deviate from accepted norms.
>> —Felony, 5 years and/or fine not less than $100 nor
>> more than $1,000.
>> —Held not to apply to private consensual adult be-
>> havior. *Com. v. Balthazar*, 366 Mass. 298, 318
>> N.E. 2d 478 (1974).

MICHIGAN

Crime Against Nature (750.158)
> Anal sex.
>> —Felony, 15 years.
>> —Held unconstitutional as applied to private, con-
>> sensual adult behavior. *Michigan Organization for
>> Human Rights v. Kelley*, No. 88-815820 CZ
>> (Wayne County Circ. Ct. July 9, 1990) (no appeal
>> taken).

Disorderly Person (750.167)
> Engaging in indecent or obscene conduct in a public place.
>> —Misdemeanor, 90 days and/or $100.

Gross Indecency (750.338 & 750.338a)
> Public attempt at an act of gross indecency, including
> masturbation.
>> —Felony, 5 years and/or $2,500.

Gross Lewdness (750.335)
> Open and gross lewdness and lascivious behavior.
>> —Misdemeanor, 1 year and/or $500.

Indecent Exposure (750.335a)
> Open and knowing exposure of one's body.
>> —Misdemeanor, 1 year and/or $500.

Soliciting (750.448)
> Accosting, soliciting, or inviting another person in public to do a lewd or immoral act.
> —Misdemeanor, 90 days and/or $100.

MINNESOTA

Indecent Exposure (617.23)
> Willful and lewd public exposure of one's body or genitals, or public gross lewdness or lascivious behavior.
> —Misdemeanor, 10 days and/or $5.

Sodomy (609.293)
> Carnally knowing any person, with their consent, by the anus or mouth.
> —Misdemeanor, 1 year and/or $3,000.

MISSISSIPPI

Disorderly Conduct (97-35-3)
> Making rude or obscene remarks or gestures, using profane language, or making indecent proposals to another person.
> —Misdemeanor, 4 months and/or $200.

Disturbance of Public Peace (97-35-15)
> Disturbing others by profane, indecent or offensive language or conduct.
> —Misdemeanor, 6 months and/or $500.

Indecent Exposure (97-29-31)
> Lewd and willful exposure of one's genitals or body in a public place.
> —Misdemeanor, 6 months and/or $500.

Unnatural Intercourse (97-29-59)
Oral or anal penetration.
—Felony, 10 years.

MISSOURI

Indecent Exposure (566.130)
Exposure of one's genitals under circumstances likely to cause affront or alarm.
—Class A misdemeanor, 1 year and/or $1,000.

Sexual Misconduct (566.090)
Any sex act involving the genitals of one person and the mouth, tongue, hand or anus of another person of the same sex.
—Class A misdemeanor, 1 year and/or $1,000.

MONTANA

Deviate Sexual Conduct (45-5-505)
Sexual conduct or sexual intercourse between two persons of the same sex.
—Felony, 10 years and/or $50,000.

Indecent Exposure (45-5-504)
Exposure of one's genitals for sexual arousal under circumstances likely to cause affront or alarm.
—Misdemeanor, 6 months and/or $500.

NEBRASKA

DECRIMINALIZED:
Private consensual adult homosexual acts. 1977 Neb. Laws, L.B. 38, § 328 (eff. July 1, 1978).

Public Indecency (28-806)
> Performance of any sex act, exposure of one's genitals intending to cause affront or alarm, or lewd fondling or caressing of another person's body in public.
> —Class II misdemeanor, 6 months and/or $1,000.

NEVADA

Confinement of Person Whose Conduct May Spread AIDS (441A.300)
> Any behavior through which the disease may be spread to others.
> —Unclassified offense, confinement at discretion of court.

Crime Against Nature (201.190)
> Anal intercourse, cunnilingus, or fellatio between consenting adults of the same sex.
> —Felony, sentence not less than 1 year nor more than 6 years.

Indecent or Obscene Exposure (201.220)
> Open and indecent or obscene exposure of one's person.
> —Gross misdemeanor, 1 year and/or $1,000.

Open or Gross Lewdness (201.210)
> Committing an act of open or gross lewdness.
> —Gross misdemeanor, 1 year and/or $1,000.

Sex Offender Registration (207.151-201.157)
> Individual convicted of open or gross lewdness or indecent exposure required to register with county sheriff or police chief within 48 hours of arrival in any county.
> —Misdemeanor, 6 months and/or $500.

Vagrancy (207.030)
>   Soliciting anyone to engage in lewd or dissolute conduct in a public place, or loitering around a public toilet to solicit any lewd, lascivious, or unlawful conduct.
>   —Misdemeanor, 6 months and/or $500.

NEW HAMPSHIRE

DECRIMINALIZED:
>   Private consensual adult homosexual acts. 1973 N.H. Laws § 532:26 (eff. Nov. 1, 1973).

Indecent Exposure and Lewdness (645:1)
>   Performing any sex act, exposing one's genitals, or performing any act of gross lewdness under circumstances likely to cause affront or alarm.
>   —Misdemeanor, 1 year and/or $1,000.

NEW JERSEY

DECRIMINALIZED:
>   Private consensual adult homosexual acts. 1978 N.J. Laws c. 95, § 2C:98-2 (eff. Sept. 1, 1979).

Lewdness (2C:14-4)
>   Exposure of one's genitals in public for sexual arousal under circumstances likely to cause affront or alarm.
>   —Disorderly person offense, 6 months and/or $1,000.

NEW MEXICO

DECRIMINALIZED:
>   Private consensual adult homosexual acts, 1975 N.M. Laws ch. 109, § 8 (eff. Jan. 1, 1976).

Indecent Dancing (30-9-14.1)
>   Indecent exposure while dancing in a public place.
>   —Petty misdemeanor, 6 months and/or $500.

Indecent Exposure (30-9-14)
> Intentional exposure of one's penis, testicles, vulva, or vagina to public view.
>> —Petty misdemeanor, 6 months and/or $500.

NEW YORK

Consensual Sodomy (130.38)
> Conduct between persons not married to each other involving the mouth or anus of one person and the penis of another, or the mouth of one person and the vulva of another.
>> —Class B misdemeanor, 3 months and/or $500.
>> —Held unconstitutional as violation of federal rights to privacy and equal protection. *People v. Onofre,* 51 N.Y. 2d 476, 434 N.Y.S. 2d 947, 415 N.E. 2d 936, *cert. denied,* 451 U.S. 987 (1981).

Lewdness (245.00)
> Intentional exposure of genitals in a lewd manner or commission of any other lewd act in a public place.
>> —Class B misdemeanor, 3 months and/or $500.

Loitering (240.35)
> Remaining in a public place in order to engage in, or solicit, conduct involving the mouth or anus of one person and the penis of another, or the mouth of one person and the vulva of another.
>> —Violation, 15 days and/or $250.

NORTH CAROLINA

Crime Against Nature (14-177)
> Anal or oral intercourse.
>> —Class H felony, 10 years and/or discretionary fine.

NORTH DAKOTA

DECRIMINALIZED:
> Private consensual adult homosexual acts. 1977 N.D. Laws ch. 122, § 1 (eff. Jan. 1, 1978).

Disorderly Conduct (12.1-31-01)
>   Soliciting sexual conduct while loitering in a public place.
>   —Class B misdemeanor, 30 days and/or $500.

Indecent Exposure (12.1.-20 12.1)
>   Exposing one's penis, vulva, or anus in a public place, intending to annoy or harass another person, or masturbating in a public place.
>   —Class B misdemeanor, 30 days and/or $500.

OHIO

DECRIMINALIZED:
>   Private consensual adult homosexual acts. 1972 Ohio Laws 134 v. H 511, § 2 (eff. Jan. 1, 1974).

Importuning (2907.07)
>   Soliciting a person of the same sex to engage in sexual activity knowing that such solicitation is offensive to the other person.
>   —First degree misdemeanor, 6 months and/or $1,000.
>   —Construed to proscribe only "fighting words," words which by their very utterance inflict injury or tend to incite immediate breach of the peace. *State v. Phipps*, 58 Ohio St. 2d 271, 389 N.E.2d 1128 (1979).

Public Indecency (2907.09)
>   Exposing one's genitals, masturbating, or engaging in sexual conduct, in a public place.
>   —Fourth degree misdemeanor, 30 days and/or $250.

OKLAHOMA

Crime Against Nature (21-886)
>   Anal or oral sex.
>   —Felony, 10 years.

Engaging in Activity Causing Another's Infection with HIV (21-1192.1)
    Engaging in any activity intended to infect or which causes infection of another with HIV.
        —Felony, 5 years.

Grossly Outraging Public Decency (21-22)
    Committing any act that openly outrages public decency or is injurious to public morals.
        —Misdemeanor, 1 year and/or $500.

Indecent Exposure (21-1021)
    Lewd exposure of one's genitals in any public place, or where others are present who would be offended.
        —Felony, not less than 30 days nor more than 10 years and/or not less than $100 nor more than $10,000.

Lewdness (21-1029)
    Soliciting or inducing another to commit an act of lewdness.
        —Misdemeanor, not less than 30 days nor more than 1 year.

OREGON

DECRIMINALIZED:
    Private consensual adult homosexual acts. 1971 Or. Laws ch. 743, § 432 (eff. Jan. 1, 1972).

Public Indecency (163.465)
    Exposing one's genitals, performing sexual intercourse or engaging in any contact involving the sex organs of one person and the mouth or anus of another, in public.
        —Class A misdemeanor, 1 year and/or $2,500.

PENNSYLVANIA

Indecent Exposure (18-3127)
    Exposing one's genitals to anyone other than one's spouse for arousal or gratification, causing affront or alarm.

—Second degree misdemeanor, 2 years and/or
$5,000.

Lewdness (18-5901)
Performing a lewd act likely to be observed by others who
would be affronted or alarmed.
—Third degree misdemeanor, 1 year and/or $2,500.

Voluntary Deviate Sexual Intercourse (18-3124)
Voluntary anal or oral intercourse between persons not
husband and wife.
—Second degree misdemeanor, 2 years and/or
$5,000.
—Held unconstitutional on equal protection grounds.
Com. v. Bonadio, 490 Pa. 91, 415 A.2d 47 (1980).

RHODE ISLAND

Crime Against Nature (11-10-1)
Engaging in any unnatural sex act, that is, fellatio, cunnilingus, or anal intercourse, or in ordinary extramarital
intercourse. Consent is no defense.
—Felony, not less than 7 years nor more than 20
years.

Disorderly Conduct (11-45-1)
Exposing one's genitals to the view of others under circum-
stances likely to cause affront, distress or alarm.
—Misdemeanor, 6 months and/or $500.

Loitering for Indecent Purposes (11-34-8)
Standing or wandering in a public place and attempting to
engage passersby in conversation, or to stop motor vehicles, for the purpose of prostitution or any indecent act.
—Petty misdemeanor, 6 months and/or fine not less
than $250 nor more than $1,000.

Soliciting from Motor Vehicles for Indecent Purposes (11-34-8.1)

>While in an auto, stopping another vehicle or pedestrian and attempting to engage in conversation for the purpose of prostitution or any indecent act.
>
>—Misdemeanor, 6 months and/or fine not less than $250 nor more than $1,000.

SOUTH CAROLINA

Buggery (16-15-120)

>Abominable crime of buggery. (No further statutory explanation given.)
>
>—Felony, 5 years and/or fine not less than $500.

Exposing Others to HIV (44-29-145)

>Knowing exchange of blood or body fluids by anyone infected with HIV without informing other person of risk of exposure.
>
>—Felony, 10 years and/or $5,000.

Indecent Exposure (16-15-130)

>Willful and malicious indecent exposure of one's person in public.
>
>—Misdemeanor, discretionary fine or imprisonment.

Lewdness (16-15-90)

>Exposing indecently one's genitals for the purpose of prostitution or other indecency, or being in a place for the purpose of lewdness or prostitution.
>
>—Misdemeanor, 30 days and/or $200.

SOUTH DAKOTA

DECRIMINALIZED:

>Private consensual adult homosexual acts. 1976 S.D. Laws, ch. 158, § 22-8 (eff. Apr. 1, 1977).

Indecent Exposure (22-24-1)

Intentionally exposing one's genitals with immoral purposes in any place where there are persons to be offended or annoyed.

—Class 2 misdemeanor, 30 days and/or $100.

TENNESSEE

Homosexual Acts (39-13-510)

Engaging in consensual sexual intercourse, cunnilingus, fellatio, or anal intercourse, with another person of the same gender.

—Class C misdemeanor, 30 days and/or $50.

Indecent Exposure (39-13-511)

In a public place, intentionally exposing one's genitals or buttocks, or engaging in sexual contact, with reasonable expectation that the act will be viewed by others and would offend them or where the act is done for arousal.

—Class B misdemeanor, 6 months and/or $500.

Prostitution (39-2-632)

Giving or receiving the body for licentious sexual intercourse without hire.

—Misdemeanor, 30 days and/or $50.

TEXAS

Disorderly Conduct (42.01)

Exposing one's anus or genitals in public.

—Class C misdemeanor, $200.

Homosexual Conduct (21.06)

Engaging in any sex act involving the genitals of one person, and the mouth or anus of another person of the same sex.

—Class C misdemeanor, $200.

—Held unconstitutional in unreported state district court opinion. See *Gay Groups Turn to State*

Courts to Win Rights, New York Times, Dec. 21, 1990, § B, 6, col. 3.

Indecent Exposure (21.08)
Exposing one's anus or genitals in public for sexual arousal or gratification.
—Class B misdemeanor, 180 days and/or $1,000.

Intentionally Exposing Another to AIDS or HIV (22.012)
Engaging in conduct likely to result in transfer of bodily fluids with intent to cause injury or death.
—Third degree felony, not less than 2 years nor more than 10 years and a fine not to exceed $10,000.

Lewdness (21.07)
Engaging in any sexual act in a public place.
—Class A misdemeanor, 1 year and/or $2,000.

UTAH

Lewdness (76-9-702)
Engaging in sexual intercourse, or acts involving the genitals of one person and the mouth or anus of another, or exposing one's genitals, or masturbation, or any act of lewdness, in public which might cause affront or alarm.
—Class B misdemeanor, 6 months and/or $1,000.

Sodomy (76-5-403)
Engaging in any sexual act involving the genitals of one person, and the mouth or anus of another, regardless of the sex of either participant.
—Class B misdemeanor, 6 months and/or $1,000.

VERMONT

DECRIMINALIZED:
Private consensual adult homosexual acts. 1977 Vt. Laws No. 51, § 3 (eff. July 1, 1977).

Lewdness (13-2601)
> Open and gross lewd and lascivious behavior.
>> —Felony, 5 years and/or $300.

Prostitution (13-2632)
> Engaging in sex for hire or offering or receiving the body for indiscriminate sexual intercourse without hire, or open and gross lewdness.
>> —Misdemeanor, 1 year or $100.

VIRGINIA

Crimes Against Nature (18.2-361)
> Carnal behavior involving the mouth or anus. Consent is no defense.
>> —Class 3 felony, not less than 5 years nor more than 20 years.
>> —Upheld as not violative of the Due Process Clause or the First Amendment. *Doe v. Commonwealth's Atty.*, 425 U.S. 901 (1976).

Indecent Exposure (18.2-387)
> Intentional obscene display of one's person or genitals.
>> —Class 1 misdemeanor, 1 year and/or $1,000.

WASHINGTON

DECRIMINALIZED:
> Private consensual adult homosexual acts. 1975 Wash. Laws 1st exec. sess., ch. 260 (eff. July 1, 1976).

Indecent Exposure (9A.88.010)
> Intentional, open, obscene exposure of one's person in a manner likely to cause affront or alarm.
>> —Misdemeanor, 90 days and/or $1,000.

WEST VIRGINIA

DECRIMINALIZED:
> Private consensual adult homosexual acts. 1976 W. Va. Acts, ch. 43 (eff. June 1, 1976).

Indecent Exposure (61-8B-10)
> Intentional exposure of one's sex organs or anus under circumstances likely to cause affront or alarm.
> —Misdemeanor, 90 days or 90 days and $250.

Lewd and Lascivious Conduct (61-8-4)
> Open or gross lewdness or lasciviousness.
> —Misdemeanor, up to 6 months and not less than $50.

WISCONSIN

DECRIMINALIZED:
> Private consensual adult homosexual acts. 1983 Wisc. Acts ch. 17, § 5.

Disorderly Conduct (947.01)
> Engaging in indecent, profane, or disorderly conduct under circumstances likely to cause a disturbance.
> —Class B misdemeanor, 90 days and/or $1,000.

Lewd and Lascivious Behavior (944.20)
> Committing any indecent act of sexual gratification knowing that others are present, or publicly exposing one's genitals or pubic area.
> —Class A misdemeanor, 9 months and/or $10,000.

Sexual Gratification (944.17)
> Performing any act of sexual gratification involving the mouth or anus of one person, and the sex organs of another, in public.
> —Class A misdemeanor, 9 months and/or $10,000.

Vagrancy (947.02)
> Soliciting another person in public to commit a crime against sexual morality.
> —Class C misdemeanor, 30 days and/or $500.

WYOMING

DECRIMINALIZED:
> Private consensual adult homosexual acts. 1977 Wyo. Sess. Laws ch. 70, § 3 (eff. May 27, 1977).

Public Indecency (4-201)

Anal or oral sex, or exposure of one's genitalia, anus, or female breast, for arousal, or contact with sexual organs through clothing, in public.

—Misdemeanor, 6 months and/or $750.

Appendix B
Excerpts from Selected Statutes, Ordinances, and Executive Orders Protecting Lesbians and Gay Men

STATE CIVIL RIGHTS STATUTES

Massachusetts (Chapter 516, Statutes of 1989):

An Act Making It Unlawful to Discriminate on the Basis of Sexual Orientation.

Be it enacted by the Senate and House of Representatives in General Court assembled, and by the authority of the same, as follows:

SECTION 1: . . . The term "sexual orientation" shall mean having an orientation for or being identified as having an orientation for heterosexuality, bisexuality, or homosexuality.

. . . .

SECTION 3: [It shall be an unlawful practice f]or an employer, by himself or his agent, because of the race, color, religious creed, national origin, sex, sexual orientation, which shall not include persons whose sexual orientation involves minor children as the sex object, or ancestry of any individual to refuse to hire or employ or to bar or to discharge from employment such individual or to discriminate against such individual in compensation or in terms, conditions or privileges of employment, unless based upon a bona fide occupational qualification.

SECTION 4: [It shall be an unlawful practice f]or a labor organization, because of the race, color, religious creed, national origin, sex, sexual orientation, which shall not include persons whose sexual orientation involves minor children as the sex object, age or ancestry of any individual, or because of the handicap of any person alleging to be a qualified handicapped person, to exclude from full membership rights or to expel from its membership such individual or to discriminate in any way against any of its members or against any employer or any individual employed by an employer unless based upon a bona fide occupational qualification.

SECTION 6: [It shall be an unlawful practice f]or the owner, lessee, sublessee, licensed real estate broker, assignee or managing agent of publicly assisted or multiple dwelling or contiguously located housing accommodations or other person having the right to ownership or possession or right to rent or lease, or sell or negotiate for the sale of such accommodations, or any agent or employee of such a person, or any organization of unit owners in a condominium or housing cooperative: (a) to refuse to rent or lease or sell or negotiate for sale or otherwise to deny to or withhold from any person or group of persons such accommodations because of the race, religious creed, color, national origin, sex, sexual orientation, which shall not include persons whose sexual orientation involves minor children as the sex object, age, ancestry, or marital status of such person or persons or because such person is a veteran or member of the armed forces, or because such person is blind, or hearing impaired . . . (c) to cause to be made any written or oral inquiry or record concerning the race, religious creed, color, national origin, sex, sexual orientation, which shall not include persons whose sexual orientation involves minor children as the sex object, age, ancestry or marital status of the person seeking to rent or lease or buy any such accommodation, or concerning the fact that such person is a veteran or a member of the armed forces or because such person is blind or hearing impaired.

SECTION 10: [It shall be an unlawful practice f]or the owner, lessee, sublessee, or managing agent of, or other person having the right of ownership or possession of or the right to sell, rent or lease commercial space: (1) To refuse to sell, rent, lease or otherwise deny to or withhold from any person or group of persons such commercial space because of race, color, religious creed, national origin, sex, sexual orientation, which shall not include persons whose sexual orientation involves minor children as the sex object, age, ancestry or marital status of such person or persons.

SECTION 14: Whoever makes any distinction, discrimination or restriction on account of race, color, religious creed, national origin, sex, sexual orientation, which shall not include persons whose sexual orientation involves minor children as the sex object, deafness, blindness or any physical or mental disability or ancestry relative to the admission of any person to, or his treatment in any place of public accommodation, resort, or amusement . . . or whoever aids or incites such distinction, discrimination, or restriction, shall be punished by fine of not more than twenty-five hundred dollars or by imprisonment for not more than one year, or both, and shall be liable to any person aggrieved thereby for such damages as are enumerated [elsewhere in the statutes]; provided, however, that such civil forfeiture shall be of an amount not less than three hundred dollars; but such person so aggrieved shall not recover against more than one person by reason of any one act of distinction, discrimination or restriction. All persons shall have the right to the full and equal accommodations, advantages, facilities and privileges of any place of public accommodation, resort or amusement subject only to the conditions and limitations established by law and applicable to all persons. This right is recognized and declared to be a civil right.

Wisconsin (Chapter 112, Laws of 1981):

An Act . . . relating to prohibiting discrimination based upon sexual orientation.

The People of the State of Wisconsin, represented in senate and assembly, do enact as follows:

. . . .

SECTION 12: It is the intent of this section to render unlawful discrimination in housing. It is the declared policy of this state that all persons shall have an equal opportunity for housing regardless of sex, race, color, sexual orientation as defined in [Section 15], handicap, religion, national origin, sex or marital status of the person maintaining the household, lawful source of income, age or ancestry and it is the duty of the local units of government to assist in the orderly prevention or removal of all discrimination in housing through the power granted [municipalities]. The legislature hereby extends the state law governing equal housing opportunities to cover single-family residences which are owner-occupied. The legislature finds that the sale and rental of single-family residences constitute a significant portion of the housing business in this state and should be regulated. This section shall be deemed an exercise of the police powers of the state for the protection of the welfare, health, peace, dignity and human rights of the people of this state.

SECTION 13: The equal rights council shall disseminate information and attempt by means of discussion as well as other proper means to educate the people of the state to a greater understanding, appreciation and practice of human rights for all people, of whatever race, creed, color, sexual orientation, national origin, to the end that this state will be a better place in which to live.

SECTION 14: The practice of denying employment and other opportunities to, and discriminating against, properly qualified persons by reasons of their age, race, creed, color, handicap, sex, national origin, ancestry, sexual orientation, arrest record or conviction record, is likely to foment domestic strife and unrest, and substantially and adversely affect the general welfare of a state by depriving it of the fullest utilization of its capacities for production. The denial by some employers, licensing agencies and labor unions of employment opportunities to such persons solely because of their age, race, creed, color, handicap, sex, national origin, ancestry, sexual orientation, arrest record or conviction record, and discrimination against them in employment, tends to deprive the victims of the earnings which are necessary to maintain a just and decent standard of living, thereby committing grave injury to them.

It is believed by many students of the problem that protection by law of the rights of all people to obtain gainful employment and other privileges free from discrimination because of age, race, creed, color, handicap, sex, national origin, ancestry or sexual orientation, would remove certain recognized sources of strife and unrest, and encourage the full utilization of the productive resources of the state to the benefit of the state, the family and to all the people of the state.

In the interpretation and application of this subchapter, and otherwise, it is declared to be the public policy of the state to encourage and foster to the fullest extent practicable the employment of all properly qualified persons regardless of their age, race, creed, color, handicap, sex, national origin, ancestry or sexual orientation. Nothing in this subsection requires an affirmative action program to correct an imbalance in the work force.

SECTION 15: "Sexual orientation" means having a preference for heterosexuality, homosexuality, bisexuality, having a history of such a preference or being identified with such a preference.

. . . .

SECTION 17: It is discrimination because of sexual orientation:

1. For any employer, labor organization, licensing agency or employment agency or other person to refuse to hire, employ, admit or license, or to bar or terminate from employment, membership or licensure any individual, or to discriminate against an individual in promotion, compensation or in terms, conditions or privileges of employment because of the individual's sexual orientation.

. . . .

SECTION 25: [A person is guilty of a Class A Misdemeanor who d]enies to another or charges another a higher price than the regular rate for the full and equal enjoyment of any public place of accommodation or amusement because of sex, race, color, creed, physical condition, developmental disability . . . sexual orientation . . . national origin or ancestry [or] gives preferential treatment to some classes of persons in providing services or facilities in any public place of accommodation or amusement because of sex, race, color, creed, sexual orientation, national origin or ancestry.

EXECUTIVE ORDERS

California (Exec. Order No. B-54-79):

WHEREAS, Article I of the California Constitution guarantees the inalienable right of privacy for all people which must be vigorously enforced; and

WHEREAS, government must not single out sexual minorities for harassment or recognize sexual orientation as a basis for discrimination; and

WHEREAS, California must expand its investment in human capital by enlisting the talent of all members of society;

NOW, THEREFORE, I, Edmund G. Brown, Jr., Governor of the State of California, by virtue of the power and authority vested in me by the Constitution and statutes of the State of California, do hereby issue this order to become effective immediately:

The agencies, departments, boards and commissions within the Executive Branch of state government under the jurisdiction of the Governor shall not discriminate solely upon the individual's sexual preference. Any alleged acts of discrimination in violation of this directive shall be reported to the State Personnel Board for resolution.

Edmund G. Brown
April 4, 1979

New York (Exec. Order No. 28, as amended by No. 28.1):

Ours is a unique government. It was created and has been preserved by people from all over the world who came here seeking one thing above all others: freedom—freedom to believe and to act on those beliefs; freedom that says that so long as an individual's conduct and actions remain a matter of personal expression and do not deprive others of their rights, they should be neither restrained nor punished by government.

Our nation values freedom so greatly, it has been written into our Constitution. We all prize that freedom and millions have fought to protect and to extend it.

Each generation has come to understand the basic wisdom of our Constitution: that only by protecting the freedom of others can we ensure it for ourselves; that to encourage or allow government to discriminate against any belief or creed or private way of life would threaten us all. This is so because we could never be sure which particular value would dominate government at any particular point in time. Only neutrality by government was deemed safe and that is what our Constitution assures.

This freedom makes us strong. It is essential to our pluralism. It protects religious believers, and agnostics, and atheists, and political dissenters, and conservatives and liberals, creating a nation and a state where the right to live as conscience dictates is enshrined as law. Because of such freedom we enjoy a cultural and religious diversity unmatched by any other nation.

The freedom our Constitution grants, however, requires that government exercise a degree of tolerance unthinkable in societies less open or diverse than ours. It demands a tolerance for the privacy of each individual, a refusal to use the state as an instrument of coercion of belief or thought, however desirable the majority regards a particular belief or thought to be.

Even when this freedom is unchallenged, it is so precious to us all that our commitment to preserve it from encroachment by government deserves constant reaffirmation and reiteration. But when this freedom is questioned or when evidence of unfair discrimination exists, then our reaffirmation is not an option— it is a simple necessity.

I have seen evidence of such encroachment. As Secretary of State, I was required to issue special regulations to prohibit discrimination against individuals seeking licenses for certain occupations or corporate privileges. Up to that time such licenses were denied on the basis of sexual orientation or even presumed sexual orientation. There is no reason to believe that the discrimination apparent in that part of government was confined there.

No one argued then against my change in the State's regulations. No one was heard to say that government had no place in fighting unfair discrimination. In fact, in recognition of this, a personnel directive against discrimination in hiring was issued during the prior administration.

I suggest, respectfully, that what was right then is right now. And I believe that there is no justification for the failure to announce freedom from discrimination as the policy, not just of the Department of State but of the entire State Government.

Indeed, the most persistent argument that has been offered in opposition to my stating the views contained in this Order does not really contradict any of them. Rather, it says, in effect, we ought not to state this constitutional truth because it may be misrepresented to be something else. Specifically, it is suggested that the argument against discrimination will be distorted into an argument promoting homosexuality.

The argument is beside the mark. There is no perfect protection against distortion. Indeed one could as easily argue that silence on this issue could be distorted into an argument promoting discrimination against homosexuals.

In this case, this statement and Executive Order are clear. Their essence is that our government cannot promote any religious creed, belief, or life-style without thereby threatening all others.

This is an argument for securing freedom by insisting on neutrality. It is a proposition that is at the very foundation of our nation's strength. We ought never be embarrassed nor afraid to repeat it.

Accordingly, for all the above reasons, I am this day reiterating the law set down by the Constitution of the United States and the Constitution of the State of New York as the policy of this Administration.

1. No State agency or department shall discriminate on the basis of sexual orientation against any individual in the provision of any services or benefits by such State agency or department.

2. All State agencies and departments shall prohibit discrimination based on sexual orientation in any matter pertaining to employment by the State including, but not limited to, hiring, job appointment, promotion, tenure, recruitment and compensation.

3. The Division of Human Rights is hereby directed to review and promulgate guidelines prohibiting discrimination based on sexual orientation to maintain an environment where only job-related criteria are used to assess employees or prospective employees of the State. The Division shall also implement a procedure to ensure the swift and thorough investigation of complaints of discrimination based on sexual orientation. Particular effort should be made to conduct investigations with due regard for confidentiality.

4. In order to assure that we understand fully the extent and nature of any discrimination that exists, I will appoint a Task Force. . . . The Task Force shall submit such reports and recommendations as it sees fit, dealing with individual's rights to the benefit of government service and opportunity for government service regardless of sexual orientation. . . .

> Mario M. Cuomo
> November 18, 1983
> as amended on April 21, 1987

Ohio (Exec. Order No. 83–64):

WHEREAS, the inalienable right of privacy for all Ohioans must be vigorously enforced; and

WHEREAS, government must not single out sexual minorities for harassment or recognize sexual orientation as a basis for discrimination;

NOW, THEREFORE, I, Richard F. Celeste, Governor of the State of Ohio, by virtue of the power and authority vested in me by the Constitution and statutes of the State of Ohio, do hereby issue this order to become effective immediately;

The agencies, departments, boards and commissions within the Executive Branch of State government and under the jurisdiction of the Governor shall not discriminate in State employment against any individual based on the individual's sexual orientation.

There shall be established, within the Department of Administrative Services Division of Personnel, an Advisory Committee, the purpose of which is to advise the Director of Administrative Services on the implementation of this Executive Order. . . .

Richard F. Celeste
December 30, 1983

CITY ORDINANCES

Aspen, Colorado (Ordinance No. 60, adopted November 28, 1977):

WHEREAS, the City Council desires to amend the Aspen Municipal Code by the addition of Section 13–98 to Chapter 13 of said Code for the benefit of the City of Aspen,

NOW, THEREFORE, BE IT ORDAINED BY THE CITY COUNCIL OF THE CITY OF ASPEN, COLORADO:

SECTION 1

That Chapter 13 of the Aspen Municipal Code is hereby amended by the addition of Section 13–98 which reads as follows:

Sec. 13–98. *Discriminatory Practices Prohibited.*
  (a) *Definitions.*
    (1) *Discrimination.* "Discrimination" or "to discriminate" means, without limitation, any act which because of race, color, creed, religion, ancestry, national origin, sex, age, marital status, physical handicaps, affectional or sexual orientation, family responsibility, or political affiliation, results in the unequal treatment or separation of any person or denies, prevents, limits or otherwise adversely affects, the benefit or enjoyment by any person of employment, ownership or occupancy of real property or public services or accommodations. Such discrimination is unlawful and is a violation of this ordinance, provided, however, that the physical condition of an existing building or structure shall not, of itself, constitute discrimination.
    (2) *Housing.* "Housing" means any building, structure, vacant land or part thereof during the period it is advertised, listed or offered for sale, lease, rent or transfer of ownership, and during the period while it is being sold, leased or rented.
    (3) *Public Services or Accommodations.* "Public services or accommodations" means any place of business engaged in any sales to the public and any place offering services, facilities, privileges, advantages or accommodations to the public.
    (4) *Person.* "Person" means any individual, firm, partnership, corporation, association, organization, unincorporated organization, labor union, government agency, incorporated society, stat-

utory or common law trust, estate, executor, administrator, receiver, trustee, conservator, liquidator, trustee in bankruptcy, committee, assignee, officer, employee, principal or agent, legal or personal representative, real estate broker or salesman or any agent or representative of any of the foregoing.

(b) *Discriminatory employment practices prohibited.* It shall be unlawful for any person who is an employer or employment agency, directly or indirectly, to discriminate against any employee with regard to application for employment, hiring, occupational training, tenure, promotion, compensation, layoff, discharge, or any other term or condition of employment except when based upon a bona fide occupational qualification.

(c) *Discriminatory housing practices prohibited.* It shall be unlawful for any person, directly or indirectly, to discriminate against or to accord adverse, unlawful or unequal treatment to any other person with respect to the acquisition, occupancy, use and enjoyment of any housing, including the sale, transfer, rental or lease thereof.

(d) *Discriminatory public services and accommodation practices prohibited.* It shall be unlawful for a person engaged in providing services or accommodation to the public to, directly or indirectly, discriminate against any other person by refusing to allow the full and equal use and enjoyment of the goods, services, facilities, privileges, advantages, including accommodations, and the terms and conditions under which the same are made available, or to provide adverse, unlawful, or unequal treatment to any person in connection therewith.

(e) *Penalties and civil liability.* Any person who violates the provisions of subsection (b) through (d) hereof shall be deemed guilty of an offense and upon conviction thereof shall be punished by a fine not exceeding Three Hundred Dollars

($300.00) or imprisonment of not more than ninety (90) days or both such fine and imprisonment, at the discretion of the court. In addition, any person claiming to be aggrieved by an unlawful discriminatory act shall have a cause of action in any court of competent jurisdiction for compensatory damages and such other remedies as may be appropriate, including specifically the issuing of restraining orders and such temporary or permanent injunctions as are necessary to obtain complete compliance with this ordinance. In addition, the prevailing party shall be entitled to reasonable attorney fees and costs.

(f) Whenever it appears that the holder of a permit, license, franchise, benefit, or advantage, issued by the City of Aspen is in violation of this ordinance, notwithstanding any other action it may take or may have taken under the authority of the provisions of this ordinance, the City of Aspen may take such action regarding the temporary or permanent suspension of the violator's City of Aspen Business License, permit, franchise, benefit or advantage as it considers appropriate based on the facts disclosed to it.

SECTION 2

If any provision of this ordinance or the application hereof to any person or circumstance is held invalid, such invalidity shall not affect other provisions or applications of the ordinance which can be given effect without the invalid provisions or application, and to this end the provisions of this ordinance are declared to be severable.

New York City (Local Law No. 2, adopted April 2, 1986):

A LOCAL LAW To amend the administrative code of the City of New York, in relation to unlawful discriminatory practices. Be it enacted by the Council as follows:

SECTION 1. Legislative Declaration. The council reaffirms its finding and declaration articulated in the law establishing the city commission on human rights that in the city of New

York, with its great cosmopolitan population consisting of large numbers of people of diverse backgrounds, beliefs and ways of life, there is no greater danger to the well-being of the city and its inhabitants than the existence of groups prejudiced against one another and antagonistic to each other. It further reiterates that prejudice, intolerance, bigotry, and discrimination occasioned thereby threaten the rights and proper privileges of the city's inhabitants and menace the institutions and foundations of a free democratic state.

The council notes that, throughout the history of the city, many New Yorkers have encountered prejudice on account of their sexual orientation. In some instances, the prejudice has impaired access to employment, housing, and other basic necessities of life leading to deprivation and suffering. In addition, it has fostered a general climate of hostility and distrust, even to the point of physical violence against those perceived to be homosexual.

The council hereby finds and declares that discrimination on the basis of sexual orientation exists, that it unjustly threatens the well-being of thousands of New Yorkers, and that it should be prohibited in regard to employment, housing, land, commercial space and public accommodations.

In doing so, the council wishes to make clear that it is not the function of this civil rights statute to promote a particular group or community; its purpose is rather to ensure that individuals who live in our society will have the opportunity to pursue their own beliefs and conduct their lives as they see fit within the limits of the law.

SECTION 2. Title B of chapter one of the administrative code of the City of New York is amended by adding a new section B1-7.2 to read as follows:

B1-7.2 Unlawful discriminatory practices—sexual orientation.

1. The provisions heretofore set forth in section B1-7.0 as unlawful discriminatory practices shall be construed to include discrimination against individuals because of their actual or perceived sexual orientation.

2. Nothing in this section shall be construed to:

a. Restrict an employer's right to insist that an employee meet bona fide job-related qualifications of employment;

b. Authorize or require employers to establish affirmative action quotas based on sexual orientation or to make inquiries regarding the sexual orientation of current or prospective employees;

c. Limit or override the present exemptions in the human rights law, including those relating to employment concerns having fewer than four employees, as provided in subdivision five of section B1–2.0; owner-occupied dwellings, as provided in paragraph (a) of subdivision five of section B1–7.0; or any religious or denominational institution or organization, or any organization operated for charitable or educational purposes, which is operated, supervised or controlled by or in connection with a religious organization, as provided in subdivision nine of section B1–7.1;

d. Make lawful any act that violates the penal law of the state of New York; or

e. Endorse any particular behavior or way of life.

3. As used in the section, the term "sexual orientation" shall mean heterosexuality, homosexuality, or bisexuality.

SECTION 3. This local law shall take effect immediately.

San Diego (Ordinance No. 0–17453, adopted April 16, 1990):

BE IT ORDAINED, by the Council of The City of San Diego, as follows:

SECTION 1. That Chapter V, Article 2, of the San Diego Municipal Code be and the same is hereby amended by adding Division 96 . . . to read as follows:

DIVISION 96

Sec. 52.9601 STATEMENT OF POLICY

Discrimination based on sexual orientation deprives the City of the fullest utilization of its resources and capacity for development and advancement. Such discrimination poses a substantial threat to the health, safety and welfare of the community. Existing state and federal restraints on arbitrary discrimination are inadequate to meet the particular problems of this City. It is hereby declared as the public policy of The City of San Diego that it is necessary to protect and safeguard the right and opportunity of all persons to be free from discrimination based on sexual orientation. Notwithstanding the intent of this ordinance to protect all citizens from arbitrary discrimination, nothing in this ordinance shall be construed as endorsing, encouraging, or approving a particular life style nor is it the intent of this ordinance to give special privileges or rights to any person based on sexual orientation.

SEC. 52.9602 DEFINITIONS

1. Business Establishments. As used in this Division, the term "business establishment" shall mean any entity, however organized, which furnishes goods or services to the general public. An otherwise qualifying establishment which has membership requirements is considered to furnish services to the general public if its membership requirements: (a) consist only of payment of fees; or (b) consist of requirements under which a substantial portion of the residents of this City could qualify.

2. Educational Institutions. As used in this Division, the term "educational institution" shall mean any entity, however organized, which engages in the developing of knowledge and makes available the processes of training and instruction.

3. Employer. As used in this Division, "employer" includes any private person regularly employing five or more persons. "Employer" shall not include any federal, state or local agencies.

4. Frivolous. As used in this Division, the term "frivolous" shall mean (a) totally and completely without merit; or (b) for the sole purpose of harassing an opposing party.

5. Individual. As used in this Division, the term "individual" shall mean the same as the term "person." Wherever this Division refers to the sexual orientation of any individual, and the individual is a group, the phrase shall mean the sexual orientation of any member of the group.

6. Person. As used in this Division, the term "person" shall mean any natural person, firm, corporation, partnership or other organization, association or group of persons however organized.

7. Reasonable. As used in this Division, "reasonable" shall mean that which a person of ordinary care and prudence would believe to be true.

8. Religious Organizations. As used in this Division, the term

"religious organization" shall mean an organization recognized as such under 26 U.S.C. section 501(c)(3).

9. Sexual Orientation. As used in this Division, the term "sexual orientation" shall mean an individual's supposed or actual sexual preference for any lawful sexual activity

SEC. 52.9603 EMPLOYMENT

A.   *Unlawful Employment Practices*

1. Employers—Discrimination. It shall be an unlawful employment practice for an employer to fail or refuse to hire, or to discharge any individual, or otherwise to discriminate against any individual with respect to compensation, terms, conditions or privileges of employment on the basis (in whole or in part) of such individual's sexual orientation.

2. Employers—Segregation. It shall be an unlawful employment practice for an employer to limit, segregate or classify employees or applicants for employment in any manner which would deprive or tend to deprive any individual of employment opportunities, or adversely affect his or her employment status on the basis (in whole or in part) of such individual's sexual orientation.

3. Employment Agencies. It shall be an unlawful employment practice for an employment agency to fail or refuse to refer for employment any individual, or otherwise to discriminate against any individual on the basis (in whole or in part) of such individual's sexual orientation.

4. Labor Organizations. It shall be an unlawful employment practice for a labor organization to fail or refuse to include in its membership or to otherwise discriminate against any individual; or to limit, segregate or classify its membership; or fail or refuse to refer for employment any individual in any way which would deprive or tend to deprive such individual of employment opportunities, or otherwise adversely affect her or his status as an employee or as an applicant for employment on the basis (in whole or in part) of such individual's sexual orientation.

5. Job Training. It shall be an unlawful employment practice for an employer, an employment agency or a labor organization to discriminate against any individual in admission to, or employment in, any program established to provide apprenticeship or other training or retraining, including any on-the-job training program on the basis (in whole or in part) of such individual's sexual orientation.

6. Advertising. It shall be an unlawful employment practice for an employer, employment agency or a labor organization to print, publish, advertise or disseminate in any way, any notice or advertisement with respect to employment, membership in, or any classification or referral for employment or training by any such organization, which indicates an unlawful discriminatory practice.

B.   Subterfuge.

It shall be unlawful to do any of the acts mentioned in this section for any reason that would not have been asserted wholly or partially, but for the sexual orientation of any individual.

C.   Bona Fide Occupational Qualification Not Prohibited; Burden of Proof.

1. Bona Fide Occupational Qualification. Nothing contained in this section shall be deemed to prohibit selection or rejection based upon a bona fide occupational qualification.

2. Burden of Proof. In any action brought under Sections 52.9609 and 52.9610 of this Division, if a party asserts that an otherwise unlawful discriminatory practice is justified as a bona fide occupational qualification, that party shall have the burden of proving (a) that the discrimination is in fact a necessary result of a bona fide occupational qualification; and (b) that there exists no less discriminatory means of satisfying the occupational qualification.

D.   Exceptions

1. Bona Fide Employment Benefit Systems. It shall not be an unlawful discriminatory practice for an employer to observe the conditions of a bona fide employee benefit system, provided such systems or plans are not a subterfuge to evade the purposes of this Division; provided further that no such system shall provide an excuse for failure to hire any individual.

2. Standards of Conduct and Dress Codes. It shall not be an unlawful discriminatory practice for an employer to establish reasonable standards of conduct and dress codes which uniformly apply to all persons, and for such employer to fail or refuse to hire, or to discharge, any individual as a result of the failure of such individual to adhere to such standards of conduct or dress code.

3. Affirmative Action Not Required. Nothing in this ordinance shall be construed as requiring affirmative action on the basis of sexual orientation.

Sec. 52.9604 Housing and Other Real Eestate Transactions

A.   *Unlawful Real Estate Practices.*

1. Transactions Generally. It shall be an unlawful real estate
practice for any person to interrupt, terminate, or fail or refuse
to initiate or conduct any transaction in real property, including
but not limited to the rental thereof; to require different terms
for such transaction; to include in the terms or conditions of a
transaction in real property any clause, condition or restriction;
or to falsely represent that an interest in real property is not
available for transaction on the basis (in whole or in part) of any
individual's sexual orientation.

2. Credit. It shall be an unlawful real estate practice for any
person to refuse to lend money, guarantee the loan, accept a
deed of trust or mortgage, or otherwise refuse to make available
funds for the purchase, acquisition, construction, alteration,
rehabilitation, repair or maintenance of real property; or impose different conditions on such financing; on the basis (in
whole or in part) of any individual's sexual orientation.

3. Tenants' Services. It shall be an unlawful real estate practice for any person to refuse or restrict facilities, services,
repairs or improvement for any tenant or lessee on the basis
(in whole or in part) of any individual's sexual orientation.

4. Advertising. It shall be an unlawful real estate practice for
any person to make, print, publish, advertise or disseminate in
any way, any notice, statement or advertisement with respect
to a transaction or proposed transaction in real property, or
with respect to financing related to any such transaction, which
unlawfully indicates or attempts to indicate any unlawful preference, limitation or discrimination.

B.   *Subterfuge.*

It shall be unlawful to do any of the actions mentioned in this
Section for any reason that would not have been asserted wholly
or partially, but for the sexual orientation of any individual.

C.   *Exceptions.*

1. Owner-Occupied and Small Dwellings. Nothing in this
Section shall be construed to apply to the rental or leasing
of any housing unit in which the owner or lessor or any
member of his or her family occupies one of the living units
and either (a) it is necessary for the owner or lessor to use
either a bathroom or kitchen facility in common with the

prospective tenant; or (b) the structure contains fewer than three dwelling units.

2. Effect on Other Laws. Nothing in this Division shall be deemed to permit rental or occupancy of any dwelling unit or commercial space otherwise prohibited by law.

SEC. 52.9605 BUSINESS ESTABLISHMENTS

A. *Unlawful Business Practice*

1. Unlawful Practices Generally. It shall be an unlawful business practice for any person to deny any individual the full and equal enjoyment of the goods, services, facilities, privileges, advantages and accommodations of any business establishment on the basis (in whole or in part) of such individual's sexual orientation.

2. Credit. It shall be an unlawful business practice for any person to deny credit to any individual on the basis (in whole or in part) of such individual's sexual orientation.

3. Advertising. It shall be an unlawful business practice for any person to make, print, publish, advertise or disseminate in any way any notice, statement or advertisement with respect to any business establishment which indicates that such establishment engages or will engage in any unlawful business practice.

B. *Subterfuge.*

It shall be unlawful to do any of the acts mentioned in this Section for any reason that would not have been asserted, wholly or partially, but for the sexual orientation of any individual.

SEC. 52.9606 CITY FACILITIES AND SERVICES

A. *Unlawful Service Practices*

1. City Facilities. It shall be an unlawful service practice for any person to deny any individual the full and equal enjoyment of, or to place different terms and conditions on the availability of the use of any City facility on the basis (in whole or in part) of such individual's sexual orientation.

2. City Services. It shall be an unlawful service practice for any person to deny any individual the full and equal enjoyment of, or to impose different terms or conditions on the availability of, any City service on the basis (in whole or in part) of such individual's sexual orientation.

3. Supported Facilities and Services. It shall be an unlawful

service practice for any person to deny any individual the full and equal enjoyment of, or to impose different terms and conditions upon the availability of, any service, program or facility wholly or partially funded or otherwise supported by The City of San Diego, on the basis (in whole or in part) of such individual's sexual orientation. This subsection shall not apply to any facility, service or program which does not receive assistance from The City of San Diego which is not provided to the public generally.

4. Advertising. It shall be an unlawful service practice for any person to make, print, publish, advertise or disseminate in any way any notice, statement or advertisement with respect to any service or facility provided by either The City of San Diego or an organization described in subsection 3 which indicates that The City of San Diego or an organization described in subsection 3 engages in or will engage in unlawful service practices.

B. Subterfuge.

It shall be an unlawful discriminatory practice to do any of the acts mentioned in this Section for any reason which would not have been asserted, wholly or partially, but for the sexual orientation of any individual.

SEC. 52.9607 EDUCATIONAL INSTITUTIONS

A. Unlawful Education Practices.

1. Admission. It shall be an unlawful educational practice for any person to deny admission to any educational institution, or to impose different terms or conditions on admission, on the basis (in whole or in part) of such individual's sexual orientation.

2. Services. It shall be an unlawful educational practice for any person to deny any individual the full and equal enjoyment of, or to impose different terms or conditions upon the availability of, any services or program offered by an educational institution on the basis (in whole or in part) of such individual's sexual orientation.

3. Facilities. It shall be an unlawful educational practice for any person to deny any individual the full and equal enjoyment of, or to impose different terms or conditions upon the availability of, any facility owned or operated by an educational institution.

4. Advertising. It shall be an unlawful educational practice

for any person to make, print, publish, advertise or disseminate in any way any notice, statement or advertisement with respect to an educational institution which indicates that such institutions engages in, or will engage in, unlawful educational practices.

B. *Subterfuge.*

It shall be an unlawful discriminatory practice to do any of the acts mentioned in this Section for any reason which would not have been asserted, wholly or partially, but for the sexual orientation of any individual.

SEC. 52.9608 FRIVOLOUS ACTION PROHIBITED

Any person who files or maintains a frivolous action under this Division shall be liable for expenses, including attorney fees, incurred in defense of the action. The liability imposed by this section is in addition to any other liability imposed by law.

SEC. 52.9609 ENFORCEMENT

a. Civil Action. Any aggrieved person may enforce the provisions of this Division by means of a civil action.

b. Injunction.

1. Any person who commits an act in violation of this Division may be enjoined therefrom by any court of competent jurisdiction.

2. An action for injunction under this section may be brought by any aggrieved person, by the City Attorney, or by any person or entity which will fairly and adequately represent the interests of the protected class.

SEC. 52.9610 LIABILITY

Any person who violates any of the provisions of this Division or who aids in the violation of any provisions of this Division shall be liable for, and the court or a jury shall award to the individual whose rights are violated up to three (3) times the amount of actual damages, but in no case less than two hundred fifty dollars ($250.00) for each and every offense as well as reasonable attorneys' fees. The court or jury may award punitive damages in a proper case.

SEC. 52.9611 LIMITATION OF ACTION

Actions under this Division must be filed within one year of the alleged discriminatory acts.

SEC. 52.9612 RETALIATION PROHIBITED

No person shall retaliate against any individual because such individual seeks the enforcement of the provisions of this Division.

SEC. 52.9613 NONWAIVERABILITY

Any written or oral agreement whereby any provision of this Division is waived or modified is against public policy and void.

SEC. 52.9614 SEVERABILITY

If any part or provision of this Division, or the application thereof to any person or circumstance, is held invalid, the remainder of this Division, including the application of such part or provision to other persons or circumstances, shall not be affected thereby and shall continue in full force and effect. To this end, the provisions of this Division are severable.

SEC. 52.9615 EXEMPTION

Religious Organizations. Religious organizations and their schools shall be exempt from the terms of this Division.

DOMESTIC PARTNERSHIP STATUTE

Seattle (Ordinance No. 114648, effective September 17, 1989):

AN ORDINANCE relating to sick leave and funeral leave use; adding a new chapter to the Seattle Municipal Code ("S.M.C.") to facilitate the identification of an individual as the spouse or "domestic partner" of a City office or employee. . . .

WHEREAS, The City of Seattle recognizes that families and other long-term committed relationships foster economic stability and emotional and psychological bonds; and

WHEREAS, the welfare of all residents of The City of Seattle is enhanced by measures that reinforce the bonds of families and long-term committed relationships and that encourage commitment to proper care for children and parents; and

WHEREAS, The City of Seattle has already established a sick leave program that may be utilized for the care of dependent children of an officer or employee, and a funeral leave program that may be used in the event of a death of certain relatives, which programs limit the circumstances in which such leave may be used; and

. . . .

WHEREAS, it is desirable to establish a policy that allows any City officer or employee to utilize accumulated sick leave for the care of his or her spouse or domestic partner or the dependent child or parent of a City officer or employee or his or her spouse or domestic partner, consistent with state law, and to define domestic partners and certain other persons as relatives for the purpose of utilizing funeral leave; and

WHEREAS, City officers and employees have expressed a willingness to transfer accumulated sick leave from their sick leave accounts to the sick leave accounts of other officers or employees who have used or are about to use all of their accumulated sick leave because the officers or employees suffer from catastrophic illnesses, injuries, impairments, or physical or mental conditions; NOW, THEREFORE,

BE IT ORDAINED BY THE CITY OF SEATTLE AS FOLLOWS:

. . . .

SECTION 6. A new chapter is added to the Seattle Municipal Code as follows:

4.30 Documentation of Eligibility for Certain Uses of Sick Leave and Funeral Leave.

4.30.010 Establishment of Eligibility for Certain Funeral Leave and Non-personal Sick Leave Uses.

A. Any officer or employee who, on or after the effective date of this ordinance:

1. Commences services for the City, or
2. Recommences City service following a break in such service, or
3. Becomes another person's spouse or domestic partner, may use sick leave under S.M.C. Ch. 4.24 for the care of his or her spouse, domestic partner, parent, or the parent of child or his or her spouse or domestic partner, and funeral leave under S.M.C. Ch. 4.28 in connection with the death of his or her spouse or domestic partner or any other person added by this ordinance, by filing with the appointing authority for his or her employing

unit, within a period specified in S.M.C. 4.30.010-C, an affidavit as contemplated in S.M.C. 4.30.020.

B. The Personnel Director shall specify by rule, what documentation, if any, that a person who is a City officer or employee immediately prior to the effective date of this ordinance and who is (1) married, or (2) participating in a domestic partnership, must provide to the appointing authority of such officer's or employee's employing unit to establish City knowledge of such officer's or employee's participation in a marriage or domestic partnership and eligibility of that officer or employee to use sick leave under S.M.C. Ch. 4.24 for the care of his or her spouse, domestic partner, or the parent of child of his or her spouse or domestic partner, and funeral leave under S.M.C. Ch. 4.28 in connection with the death of a spouse or domestic partner or any other person added by this ordinance.

C. An officer or employee may file the documentation required under S.M.C. 4.30.010-A or -B only:

1. Within the first thirty (30) days after the commencement date of his or her marriage or domestic partnership;
2. Within the first thirty (30) days after the commencement or recommencement of such officer's or employee's service; and
3. During an open enrollment period of ninety (90) days as specified by the Personnel Director following the effective date of this ordinance and, thereafter, during a regular annual open enrollment period as specified by the Personnel Director.
4. 30.020 Affidavit of Marriage/Domestic Partnership.
   The documentation sufficient to qualify an officer or employee to use sick leave or funeral leave as contemplated in S.M.C. 4.30.010-A shall consist of an affidavit in a form prescribed and furnished by the Personnel Director, on which such officer or employee dates and signs his or her name and:

A. Attests:

1. If married, that he or she is currently married to the individual identified by name on said form; or
2. If participating in a domestic partnership, that:
   a. He or she and his or her domestic partner (who shall be identified, by name, on said form) share the same

regular and permanent residence, have a close personal relationship, and have agreed to be jointly responsible for basic living expenses incurred during the domestic partnership;

b. They are not married to anyone;

c. They are each eighteen (18) years of age or older;

d. They are not related by blood closer than would bar marriage in the state of Washington;

e. They were mentally competent to consent to contract when their domestic partnership began;

f. They are each other's sole domestic partner and are responsible for each other's common welfare; and

g. Any prior domestic partnership in which he or she or his or her domestic partner participated with a third party was terminated not less than ninety (90) days prior to the date of said affidavit or by the death of that third party, whichever was earlier, and, if such earlier domestic partnership had been acknowledged pursuant to S.M.C. 4.30.010-A or -B, that notice of the termination of such earlier domestic partnership was provided to the City pursuant to S.M.C. 4.30.030 not less than ninety (90) days prior to the date of said affidavit;

B. Agrees to notify the City if there is a change of the circumstances attested to in the affidavit; and

C. Affirms, under penalty of law, that the assertions in the affidavit are true.

4. 30.030 Notice of Termination of Domestic Partnership.

For the purposes of this chapter, a domestic partnership that has been acknowledged as contemplated in S.M.C. 4.30.010-A or -B shall be effectively terminated upon the death of a domestic partner or on the ninetieth (90th) day after notice of the termination thereof was provided to the City in the form prescribed therefor by the Personnel Director, whichever is earlier.

AIDS DISCRIMINATION STATUTE

Florida (Fla. Stat. § 760.50 [1989]):

DISCRIMINATION ON THE BASIS OF ACQUIRED IMMUNE DEFICIENCY SYNDROME, ACQUIRED IM-

MUNE DEFICIENCY SYNDROME RELATED COM-
PLEX, AND HUMAN IMMUNODEFICIENCY VIRUS
PROHIBITED.—

(1) The Legislature finds and declares that persons infected
or believed to be infected with human immunodeficiency virus
have suffered and will continue to suffer irrational and scien-
tifically unfounded discrimination. The Legislature further
finds and declares that society itself is harmed by this discrimination, as otherwise able-bodied persons are deprived of the
means of supporting themselves, providing for their own health
care, housing themselves, and participating in the opportunities otherwise available to them in society. The Legislature
further finds and declares that remedies are needed to correct
these problems.

(2) Any person with or perceived as having acquired immune
deficiency syndrome, acquired immune deficiency syndrome
related complex, or human immunodeficiency virus shall have
every protection made available to handicapped persons.

(3)(a) No person may require an individual to take a human
immunodeficiency virus-related test as a condition of hiring,
promotion, or continued employment unless the absence of
human immunodeficiency virus infection is a bona fide occupational qualification for the job in question.

(b) No person may fail or refuse to hire or discharge any
individual, segregate or classify any individual in any way which
would deprive or tend to deprive that individual of employment
opportunities or adversely affect his status as an employee, or
otherwise discriminate against any individual with respect to
compensation, terms, conditions, or privileges of employment
on the basis of knowledge or belief that the individual has
taken a human immunodeficiency virus test or the results or
perceived results of such test unless the absence of human
immunodeficiency virus infection is a bona fide occupational
qualification of the job in question.

(c) A person who asserts that a bona fide occupational
qualification exists for human immunodeficiency virus-related
testing shall have the burden of proving that:

1. The human immunodeficiency virus-related test is necessary to ascertain whether an employee is currently able to
perform in a reasonable manner the duties of the particular
job or whether an employee will present a significant risk of

transmitting human immunodeficiency virus infection to other persons in the course of normal work activities; and

2. There exists no means of reasonable accommodation short of requiring that the individual be free of human immunodeficiency virus infection.

(4)(a) A person may not discriminate against an otherwise qualified individual in housing, public accommodations, or governmental services on the basis of the fact that such individual is, or is regarded as being, infected with human immunodeficiency virus.

(b) A person or other entity receiving or benefiting from state financial assistance may not discriminate against an otherwise qualified individual on the basis of the fact that such individual is, or is regarded as being, infected with human immunodeficiency virus.

(c) A person who asserts that an individual who is infected with human immunodeficiency virus is not otherwise qualified shall have the burden of proving that no reasonable accommodation can be made to prevent the likelihood that the individual will, under the circumstances involved, expose other individuals to a significant possibility of being infected with human immunodeficiency virus.

(d) A person may not fail or refuse to hire or discharge any individual, segregate or classify any individual in any way which would deprive or tend to deprive that individual of employment opportunities or adversely affect his or her status as an employee, or otherwise discriminate against any individual with respect to compensation, terms, conditions, or privileges of employment on the basis of the fact that the individual is a licensed health care professional or health care worker who treats or provides patient care to persons infected with human immunodeficiency virus.

(5) Every employer who provides or administers health insurance benefits or life insurance benefits to its employees shall develop and implement procedures to maintain the confidentiality of all records and information in its possession relating to the medical condition or status of any person covered by the health insurance benefits or life insurance benefits which it provides or administers. An employer shall be liable in damages to any person damaged by its failure to implement such a procedure.

(6)(a) Any person aggrieved by a violation of this section shall have a right of action in the circuit court and may recover for each violation:

1. Against any person who violates a provision of this section, liquidated damages of $1,000 or actual damages, whichever is greater.
2. Against any person who intentionally or recklessly violates a provision of this section, liquidated damages of $5,000 or actual damages, whichever is greater.
3. Reasonable attorney's fees.
4. Such other relief, including an injunction, as the court may deem appropriate.

(b) Nothing in this section limits the right of the person aggrieved by a violation of this section to recover damages or other relief under any other applicable law.

Appendix C
A List of Statutes, Ordinances, and Executive Orders

State City	Civil Rights Act or Order Prohibiting Discrimination Based on Sexual Orientation	Statewide Hate- or Bias-Crime Legislation That Explicitly Includes Sexual Orientation
ALABAMA		
ALASKA		
ARIZONA		
Tucson	Ch. 17, 1977 Code	
ARKANSAS		
CALIFORNIA	Civil Code § 51 Exec. Order B-54-79‡	422.6–7, 1170.75
Berkeley	Ch. 13.28 et seq.	
Cathedral City	Ch. 11.66	
Cupertino	Res. No. 3833*	
Davis	Ch. 7A	
Laguna Beach	Ch. 1.07	
Long Beach	Ch. 5.09	
Los Angeles	Ch. IV, art. 12	
Mountain View	Res. No. 10435*	
Oakland	Art. 20; Ord. No. 10427	
Sacramento	Ch. 14; Ord. No. 86-042	
San Diego	52.9601 to .9615	
San Francisco	Admin. Code 33-3301 et seq.	
San Jose	Res. No. 58076*	
Santa Barbara	Chs. 9.126, 9.130	
Santa Cruz	Res. No. 15–246*	
Santa Monica	Res. No. 781–81 Ch. 9; §§ 4900-10	
West Hollywood	Ord. Nos. 7, 22, 77U	

COLORADO	Exec. Order 90-	
Aspen	13–98	
Boulder	City Charter, Title 12	
Denver	28–91 et seq.	
CONNECTICUT	Public Act 91–58	29–7m†
Hartford	2–276	
New Haven	Citation unavailable	
Stamford	Ord. 667 (Supp.)	
DELAWARE		
DIST. COLUMBIA	1–2541(c)	22–4001–4
FLORIDA		877.19
Hillsborough County	Human Rights Amend. 91-9	
Palm Beach County	Citation unavailable	
Tampa	Ord. 91-88	
GEORGIA		
Atlanta	City Charter (1973 Ga. Laws 2188)	
HAWAII	1991 Haw. Sess. Laws Act 2	
Honolulu	Ord. No. 88–16‡	
IDAHO		
ILLINOIS	Civil Service Rule‡	38–110–5
Champaign	Ch. 13; Ord. No. 77–222	
Chicago	Ch. 199 et seq.	
Evanston	Ch. 5 (Housing)	
Urbana	12–1 et seq.	
INDIANA		
IOWA		80.40†
Iowa City	18–1 et seq.	
KANSAS		
KENTUCKY		
LOUISIANA		
New Orleans	Citation unavailable	
MAINE		
MARYLAND		
Baltimore	Art. 4, §§ 9(16), 12(8)	
Montgomery County	27–1 et seq.	
Prince George's County	Citation unavailable	
Rockville	Ch. 11	

MASSACHUSETTS	Chs. 151B, 272	1990 Mass. Acts 434
Boston	Title 12, Ch. 40	
Cambridge	Ord. No. 1016	
Malden	Art. IV, § 16.13	
MICHIGAN	Civil Service Rule‡	
Ann Arbor	Title IX, Ch. 112	
Detroit	Ch. 27	
East Lansing	Ch. 4, § 1.120 et seq.	
Flint	Ch. 2	
Ingham County	EOE Plan (5/26/87)‡	
Lansing	Chs. 296, 297	
Saginaw	Art. 3	
MINNESOTA	Exec. Order 86–14‡	Numerous provisions
Hennepin County	EEO Policy (1974)‡	
Minneapolis	Title 7, Chs. 139, 141	
St. Paul	Ch. 183	
MISSISSIPPI		
MISSOURI		
Kansas City	EOE Plan‡	
MONTANA		
NEBRASKA		
NEVADA		207.185
NEW HAMPSHIRE		651:6(g)
NEW JERSEY	Rev. Stat. 10:2-1 & 11:17-1	1990 N.J. Laws 87
	Exec. Order 91-39‡	
NEW MEXICO	Exec. Order 85–15‡	
NEW YORK	Exec. Orders 28, 28.1‡	
Alfred	Art II, § 1 (5/74)	
Brighton	Citation unavailable	
Buffalo	EEO Ord. (3/84)‡	
East Hampton	Affirmative Action Plan	
Ithaca	Chs. 28 & 29	
New York City	Admin. Code B1–7.2	
Rochester	83–58	
Suffolk County	89–1 et seq.	
Syracuse	Citation unavailable	
Tompkins County	Art. 24	
Troy	2–20‡	
NORTH CAROLINA		
Chapel Hill	Article IV	

Durham	Proclamation (6/25/86)	
Raleigh	4–1004	
NORTH DAKOTA		
OHIO	Exec. Order 83–64‡	
Columbus	Ch. 2325	
Cuyahoga County	Aff. Action Res. (12/21/81)‡	
Yellow Springs	Town Charter, § 29	
OKLAHOMA		
OREGON		166.155 & .165
Eugene	4.730, 4.780	
Portland	Res. 31510 (12/74) Ord. No. 159639 (5/7/87)	
PENNSYLVANIA	Exec. Order 1/20/88‡	
Harrisburg	Art. 725	
Philadelphia	Fair Practices Ord. (1982)	
Pittsburgh	Title VI	
RHODE ISLAND	Exec. Order 85–11‡	
SOUTH CAROLINA		
SOUTH DAKOTA		
Minnehaha County	Employee Policy Manual‡	
TENNESSEE		
TEXAS		
Austin	Ch. 7–4, Arts. II, III, IV	
UTAH		
VERMONT		13-1454–57
VIRGINIA		
Alexandria	Ord. No. 3498	
Arlington County	Citation unavailable‡	
WASHINGTON	Exec. Order 85–09‡	
Clallam County	Article X	
King County	Ch. 12.18	
Olympia	Ord. No. 4692	
Pullman	Ord. No. B–271*	
Seattle	Chs. 14.04 & 14.08; Ord. No. 111714	
Tacoma	1.29.010 et seq.	
WEST VIRGINIA		

WISCONSIN	Ch. 112, Laws of 1981	939.645
Dane County	Chs. 19 & 31	
Madison	3.23	
Milwaukee	Ch. 109-15	
WYOMING		

Note: Unless otherwise noted, references are to the relevant state, county, or municipal code.

* Affirmative action policy.

† Authorizes collection of statistics only.

‡ Prohibits discrimination by government and its employees only.

Appendix D
Selected Organizations Providing Legal Assistance

American Civil Liberties Union
AIDS Project and Lesbian and Gay Rights Project
132 West 43d Street
New York, NY 10036
212/944–9400, ext. 545

Center for Constitutional Rights
666 Broadway, 7th Floor
New York, NY 10012
212/614–6464

Gay and Lesbian Advocates and Defenders
P.O. Box 218
Boston, MA 02112
617/426–1350

Lambda Legal Defense and Education Fund, Inc.
666 Broadway, 12th Floor
New York, NY 10012
212/995–8585

606 South Olive Street, Suite 580
Los Angeles, CA 90014
213/629–2728

Michigan Organization for Human Rights
2000 Town Center, Suite 600
Southfield, MI 48075
313/358–0080

National Center for Lesbian Rights
1663 Mission Street, 4th Floor
San Francisco, CA 94103
415/621–0674

Texas Human Rights Foundation
2201 North Lamar, #203
Austin, TX 78705

Appendix E
State, Regional, and National Offices of the ACLU

ALABAMA

POB 447
Montgomery, AL 36101
205/262–0304

ALASKA

POB 201844
Anchorage, AK 99520–1844
907/276–2258

ARIZONA

POB 17148
Phoenix, AZ 85011
602/650–1967

ARKANSAS

103 W. Capitol, #1120
Little Rock, AR 72201
501/374–2660

CALIFORNIA

No. California
1663 Mission St., #460
San Francisco, CA 94103
415/621–2488

So. California
1616 Beverly Blvd.
Los Angeles, CA 90026
213/977–9500

San Diego
1202 Kettner Blvd., #6200
San Diego, CA 92101
619/232–2121

COLORADO

815 East 22d Ave.
Denver, CO 80205
303/861–2258

CONNECTICUT

32 Grand St.
Hartford, CT 06106
203/247–9823

DELAWARE

702 King St., #600A
Wilmington, DE 19801
302/654–3966

DISTRICT OF COLUMBIA

(See NATIONAL CAPITAL AREA)

FLORIDA

225 NE 34th St., Ste. 102
Miami, FL 33137
305/576–2336

GEORGIA

233 Mitchell St., SW, #200
Atlanta, GA 30303
404/523–5398

HAWAII

POB 3410
Honolulu, HI 96801
808/545–1722

IDAHO

POB 1897
Boise, ID 83701
208/344–5243

ILLINOIS

20 East Jackson Blvd.
Suite 1600
Chicago, IL 60604
312/427–7330

INDIANA

445 N. Pennsylvania St.
Suite 911
Indianapolis, IN 46204
317/635–4056

IOWA

446 Insurance Exchange Bldg.
Des Moines, IA 50309
515/243–3576

KANSAS & WESTERN MISSOURI

201 Wyandotte St., #209
Kansas City, MO 64105
816/421–4449

KENTUCKY

425 W. Muhammad Ali Blvd.
Suite 230
Louisville, KY 40202
502/581–1181

LOUISIANA

921 Canal St., #1237
New Orleans, LA 70112
504/522–0617

MAINE

97A Exchange St.
Portland, ME 04101
207/774–8087

MARYLAND

2219 St. Paul St.
Baltimore, MD 21218
410/889–8555

MASSACHUSETTS

19 Temple Place
Boston, MA 02111
617/482–3170

MICHIGAN

1249 Washington Blvd.
Suite 2910
Detroit, MI 48226–1822
313/961–4662

MINNESOTA

1021 W. Broadway
Minneapolis, MN 55411
612/522–2423

MISSISSIPPI

921 N. Congress St.
Jackson, MS 39202
601/355–6464

MISSOURI

Eastern Missouri
4557 Laclede Ave.
St. Louis, MO 63108
314/361–2111

Western Missouri
(See KANSAS)

MONTANA

POB 3012
Billings, MT 59103
406/248–1086

NATIONAL CAPITAL AREA

1400 20th St., NW., #119
Washington, DC 20036
202/457–0800

NEBRASKA

POB 81455
Lincoln, NE 68501
402/476–8091

NEVADA

418 S. Maryland Parkway
Las Vegas, NV 89101
702/366–1226

NEW HAMPSHIRE

11 South Main St.
Concord, NH 03301
603/225–3080

NEW JERSEY

2 Washington Place
Newark, NJ 07102
201/642–2084

NEW MEXICO

POB 80915
Albuquerque, NM 87108
505/266–5915

NEW YORK

132 West 43d St. 2d Fl.
New York, NY 10036
212/382–0557

NORTH CAROLINA

POB 28004
Raleigh, NC 27611
919/834–3390

OHIO

1223 West 6th St., 2d Fl.
Cleveland, OH 44113
216/781–6276

OKLAHOMA

1411 Classen
Suite 318
Oklahoma City, OK 73106
405/524–8511

OREGON

705 Board of Trade Bldg.
310 SW 4th Ave.
Portland, OR 97204
503/227–3186

PENNSYLVANIA

POB 1161
Philadelphia, PA 19105
215/923–4357

Pittsburgh Chapter
237 Oakland Ave.
Pittsburgh, PA 15213
412/681–7736

RHODE ISLAND

212 Union St., Rm. 211
Providence, RI 02903
401/831–7171

SOUTH CAROLINA

Suite 104 Middleburg Plaza
2712 Middleburg Drive
Columbia, SC 29204
803/799–5151

TENNESSEE

POB 120160
Nashville, TN 37212
615/320–7142

TEXAS

1236 W. Gray
Houston, TX 77019
713/524–5925

Dallas Chapter
POB 215135
Dallas, TX 75221
214/823–1555

Houston Chapter
1236 West Gray
Houston, TX 77019
713/524–5925

UTAH

9 Exchange Place
Suite 419
Salt Lake City, UT 84111
801/521–9289

VERMONT

100 State St.
Montepelier, VT 05601
802/223–6304

VIRGINIA

6 North 6th St.
Suite 400
Richmond, VA 23219–2419
804/644–8022

WASHINGTON

705 Second Avenue, 300
Seattle, WA 98104
206/624–2180

WEST VIRGINIA

POB 3952
Charleston, WV 25325
304/345–9246

WISCONSIN

207 E. Buffalo St., #325
Milwaukee, WI 53202
414/272–4032

WYOMING

POB A
Laramie, WY 82070
307/745–4515

REGIONAL OFFICES

Mountain States Regional Office
6825 E. Tennessee Ave.
Bldg. 2, Suite 262
Denver, CO 80224
303/321–4828

Southern Regional Office
44 Forsyth Street, NW
Suite 202
Atlanta, GA 30303
404/523–2721

NATIONAL OFFICES

Principal National Office
132 W. 43d St.
NY, NY 10036
212/944–9800

National Legislative Office
122 Maryland Ave, NE
Washington, DC 20002
202/544–1681

National Prison Project
1875 Connecticut Ave., NW
Suite 410
Washington, DC 20009
202/234–4830

Appendix F
A Brief Bibliography

There are now many books and articles about gay people and the law, such that a complete listing would overwhelm the reader. The following are books we especially recommend for their clarity and practicality.

R. Achtenberg (ed.), *Sexual Orientation and the Law* (1985) (updated regularly).

American Civil Liberties Union, *Epidemic of Fear: A Survey of AIDS Discrimination in the 1980s and Policy Recommendations for the 1990s* (1990).

H. Dalton and S. Burris (eds.), *AIDS and the Law* (1987).

J. D'Emilio and E. Freedman, *Intimate Matters: A History of Sexuality in America* (1988).

K. Dyer (ed.), *Gays in Uniform: The Pentagon's Secret Reports* (1990).

Harvard Law Review, *Sexual Orientation and the Law* (1990).

N. D. Hunter and W. B. Rubenstein (eds.), *AIDS Agenda: Emerging Issues in Civil Rights* (forthcoming 1992).

R. Jarvis, M. Closen, D. Herman, and A. Leonard, *AIDS Law in a Nutshell* (1991).

T. P. McCormack, *The AIDS Benefits Book* (1990).